MY MEMOIRS

Fifty Years of Journalism,
from Print to the Internet

BERNARD GWERTZMAN

Printed in the United States of America.

ISBN   Paperback   978-1-64361-094-8
              Hardback   978-1-64361-095-5
              eBook   978-1-64361-096-2

Westwood Books Publishing LLC
10389 Almayo Ave, Suite 103
Los Angeles, CA 90064

www.westwoodbookspublishing.com

CONTENTS

PREFACE

When I was about ten years old, I fell in love with a radio show called "The Big Story" which each week featured as its hero a reporter from a newspaper, who broke a story that ended up sending a crooked official to jail, or rewarding a good citizen. At the end of the program the reporter received a $500 prize from Pall Mall cigarettes which sponsored the show.

I grew up in New York City, which always had many newspapers. In our modest household in the Bronx, we got PM, a very liberal sheet which took no advertising, The New York Times, The New York Post, and the World-Telegram and Sun. The Post and the World-Telegram then were afternoon papers.

I liked to look at the Daily News or the Daily Mirror and the Journal American. I loved baseball, and used to read the sportswriters with abandon. When we moved to New Rochelle, N.Y., a nearby suburb, I was taken under the wing of Charles Russell, who was the faculty adviser for HighLights, the Junior High School newspaper of Albert Leonard Junior High, and he made me Managing

Editor. My job was to make sure the paper came off the presses on time each month, and I fell in love with the allure of printer's ink at the local print shop that did work.

I was thrilled when I was hired to cover New Rochelle High School sports for the local newspaper, the New Rochelle Standard Star, which like so many afternoon newspapers today, is no more. To me, it was like covering the Yankees for the New York Times.

After high school, I got into Harvard, and spent 80 percent of my time on the Harvard Crimson newspaper. I enlisted in the Army Reserves for six months active duty, to meet the obligation insisted upon by the Washington Evening Star and the rest is history which I try to lay out in this book of Memoirs. I loved the romance of the profession. How my first city editor used to tell me how important it was to find the nearest pay phone to call in a breaking story. How I graduated to covering President Johnson's cross Pacific trip and was sent by the Star to Eastern Europe and Russia to write about life behind the Iron Curtain; how the New York Times hired me to hold the fort in Moscow.

I got to know Henry Kissinger well, and watched him put together the first Middle East accords, and then Carter at Camp David, and then Cyrus Vance quitting over the failed effort to free hostages in Iran. And then I was promoted to being an editor, and as Foreign Editor, I was supervising a great team as we reported on the end of

Communism in Eastern Europe and the breakup of the Soviet Union on Christmas Day 1971.

All this, a build-up to the slow collapse of printed newspapers, the rise of web journalism, and how I chose to be part of the first wave of editors in the new field. In part, it was due to my son, James, who so loved tinkering with his computers. But in 1995-96 when we started the NY Times on the Web, I was hiring anyone who knew anything at all about the web. Who would have thought that by 2018, the paper is dependent on the web for survival.

This book is an effort to tell the story of how journalism has evolved in the past fifty or so years from the fabled print papers made famous by the play "The Front Page," that I grew up with to the internet products we are now living with. I would like to thank the many, many. people who have inspired me through the years. Unfortunately, many of them are no longer living, but I want to mention them anyway. In particular, I want to thank Newbold Noyes, who hired me for the Washington Evening Star, Charles Seib, Burt Hoffman, I. William Hill, Sid Epstein, and many others who helped me learn the business of journalism.

I would also like the many, many people on the The New York Times who helped me along. These include Seymour Topping, who hired me for the foreign desk, Joe Lelyveld., who was my boss on the foreign desk until I succeeded him as Foreign Editor, Tom Feyer,

Jeanne Pinder, Nancy Kenney, Cynthia Latimer, Marie Courtney, and Kevin McKenna, who later was part of the team that started The New York Times on the Web. In recent years, The Times has abolished desks for the different departments, but I have to say a word for all the copy editors we had on the foreign desk, who performed so well under times of stress.

I would like to thank Henry Kamm, a great journalist, who introduced me to Moscow when I joined his crew there. And a word of thanks to Boris, Sara and Ivan, our Moscow staff, and Shura, our friend and maid.

Special thanks to Martin Nisenholtz, who was the president of the New York Times on the web enterprise, and to the long list of people who worked so hard to get the New York Times on the Web off the ground. I would like to single out Meredith Artley and Naka Nathaniel, who met at the web site and got married, and Fiona Spruill and David Gallagher, who also met working on our web site and got married.

I look back with great affection to the early players on the web for us: Elizabeth Osder. Beth Flynn, Laura Noueihed, Mo Krochmal, and Lisa Napoli.

After I was asked to take a buyout from The Times in 2002, I spent the next 13 years on the web site of the Council on Foreign Relations as a consulting editor and I did more than 1,000 interviews for the web in that period. I was initially hired by Les Gelb, who was the Council's president then. I want to thank Richard Haass, who succeeded Les in that job, and James Lindsay, his deputy, who supported me in my work. And I want to thank Bob McMahon who was my editor in my final years on the Council's website.

And there is a special word of thanks to my wife of 49 years, Marie-Jeanne Gwertzman, who was with me in Moscow and ever after and who is my dearest friend, and my partner in life.

My Love for Newspapers Is Born

Ever since I was a young boy, I was fascinated by reporting. I can remember during World War Two, listening to the war correspondents filing their pieces on the radio, and imagining I was there. I read avidly the glaring headlines in the newspapers reporting the good and bad news. My mother who had hoped to be an actress, but ended up a Latin major and school teacher, wrote articles for the Hunter College magazine as an undergraduate and loved to dig them out and show them to me, and I guess I felt journalism was in my blood. My father, a successful trial attorney hoped I would go into law, but I did not have any interest in doing so. CBS on radio had a series "CBS Is There" recreating historical events with correspondents reporting as if they were there, and I loved the show. I became mesmerized by a radio show called "The Big Story" which began on NBC in 1949 which rewarded each Friday night an enterprising reporter with a $500 check for uncovering a murderer or a crooked official. I loved Jimmy Stewart, no less so when I watched him as an enterprising reporter in the 1948 film "Call Northside 777" in which he helps free an unjustly imprisoned person from jail.

In 1949, my family moved from the Bronx, in New York City, to New Rochelle, a nearby suburb, and I entered the ninth grade at Albert Leonard Junior High School. There had just been a restructuring of the school system in the city, and this was the first year of this junior high school as such, so the first year of the ninth grade in the new school. There were try outs for the school monthly newspaper High Lights, and I was chosen as Managing Editor. The Faculty Advisor was Charles Russell, and he had a strong influence on me, encouraging my love for journalism. My life long friend Jerry Greenspan was the editor in chief. And I was responsible each month for spending time at the printers downtown making sure everything worked and the paper came off the flatbed presses okay. Many of my friends from those ninth grade days are still close to me.

In the tenth grade, we all moved to the larger New Rochelle High School and I joined the school newspaper. But I also had my eye on a different journalistic job, that of being the sports reporter for the New Rochelle Standard Star. The Star was located in the center of the city in a relatively small building from which its presses published an afternoon newspaper six days a week. There were three high schools in the city, New Rochelle, Blessed Sacrament, and Iona Prep. Each had a high school sports reporter who worked for The Star. I was lusting for the New Rochelle job. Meanwhile, I joined the school's basketball team as an assistant manager, meaning I went on the team bus to all games, helped put the dirty uniforms in baskets for the cleaners, and otherwise made myself useful to Coach Dan O'Brien. In that year, the team was mediocre, winning a few more than it lost. As the end of the season neared, the coach asked me if I would like to be "the" manager next season. I thanked him for the honor but explained that I was going to try to become the sportswriter.

He, of course, was surprised because he neither knew of my ambitions or of my talents. But the coach, who on the outside seemed rather gruff, did not laugh at my plan. He said to me that tomorrow [Saturday] he was entering a mile relay team in the Millrose Games at Madison Square Garden, and I should go with him there and cover the event, write about it, and turn in my copy to him on Monday. I did as he suggested, and sat in the mezzanine in fairly good seats at the Garden, and wrote my story from home, and brought it to him on Monday. I was really shocked when O'Brien told me a few days later that "You have the job." He said go to the Star and meet with Elmer H. Miller, the editor in chief of the paper. Obviously, O'Brien must have used his influence to get me the job. In any event, as soon as school let out, I rushed down to the Star building and met with Miller. But after shaking my hand, and a few kind words, Miller asked me how old I was. When I told him I was 15 ½, he said I had to be 16 before I could start. So when I turned 16 two months later, on May 3, 1951, I rushed back down to The Star and signed the necessary documents. I would get $.75 an hour, then the federal minimum wage. I met with Pat McGowan, the sports editor, and I started covering sports that spring, and I did it until I graduated in June 1953.

Pat was a very gracious editor. He let my copy appear with clichés galore. In fact I kept a scrapbook of all my stories and I am a bit red-faced when I read them today. But how else do you learn? Since covering New Rochelle High School sports for the Standard- Star was like covering the Yankees for the Times, I got incredible play for my stories. For instance, on October 4, 1952, a Saturday paper, there was a banner headline on the sports page saying "Huguenot Gridders Rout Heavier DeWitt Clinton 16-0". My story, under the byline, "By Bernie Gwertzman" read:

> "An inspired New Rochelle High completely outplayed and outfought a bigger DeWitt Clinton High eleven of the Bronx last night and picked up their first win of the young season, 26-0, under McKenna Field arcs."

I covered the biggest game of the year, the annual Thanksgiving game between Iona Prep and New Rochelle High which ended in a tie: My lead paragraph hurts to read today:

> "The fighting Huguenots of New Rochelle High took all favored Iona Prep could muster and then on the shoulders of an inspired forward wall battled back to tie the Irish for the city title. 6-6, at McKenna Field yesterday. New Rochelle has won or tied for the mythical crown for four straight years."

In those days, applying to college was not the traumatic event it has been in more recent years, but it still had its drama attached. My high school tried to limit us to three applications. Because my grade average was about an "A" I did not worry much about it. I applied to three colleges which had good college daily newspapers: Harvard, Yale and Cornell. The city editor of The Standard-Star in fact was a Harvard alumnus and was a big booster of his school. In my own mind, Harvard was my first choice. But when the results arrived, Harvard put me on the waiting list, Yale rejected me, and Cornell accepted me. Since I also won a New York State scholarship, I assumed I would go to Cornell where a close friend of mine, Steve Weiss was an avid booster. I remember driving up to Ithaca with some other New Rochelle graduates who had been accepted to Cornell and buying sweatshirts and car stickers in advance of our arrival in the fall.

I later learned that the city editor had resigned from the Harvard Club of Westchester because I had not been accepted, He had been the club's secretary. But he did not tell me this. The day after graduation, a Saturday, as I recall, my father burst into my bedroom with a thick letter from Harvard, and when I opened it, it announced that I had been accepted after all. I decided to attend. And so in the fall of 1953, I joined the Class of 1957, and later that fall, joined the freshmen candidates seeking to become editors of the Harvard Crimson.

Ironically, the person directing the "competition," as it was called, was Jack Rosenthal, Class of 1956, an aspiring journalist also, from Portland, Oregon. In later life, Jack became an assistant to Robert Kennedy, when he was Attorney General, and also for Nicholas Katzenbach, who succeeded Kennedy in that post. Jack's initials at the Crimson were JR2. Jack, who became the editorial board chairman of the Times, and later directed the paper's charitable efforts, died in August 2017. Two other important editors on the Crimson in those days were David L. Halberstam (DLH) from Connecticut who like me, loved sports, and later won a Pulitzer Prize for The Times for his coverage in Vietnam, in the first years of American entry into the war and J. Anthony Lukas. (JAL), who won the Pulitzer

Prize for an article about a teen age girl in Connecticut who committed suicide after being caught up in drugs and hippies. Halberstam died in a car crash in a car driven by a student in Menlo Park, California, where he was giving a speech in April 2007. Lukas committed suicide in 1997.

I wrote dozens of articles for the Crimson and became managing editor for the 1956-57 year. The Crimson building was then as it is today at 14 Plympton Street in Cambridge. At that time is was a small townhouse, with its business and editorial offices on the main floor. The "printing plant" consisted of two linotype machines and a flatbed printing press which could publish a four-page paper every night. The papers would be delivered in the morning to the various living quarters on campus to the paying subscribers. If we wanted a six-page paper, or larger, the extra pages had to be prepared ahead of time.

I found that being managing editor was a full-time job and it was miraculous that I was still able to do a senior thesis on a virtually unknown British writer, Thomas Lovell Beddoes. I eventually graduated cum laude.

In the spring of 1957, Newbold Noyes Jr., the editor of the Washington Evening Star, paid a visit to Harvard looking to recruit some writers for his newspaper, which at that time was the leading afternoon newspaper in D.C. The Noyes family was one of the founding families of that newspaper which was solidly entrenched in Washington with a high-rise building on Eleventh Street and

Pennsylvania Avenue, N.W., in the heart of the downtown. I explained to him that that I might have to fulfill my military commitment first— there still was a military draft—with the option of volunteering for six months active duty in the reserves and five and a half years in reserve duty to follow.

I still have Noyes' telegram to me, offering me a job: "Subject to solution of problem of your military obligation am happy to inform you of your selection from among twenty-five college applicants as news department trainee under terms you and I discussed. We would like you to report for work around January 1 after completing six months of active service with National Guard or Reserve."

I joined a Civil Affairs Army Reserve unit from Boston. I was persuaded by a recruiter who came to Harvard that in time of conflict, we in the unit would go to a town and help the people get their lives back to normal. Editors would help get newspapers rolling again, etc. I thought that might be interesting, but once I joined the unit, I found that people with my lowly rank of private could only be clerks or drivers. Anyway, after six weeks of basic training in Fort Dix, N.J., my whole unit was taken in a convoy of buses to Fort Devens, Mass., where the base's personnel people were not sure what to do with us. The base was normally used to train advanced infantry troops. I told the personnel interviewer that I was interested in journalism, and I was quickly assigned to the public information office on base which published the weekly "Devens Dispatch."

That was a very pleasant assignment indeed. It was essentially run by a sergeant who was anti-military and just wanted to make sure we stayed out of trouble. This was the height of the cold war, of course, and each week, the Pentagon would send us a package of "suggested" material we could use on how bad Red China was or something like that,

At the end of December, I drove down to Washington, and with the help of my old friend, Michael Sweedler, I found a room in a rooming house near George Washington University for which I paid about $15 a week, My salary at the Star was $58 a week, which I was paid in cash each week, I could buy a meal for about a dollar at a cafeteria nearby. I love to tell people that my freshman year's tuition at Harvard was $750. It went up to $1,500 after that. My father gave me a check before I left for Harvard of about $2,000 which I deposited in a bank in Harvard Square to pay my expenses. That's just to say that in 1958, a dollar went a long way.

The newsroom for The Star was on the seventh floor of the rather majestic building at the corner of Pennsylvania Avenue and Eleventh Street, N.W. Its city editor was Sidney Epstein, who was very familiar with the nuts and bolts of covering Washington. Soon after I arrived, he said to me something like: "Kid, I want you to memorize overnight the locations of the city's police precincts." It's interesting. I can still remember that at that time, there were thirteen such precincts. I was able to pass his "test" the next day and then I asked him why it was necessary to know the locations. He replied in this way: "We are an afternoon paper, so we need the news fast. Say you are taking a cab to a murder scene and the cops have all gone. You have to get to the nearest precinct and the cabby doesn't know so you can tell him."

He was describing the reality of working for The Star then. Like other big city PM papers, the Star prided itself in getting the news in its pages before the Post did in the next morning's editions. The newsroom of The Star was populated by mostly male reporters, but there were some outstanding women reporters as well. When I arrived on the scene, The Star was in the midst of winning three consecutive Pulitzer Prizes for Reporting: George Beveridge, who specialized in urban planning, won it in 1958. Mary Loo Werner, who covered Virginia politics, won it in 1959. And Miriam Ottenberg, who was the paper's investigative reporter, won in 1960.

The atmosphere in and around the newsroom was right out of an old-time movie. Many reporters and editors smoked (I luckily did not until I picked up smoking a pipe when in graduate school, still to come in this narrative). Since the paper pretty much closed down by 5 pm many of the reporters —and that included some younger reporters as well—would congregate at a local bar or restaurant to relax and gossip. It was a great way for a young journalist like myself to pick up some tricks of the trade.

My first real job was as the night dictation typist. I would come to work around 5:30 p.m., just as the daily paper was closing up shop for the day. The newsroom would be empty in the evening, except for the night city editor who would edit copy destined for the next day's paper, primarily the first edition which hit the streets around 10:30 a.m., in time for people to buy a copy and take it to lunch. That edition would usually have a lot of analytical pieces and breaking wire stories [when I joined the paper in 1960, the paper only subscribed to the Associated Press; later it took United Press as well]. The second edition which was meant for home delivery in the suburbs, came out around 2:30 p.m. The next two editions, which were meant for people going home at night, were supposed to have whatever breaking news we could muster. It had mid-afternoon stock tables, early afternoon baseball game scores, et al.

The night city editor at the time I was breaking in was past his prime and when he had finished the copy in front of him, used to take a "lunch break" around 10:30 or 11 p.m. at an Italian restaurant across the street that everyone called "The Chicken Hut" which had been the name of the previous tenant. The editor liked to have me keep him company. I didn't mind, but I had to fight off his efforts to persuade me to accompany him home. He wanted me to accompany him because inevitably he would have two or three martinis at dinner and his wife would inveigh against his drinking. He hoped that if I came home with him, she would not be so tough. It was embarrassing to say the least. I usually had one beer at dinner.

The "staff" at night also included a night reporter and a night photographer. During my stint as the dictationist, if a murder occurred [we could hear the police radio], I might be sent out to cover it, along with the photographer, if the reporter was otherwise tied up.

I might add that at this particular time in newspaper history, afternoon papers like The Star were the rule in American cities. It's hard to visualize today when there are no longer any P.M. papers for sale. But in those days, the 1950s and early 60's, were marked by competing papers. In New York, there was the World Telegram, the New York Sun, the Journal-American, The New York Post. The Star's afternoon competition in Washington was the Washington Daily News, a Scripps Howard tabloid, aimed at government workers.

The Star's newsroom was a noisy place during the day. There was no air conditioning. On a hot day, the windows would be open. You could hear typewriters clicking. When you were writing close to a deadline, you would shout "Copy" after each page was finished. A copy boy would come and pick up a copy of the page just typed and bring it to the correct desk to be edited. When that desk was finished with it, it would go the main copy desk where it got a scan and then sent by pneumatic tube to the composing room. Once it got there, it would be re-typed on a linotype machine which transformed molten lead into readable copy. When a story was finished, the lead would be fitted onto a page, and then transformed into a stereo mat. Eventually, the completed pages made their way to the printing presses downstairs as stereo mats.

My first "big story" for The Star occurred while I was working at night. There had been a holdup of a family of a well-known liquor stores owner by two men who had barged into the house with guns. But they did not know that the family daughter was upstairs and when she heard what was happening downstairs she called the police. The police came promptly and arrested the intruders. It was a front page story, but I did not get a byline. It was a break for me. I still have the clipping: "At least seven victims of recent holdups will look over two men seized in a Northwest Washington home last night, trapped by a seventeen-year-old's phone call." And then, I remember helping out the coverage of a major fire on Fourteenth

Street in Washington. We had a phone book in the office which placed people by geography, so I could see who lived across the street from the fire. I was told how to do it.

I would call people across the street and say, "Hello, 'pa-leese,' what do you see across the street?" Obviously, I was trying to persuade people that I was the police calling.

My first byline in The Star resulted from covering a citizens' association meeting the previous night (to earn a few extra dollars).

"Rats Are Robbers Too, Each Takes Six Dollars
a Year"

By Bernard M. Gwertzman
Star Staff Writer

"A rat is apparently not only a pest, but an expensive and very tough one at that. A district housing official said last night that each rat in the community not only costs the populace $6 but can probably kill an ordinary alley cat if he has to.

"S. Tudor Strand, assistant superintendent of the District's housing division, said, "Rats are a drain of the community's money."

I eventually was moved to the day side where the action of course was more furious and I took rapid-fire dictation from reporters like Bill Hines, the science reporter, who was covering space launches from Cape Canaveral. I think I drove the national editor to distraction because I repeatedly misspelled "missile" as "missle." By May, I was enrolled in a three months trial reporters' assignment., in which I was given an assortment of stories, ranging from religious page features, to crime stories. I remember being sent to Bethesda, Md. Because a young woman had called the city desk claiming that her three-year old son was able to read the newspaper. My photographer and I soon discovered that her precocious son was really not very precocious, and we departed the scene without hurting the mother's feelings too badly.

At the end of July, I was notified by Noyes that I had been accepted on the staff as a general assignment reporter. I did not tell him that I had been thinking of leaving The Star and going back to Harvard Graduate School to study Russian affairs, I had entered Harvard College in September 1953, only six months after Stalin had died, and as a result, Soviet affairs were on the minds of almost everyone at Harvard in my first years. In my freshman year, I took Government 1, the introductory course in political theory which included discussions on Communism led by a very young teaching fellow from Poland, Zbigniew

Brezinski, and I took a course in Soviet Government given by Merle Fainsod, the school's top Russian expert. After I joined the Crimson staff I did a week long series of articles on the Russian Research Center, which was loosely attached to the Graduate School of Arts and Sciences. It was then headed by Professor Adam Ulam and the deputy was Marshall Shulman, an expert on Soviet foreign policy, who later moved to Columbia University where he headed the Harriman Institute for years.

I became quite friendly with Shulman, who had been a journalist in his younger days and who said that he was quite eager to get more journalists into his Institute, so that those who went to Moscow on assignment as correspondents would have a solid background.

In May 1957, as I was preparing to graduate, I was invited to a farewell party at the home of McGeorge Bundy, who was at that time, dean of the Faculty of Arts and Sciences at Harvard. He was giving a party for Arthur J. Langguth, who was a former Crimson president (AJL) and who was about to be drafted, and who had worked for Bundy that year. Langguth, who died in 2014, later became a prominent correspondent for The New York Times and then a professor at the University of Southern California. Bundy, who was in a cheerful mood, said to me: "Gwertzman, where are you going to graduate school?" I replied: "Mr. Bundy, I'm not. I'm going into the army and then I'm going to work for the Washington Star." He then replied: "Everyone goes to graduate school. If you change your mind, let me know, and I'll help you. I'll give you a recommendation."

To make a long story short, I kept seeing headlines in the Star about President Eisenhower and Nikita S. Khrushchev, the Soviet leader, exchanging warnings about the Middle East. There had been a Big Four summit in Geneva in 1955 and I was following events as best I could. And to be candid, I had a girl friend at Radcliffe with whom I had lost touch and I thought perhaps if I went back, I could rekindle our romance [I failed]. I wrote Shulman and asked if there was any chance of getting into the Russian program this late. He encouraged me, but said I would need another recommendation or two, besides his own. So I wrote Bundy and Ulam. Sure enough, I got a letter from Harvard at the end of August 1958, notifying me that I had been accepted into the program.

But when I asked Noyes for a leave of absence, he was shocked and told me I was making a mistake. He told me The Star would just have to sever relations. When I got to Harvard and paid respects to Bundy and Ulam to thank them for their recommendations, I realized they both had confused me with Milton S. Gwirtzman, Class of 1956, who had been editorial board chairman of The Crimson, and who graduated summa cum laude. I did not correct them, but merely thanked them. Several years later, I told the story to Milt, who enjoyed it immensely. He died in 2011.

CHAPTER 2

My Introduction to Russia

In the summer of 1958, on the advice of Shulman, I signed up for a night course at George Washington University in elementary Russian. I found it a very difficult language to learn, and I realized when I got to Harvard's Graduate School, I would have some serious work to do, since one of the requirements to receive the MA degree was proficiency in Russian. I signed up for an accelerated Russian course which I did my best to master. I passed the course, but with difficulty, as I recall. I studied Soviet economics with Abraham Bergson, a leading expert; Russian history with Richard Pipes and Russian literature with several experts.

Like most graduate students, I found a second home in Widener Library, and used to like to read in that part of the library where one could smoke a pipe. It was an affectation I had developed at the Star, but luckily I did not inhale. My home that first year was in a rooming house on Lee Street, close to Central Square, about as far away from Harvard psychologically as one could get. I spent some time schmoozing at the Crimson with friends I knew from the past. In fact, the Crimson asked me to do a special takeout on the six months army program I had recently done in the army. I gave it good marks.

As for my romantic life, I contacted Elizabeth Stein, but we did not date, She had other interests and eventually married another Crimson editor. Many years later, we met in Washington. She had divorced and had a good job in the government and two grown children. She died in 2009.

In the spring of 1959, I noticed a circular asking for volunteers to join the second U.S. Youth Cultural Exchange delegation to the Soviet Union that summer. It was sponsored by the Lisle Fellowship Organization. This was part of the first U.S,-Soviet Cultural Exchange Agreement signed in 1958. A lot of publicity had been given to the tour of the New York Philharmonic under Leonard Bernstein in 1958, but the exchange of youth was a novelty and it included opening up universities to graduate students.

I applied and was accepted by Lisle.

There were about 25 of us, mostly graduate students, and we sailed from Montreal aboard a student charter ship

—then the cheapest way to get to Europe—to Hamburg and then by train to Berlin. There had been no wall put up yet. We visited East Berlin. I remember sampling Beliner Weisse beer, and then by train to Warsaw, which was still pretty much devastated from World War II. I was fully aware of the failed uprising by Polish Jews in the Warsaw Ghetto which was crushed by the Nazis and paid a visit to the area. And from Warsaw, we took another train to Moscow. We were put up in a student dormitory on the outskirts of the city, as I recall. But there were no Russian students around. In Moscow, however, there was quite a lot of anticipation about an improvement in relations.

A very large Soviet exhibition had opened earlier in June at the Coliseum Building in New York City. In Moscow, we happened to be there at the same time as the opening of a vast U.S. exhibition in Sokolniki Park on July 26. Sokolniki Park is comparable to Central Park in New York. This was a exhibition which the U.S. Government had spent millions of dollars in building. They put up a "typical American house" in this exhibit and in that typical American house, Vice President Richard Nixon, in showing Premier Nikita Khrushchev around, got into his famous argument with Khrushchev that caused a lot of publicity in which they ended up arguing about such things as a captive nations resolution that had been passed by the U.S. Congress and which country was further ahead in technology. Nothing was really accomplished but it won a lot of publicity for Vice President Nixon. I didn't see that argument of course. We hadn't yet arrived at the exhibit.

Our group arrived at the exhibit the next day when it formally opened to the public and it was quite an amazing show for us. There was an exhibit of PepsiCola. At that time, there were no carbonated beverages available to Russians. If a Russian wanted a cold drink in the street, he went to a machine that provided a beverage called Kvass, which was a kind of fermented beverage like apple cider. It just wasn't soda. PepsiCola was giving away free drinks of Pepsi to Russians and Russians were lining up around the building to get free cups of Pepsi. There were communist kids around drinking Pepsi and then spitting it out as if to discourage Russians from drinking it and that didn't do them much good. I might add now that Pepsi is a major bottler of beverages in Russia as is CocaCola. There were all sorts of American modern automobiles being shown at this exhibit, which were again very popular for Russians to look at since there were no foreign cars for sale in Moscow in those days.

When I became a correspondent in Moscow ten years later, I had a Chevrolet Impala which I bought for The Times in Helsinki and people often would stop when I parked my car and come up and talk to me about it. At that time Americans were very popular in Moscow. There was a kind of post-Stalin euphoria in the Soviet Union. This was after all just six years after Stalin had died. People wanted consumer goods in the worst way.

After we'd been in Moscow for just a couple of days, we were taken to a movie theatre to see a documentary about the accomplishments of the Soviet Union. I decided to take a trolley back to the dormitory afterwards and a young man came up to me and asked me in Russian how much my short sleeve Dacron shirt cost.

He was talking to me in Russian and I replied, "okolo pyat dollarov" [about five dollars] He replied, "No, in rubles." He wanted to buy it off my back. I had to explain to him that I couldn't sell it since I needed it. I asked him why he wanted to buy it since I had seen a lot of t-shirts in GUM – that was the Soviet department store in Red Square. He explained, "They didn't have that kind of material."

It was a very interesting trip. We met with all kinds of students. We stayed in Soviet student dormitories, but of course the Soviet Union was very wary of too much interplay. So even though we stayed in Soviet student dormitories, there weren't any Soviet students staying in them with us. We were segregated at that time. We had meetings with members of Soviet youth groups. They had some dances set up. But the best times we had were informal meetings with Russians. I'll tell a few anecdotes just to give you some sense of it.

In Leningrad (now St. Petersburg), we went to a White Nights Festival in a public park. There I met a young woman, who was a student, and who was fascinated to meet an American. We started talking and she took pity on my poor Russian. We agreed to meet the next night (a Sunday) and go out to dinner,

Meanwhile, I knew the Nixon party was now in Leningrad and staying at the Astoria Hotel. I was hoping to meet some member of the press corps just to chat, but while I was in the lobby, a woman from Intourist, the Soviet travel agency, came up to me and asked "Are you an American?" When I said "Yes" she handed me two tickets to the Kirov ballet (now the Marinsky) and said Nixon would be attending the ballet. I was very pleased because I knew Russians love ballet and I was sure my Russian "date" would like to attend.

The ballet that night was "Spartacus" by Aram Khachaturian. When we got to the theatre, I could see why I was given free tickets. Almost all the seats were filled with foreign tourists, dressed in Western finery. I was afraid that my "date" might have been intimidated by being so underdressed for the performance. At the first intermission, I followed a horde of correspondents to the balcony level where Nixon was sitting in the royal box, He came out and was asked how he liked the ballet. He said he liked it, but then asked, "Where are the Russians?"

At that point, I stepped forward and introduced my date. "Here is a young Russian woman, Mr. Vice President," I blurted out. There is one footnote to this story. Years later, on November 7, 1980. I am diplomatic correspondent for The New York Times in Washington, attending the annual Nov. 7th party at the Soviet embassy. In walks Nixon, six years after he had resigned as president over the Watergate scandal, accompanied by Henry Kissinger, A crowd of diplomats and others crowded around Nixon who usually had not attended such functions. At one point, I asked him if he remembered his visit to the Kirov in Leningrad. He replies, "I bet you can't remember the name of the ballet." I answer: "It was Spartacus." "You're right," he says.

I later wrote some articles about my trip for the *Washington Star*. They ran three articles in their "teen" section, which was supposed to be about what life was like for Soviet teenagers. But they were really about Soviet youth.

One episode which I did not write about in these articles.

We were on an overnight train ride from Moscow to Kiev. On the Soviet trains, like European trains, you stay in compartments. I ended up in a compartment with a Russian family. It was a man and a woman and their young son. We chatted. My Russian at that time was passable, but not fluent. It was not a very exciting conversation. What he had to say was okay – but he was very defensive of Soviet life. He had no criticisms to make about the Soviet Union. He was a defender of the Soviet system. And I was not about to criticize anything. So it was kind of boring. As we got nearer to Kiev, somehow it came out that I was Jewish. And he said to me – "You're Jewish?" The word Jewish in Russian is ""Yevrei"." I said yes, and he said "we are all Yevrei." And he got very excited. And his wife got very nervous. But he hushed her up and took me out into the hallway on the train and then proceeded to tell me how tough life was for Jews in the Soviet Union. They couldn't travel to Israel, etc. which I had heard about. And so I found that quite interesting. Later when I was a correspondent in Moscow I heard many stories like that. But this was the first and very interesting conversation of its kind that I had had.

I'll relate one more story here. Our last stop on this forty day trip that our delegation took was to a World

Youth Communist Congress. This was in a place called Gurzuf in the Crimea. This was not far from Yalta where, of course, during World War II there was a famous meeting of Roosevelt, Stalin, and Churchill. At this camp were Communist youth groups from Communist countries as well as from capitalist countries like Britain and France. We were treated as non-Communist visitors from the United States. When we arrived by bus from the train station we were greeted by three Soviet counselors from the camp who presented us with flowers and welcomed us. The first thing they asked was, "would you like to have a volleyball match tomorrow?"

We, not knowing any better, said sure, why not! This will be a co-ed volleyball match, we had 20 odd people in our group. None of us was particularly known for his or her volleyball prowess. The next thing we know is that in the morning, posted around the town of Gurzuf are posters in Russian "international volleyball match, U.S.A. versus the USSR at 3pm." It was to take place in a little outdoor court with seats – not quite a stadium.

Out comes this Soviet team of gym teachers all in their twenties, a little older than us, and obviously they are well-trained and they killed us like fifteen to one. They had a good time, we were slaughtered. In retaliation, we insisted on playing them in ping pong the next day and we won the ping pong matches. That was fun.

The camp was rather loosely organized. The camp organizers didn't bother with us much. We went on an overnight hike, but everyone loved the beach. The beach was a rocky beach sort of like at the city of Cannes in France. I'm sitting on the beach with some of my American friends and some Russians one day taking in the sun and along comes a very tall Russian young man. He looked about – I was then twenty- four – he looked about twenty-eight or twenty-nine. He comes up to me and he leans over. And speaks in English and says to me in good English, "Hello, are you Jewish?" And I said, "yes, I am." That seemed to reassure him. He shook my hand and introduced himself. Unfortunately I do not remember his name. He explains that he is a professor at Moscow University and his specialty was cancer research of the eye. And he has specialized in this particular specialty for some time. His father was also a noted scientist who had been arrested by Stalin and was put into prison and was one of those in this so-called "doctors plot" against Stalin, who had been freed at the time of Stalin's death. He would have probably been executed if Stalin had lived. Stalin in his last years had become very anti- Semitic. The young man explained that his specialty was one that very few scientists in the world were involved in.

He told me that there was one professor at Columbia University in New York who also had written on the subject. He did not think that this American professor knew anything about the research that he had done on this subject. But that because of Soviet restrictions, if he had sent this professor a letter through the open mail with a reference to his articles or translations of his article out of the blue, he could get in trouble because the Soviet censors would spot it and he might be penalized.

But if the American professor were to read what he had written in a Soviet journal and to send him a note and comment on his article, then he would be permitted to answer this professor and then they could get into a dialogue. That would be permitted.

In other words, that would be permitted under the loosened exchanges going on in 1959. This young professor talked to me at great length and we agreed to meet at night.

Gurzuf was an interesting town. Besides the world youth conference going on, there were lots of Russians that just came down to this small town, rented rooms in people's houses, and just had a good time relaxing in the sun. This professor was one of those. And he took me around to little restaurants and places and we met some Russians.

We had a good time. And at the end of a few days of this, as I was about to leave, he gave me a letter to this Columbia professor written in English. He asked me if I could smuggle this letter out and deliver it to the Columbia professor. I did. I unfortunately do not remember his name or the Columbia professor's name.

I probably should have followed up on it, but I never did.

When I got back to the United States, I went to the Columbia professor's office and I delivered the letter. The Columbia professor took the letter. I hope the two got in touch with each other. That's the end of that story.

When I got back to the States, ironically, Khrushchev was invited by Eisenhower to come to the United States for a visit. In addition to selling the *Star* on this three-part series about Soviet teenagers, I came down to Washington and helped cover the arrival of Khrushchev by reporting on the Soviet journalists who came with him to Washington. It wasn't much of a story. I just wrote about them and then I went back to Harvard for my second year.

While at Harvard, I became engaged to a graduate student in Romance Languges, Jacqueline Tabachnick, but after I came down with mononucleosis, she broke off the engagement, not because I was sick, but because she did not want to move to Washington, where the Star had rehired me. By this time, the *Star* was interested in using me more and I gradually worked my way into becoming its chief diplomatic correspondent.

The Star at that time had a coterie of experienced Washington reporters who knew their "beats" well. There was William "Bill" Hines, who covered science and in particular, in those years, the space program, Cecil Holland, who covered the Senate, Garnett "Jack" Horner, a veteran White House correspondent, Richard Fryklund, the Pentagon correspondent, who was a World War II Air Force veteran, J.A, O'Leary, a veteran reporter who had covered Capitol Hill for years, and his son, Jerry O'Leary, a former Marine, who covered Latin America.

Earl Voss was the State Department reporter, whom I eventually replaced. There were a few but important women reporters, Miriam Ottenberg, an investigative reporter, and Mary Lou Werner, a Virginia correspondent, both of whom won Pulitzer Prizes. David Broder, who later became a prominent political analyst for The Post, started at The Sar. And Mary McGrory, a Bostonian, whose beautiful writing captivated Washington, launched her career at The Star and also won a Pulitzer, as did Haynes Johnson, a political reporer, with whom I co-authored a biography of J. William Fulbright called "The Dissenter."

CHAPTER 3

Return to Washington

I returned to Washington, D.C. in June of 1960 after completing my two years as a graduate student at Harvard. By then, I had an MA graduate degree, I had recovered from a bout of mononucleosis, and I had of course completed my first trip to the Soviet Union as a student and had published my experiences in the *Evening Star* in the "teen" section. The *Star* was interested in having me back.

This time, instead of moving into another boarding house, I moved in with my close friend, Mike Sweedler, who was then attending George Washington University Law School at night while working during the day for the Patent Office. Our apartment was in Arlington, Va. What was most shocking about my return to Washington was to see that The Star had moved from the historic headquarters on Pennsylvania Ave, to a new, industrial type building in Southeast Washington, to make it easier for delivery trucks.

One of my first articles for the *Star* in my new job was headlined "Red Diplomats Live Well but Chafe Under Restrictions." And the lead was:

> For 332 Russians attached to the Soviet Embassy in Washington, life may be extremely plush but it is not necessarily popular. Luxury apartments, expensive cars, parties – all the frills of embassy existence – go over pretty well with the Russians. Other factors, ranging from travel restrictions to Washington's lack of theaters, often irk them

In the same type of article, I was asked to do one about Russian tourists, who were in Washington since I had been a similar tourist in Moscow. I did a piece saying, "Red Tourists See City but on Rigid Schedule." And my lead was:

> As the big bus headed up sixteenth street northwest toward Silver Spring, one of the Russians inside called out in disgust to the guide, "Why do we have to go into the country?" And then under his breath, "I'd rather go to the National Gallery." The Soviet Intourist guide consulted the American hosts on the bus and then shot back the answer loud enough for all to hear, "Comrades, we are going somewhere not

usually seen by our tourists. It has been arranged especially for us. We are going to see the new areas where many Americans now live."

"Ah" another Russian added, "Like the new area of Moscow." This is the way that the most recent of approximately two hundred Soviet tourists who have seen Washington this year gain their impressions of American life. Another two hundred are expected before the end of the year. And undoubtedly as tourists, several will also prefer the National Gallery to a shopping center. Yet as Soviet tourists, they will have to abide by the subtle propaganda war that the two sides wage to show each other how well the other half lives.

The paper didn't quite know what to do with me for the first few months. On the weekends, I was allowed, even encouraged, to do "think" pieces for the Sunday review section. I did an article on Soviet law after the U.S. pilot Francis Gary Powers had been shot down flying a U-2 plane over Sverdlovsk and went on trial on August 17 for espionage. I explained there was a three-court judge. Powers had been charged with espionage, etc. My lead was:

When U-2 Pilot Francis Powers goes on trial on August 17 in Moscow for espionage, legal experts throughout the world will be getting a firsthand look at the operations of the new Soviet criminal code. First adopted in December of 1958, the Soviet criminal code was recorded at the time by many legal commentators as a step toward the creation of an independent legal system.

I have to explain that I had taken a course in Soviet law at Harvard Law School during my two-year stint getting a master's degree in Soviet studies.

I had a rather humorous experience of covering the visit of Patrice Lumumba to Washington. Patrice Lumumba was the first Prime Minister of the independent Congo Republic. And Joseph Kasavubu, a fellow nationalist, but not a member of Lumumba's party, became president. It was one of the first African states to become independent. Before that time it had been a Belgian property and it had gotten its independence suddenly on June 30. But Belgian troops remained in the country and more were sent in to restore order after there were mutinies.

Soon, with the encouragement of the Belgians, Moise Tshombe, a Congolese soldier, declared the independence of the rich copper region of Katanga, which produced one half of Congo's exports.

At this crucial time, we now know that Washington feared that Lumumba was showing symptoms of becoming another Castro. But they welcomed a visit by him to the United States. Lumumba made a trip to New York and Washington in July looking for support from the international community to expel the Belgians. There was great apprehension at that time in Washington about how stable Lumumba's government would be and whether he was too pro-Soviet.

I was asked to cover Lumumba's visit without much information on the behind-the-scenes concerns. What made this story amusing to me was that Lumumba was given a tour of Washington and it started at the Lincoln Memorial in Washington. And then he visited, among other places, Mount Vernon – where George Washington had lived. And he was told that George Washington fought the English colonialists. Lumumba smiled and was intrigued to know that Mr. Washington had such a comfortable home. He asked in French, "What was the attitude of the English toward him?" He was told, they treated him with respect. With a smile, the Prime Minister said, according to my article, "Modern day colonists are not as gallant."

Interestingly, Eisenhower did not meet with Lumumba. He did meet with Secretary of State Christian Herter and Herter's deputy, C. Douglas Dillon. He came away with no promises of U.S. assistance. The Congo situation went back and forth all summer and fall, with Lumumba eventually being arrested and executed by forces loyal to Joseph Mobutu in Katanga, even though Khrushchev himself had expended much energy on his behalf. When Khrushchev returned home from the United Nations that fall he brokered no questioning about Soviet policy toward Lumumba and the Congo. "The Congo policy is to our advantage," he said. "It discredits the imperialists and discredits the U.N."

I continued to do a variety of stories for the city desk and commentaries for the Sunday review section. I did a piece in September giving short biographies of the six Communist bloc leaders who would be coming to the United Nations General Assembly to back up Nikita Khrushchev, who was also coming to the U.N. General Assembly to speak, following up on his trip to the United States in 1959.

There was a highly publicized meeting at the U.N. that fall of the Communist bloc. The leaders of Bulgaria, Poland, Czechoslovakia, Hungary, Romania, and Albania were all coming to speak to back up Khrushchev. I wasn't able yet to actually cover what went on. I was just providing background. So after Khrushchev had his famous scene at the U.N. where he banged his shoe, I did a background piece that said "Khrushchev Antics and Tradition, Set by Lenin."

Khrushchev's desk-pounding shoe-waving behavior at the United Nations was not original or irrational. But rather an up-to-date version of tactics first set forth over forty years ago by the founder of the Soviet Union. When he saw that the Communist side could not control the actions of the General Assembly, Mr. Khrushchev, experts believe, looked to the past to find some measure of dealing with what parliamentarians would consider a defeat. Whether he planned it that way or not, Mr. Khrushchev was the first Soviet leader since Lenin who took part in an assembly in which the Communist position could be and was assailed by "bourgeois" critics.

Stalin was rarely seen in public and never attended the United Nations. Thus he never had to face a hostile majority as both Lenin and now Khrushchev did. Despite his apparent lack of erudition, Khrushchev has proven himself to be well-versed in party dogma and tradition. Experts have no doubt but that he was familiar with the way that Lenin faced similar problems.

Of course, in the United States, the summer and fall of 1960, were focused on the presidential election between Vice President Richard M. Nixon and the youthful Senator

John F. Kennedy. Jack Kennedy of course won the election and there was a certain feeling of enthusiasm among young people including me at that time in Washington, D.C. The *Star* asked me and Haynes Johnson to help cover events leading up to the inauguration. I did my share of stories. I did such pieces as "Five Thousand Inaugural Visitors to Sleep in Pullman Cars." I did one on, TV disputes:

"A behind the scenes squabble between the inaugural committee and the major television networks apparently has been settled. NBC, CBS, and ABC had refused a request by the inaugural committee to contribute to the cost of stands being constructed along Pennsylvania Avenue for television, movie, and still camera coverage of the inaugural parade. The committee had asked the networks to split the cost, which in 1957 rang up to forty- thousand dollars. But the television companies refused stating that neither the press nor photographers were required to pay similar costs. As a compromise move, however, the network officials said yesterday the networks will probably make contributions to the general Guarantee Fund (GF) together with other large corporations and this way the networks will meet the request of the committee that they share some of the cost of the inauguration but did not have to yield on the important question as to whether or not television in the case of the inauguration is a news medium."

I interviewed workmen building the stands. I did a story on the inaugural concert having a more serious tone.

"Kennedy's choice of program elates members of the [Washington] National Symphony. President elect Kennedy has selected a program of serious music for this years' inaugural concert. The program is divided into two parts and features an original work done by the Pulitzer Prize winning John LaMontaine, which will be presented by the National Symphony under the direction of Howard Mitchell on the evening of January 19th in Constitution Hall. Symphony officials pointed out today that the program chosen by Kennedy is in sharp contrast to the pop concert favored by President Eisenhower in 1957."

I had a piece:

"23,000 standees will be allowed on plazas to see Kennedy take the oath."

The *Star* sent me up to Harvard to do some background on Kennedy's time there as a student. There was great interest in what kind of a Harvard student Kennedy was. So I spent three days up at Harvard doing some research and I did several pieces about his time in Cambridge. I did one long piece on him. It was called:

Kennedy as a Student.

Cambridge, MA. Jan 20. It is the irony of John F. Kennedy's life that this man who has been so identified with Harvard never wanted to go there in the first place. Instead, fresh out of Choate, 18-year old Jack entered Princeton with his two best friends in the fall of 1935 only to withdraw at Christmas time with a bad case of hepatitis. After recuperating from his illness, he decided in September 1936 to enter Harvard as a freshman and thus keep his family's Harvard ties, alive. His father was a member of the class of 1912, and his brother Joe was entering his junior year that fall, a star football player, a leading campus politician, and above average student. Weighing only 163 pounds, and standing six foot one inch, Jack gave a very frail wiry appearance. Despite his physique, he went out for the freshman football team as soon as he had registered as a student."

The article pointed out, he did play football at Choate. It then says:

"He was an end for the freshman team. And his roommate Torbert MacDonald later captain of the varsity and still later Congressman from Massachusetts recalls that Kennedy was an excellent team player. The review of his freshman season which resulted in a 0-4-1 record had this to say of Kennedy: "the most adept pass catcher was John Kennedy, but his lack of weight was a drawback." MacDonald was also quoted as saying, "Jack was interested in dating and in making his mark on the campus." Apparently Jack was convinced his mark on the campus would best be made through extracurricular activities. He won a spot on the swimming team where he was one of the squad's backstrokers, earning himself a set of numerals. He ran for freshman class president, one of thirty-five candidates for the office, but he finished well back in the race. Jack apparently was not worried about grades his freshman year, pulling in all C's except for a B in elementary economics. At the end of their freshman year, Torbert and Jack decided on the most popular house at the time, Winthrop. Winthrop then was best known for its large number of athletes.

In addition to that, Jack was likely to pick Winthrop since his brother Joe was entering his senior year there… Jack didn't make the varsity football team because of a bad back. He again tried swimming but failed to make the varsity team…Varsity Coach Herald Ulen remembers him as a "fine kid, frail, and not too strong, but always giving it everything he had." He ran for student council his sophomore year, but once again failed to muster enough votes to win a place. His brother, by contrast, won the class day election– one of the highest honors for a senior. After a brief tryout period, Jack was named to the business board of the Crimson in May, but this was not one of his major interests and apparently he never contributed much time or effort to the same paper for which Franklin Roosevelt, class of 1904, worked so hard as President. His grades at the end of the year were worse than freshman year, all C's and one D

Just a passing average. If it weren't for the fact that in June he and a friend Reid won the intercollegiate sailing trophy, it would have been a very frustrating year indeed for young Kennedy. As junior year began in the fall of 1938, Jack took a course called "Government" given by Professor Arthur Holcombe. This course had a profound effect.

It was apparently the one course that really interested him and spurred him on to a more serious effort in his remaining time at Harvard.

Holcombe assigned each student to a Congressman and Holcombe said he assigned Kennedy to a New York Republican Congressman named Bertrand Snell who represented conservative up-state interests. "I picked him because I wanted to see what a Massachusetts Democrat would do with such a man," Holcombe said. In later life Kennedy said, "I have known many great teachers at Harvard, many who excelled in showing the enchantment of thought to young men who in this springtime of youth were more enchanted with life itself. But the teacher known to generations of Harvard students who stands out in my memory and personal affection is Arthur Holcombe. Under his direction, I discovered for the first time, the distractions of the Congressional record."

Kennedy took time off in his junior year and went overseas to Europe. This was just as war was close to breaking out. As a result of that, he wrote a senior thesis which he called "Appeasement at Munich: The Inevitable Result of the Slowness of Conversion of the British Democracy from a Disarmament t o a Rearmament Policy." His thesis was later published as a book *Why England Slept* and this was the first of three books under his name and Kennedy then became a serious student and changed his whole life.

I wrote a couple of other pieces in that series for the *Star*. One was about how JFK was deeply affected by his older brother Joe's death. Joe was killed in World War II in an airplane crash. Jack Kennedy had commanded a PT boat in the Pacific. On the day of the Inaugural Parade there was a very heavy snowfall in Washington, and the government called out U.S. troops with flamethrowers to help clear the parade route.

I slept the night before in the Star's newsroom, so I could get up early and interview West Point cadets who had come in by train to attend the Inaugural. Then I headed out to start interviewing people along the parade route, along with Haynes.

I did a post-parade analysis; and I interviewed the parade director.

Then I was asked to cover the FTC – Federal Trade Commission and census bureau, while continuing to do articles about the Soviet Union.

I was sent out to Kansas in March of 1961because Congress had passed an amendment to allow the District of Columbia the right to vote in presidential elections and the amendment needed to be ratified to give District residents the right to vote for president in 1964. It turned out we were waiting for the last state to ratify, Kansas was waiting for Ohio to vote. Finally, the Kansans moved fast and they at last voted after I informed the leader of the Kansas assembly that Ohio was about to vote. That was a big victory for Kansas. They got the vote and I got to visit Topeka Kansas for the first and last time in my life.

Eventually the *Star* decided they wanted me to work on its Sunday Review section, which was a kind of poor man's version of the *New York Times* Sunday "Week in Review" section. It was put out every Sunday as the *New York Times'* was. But unlike the *New York Times* which at that time had a staff of several people who actually wrote pieces on different subjects reviewing the news of the week and having staff writers writing interpretive pieces, the *Star*'s Week in Review section was written essentially by two people, me and a colleague named L. Edgar Prina. It was edited by Ed Tribble.

That marked a big change in my existence at the *Star/*. The first piece I did was:

> President Kennedy made final preparations for his trip to Europe this week. He will meet President de Gaulle in Paris on Wednesday, Thursday and Friday, and then travel to Vienna for weekend

talks with Soviet Premier Khrushchev. He will fly to London to confer with Prime Minister Macmillan before returning here.

We now know of course that the talks with Khrushchev were very tough.

Troubling the President is Russian intransigence at the Geneva talks on banning nuclear testing…the Soviet Union is echoing the veto doctrine that Mr. Khrushchev first enunciated at the U.N. last fall. The doctrine states that the Communist Bloc, Western Powers, and the neutral countries should be represented on any international control group. Any decision of the group would have to be unanimous. Thus the nuclear test ban talks have bogged down because Soviet negotiators demand a veto on any control machinery that might be set up. The United States prefers a neutral tsar to administer the machinery.

At that time, of course, Khrushchev considered Kennedy as an inexperienced president who had blundered into the Bay of Pigs fiasco in his first months in office, and we were to find out later that their initial meeting had jolted Kennedy.

CHAPTER 4

Reviewing the World

My introduction to writing on foreign affairs on a regular basis began in June, 1961 when I became a writer for the Star's Sunday Week in Review section. By a happy coincidence, this occurred when there was a developing crisis over Berlin, and I did not have to search for material to write about.

Back then, of course, Jack Kennedy had only been in office for a few months. In those first few months in office, there had been the crisis over the failed Bay of Pigs invasion where he inherited a situation in which some 1700 Cubans who had emigrated to the United States, had been trained by the CIA under the Eisenhower administration and had been launched in April to invade Cuba and were quickly captured and defeated, many of them killed, by the Castro forces.

The CIA plans were a fiasco. It was a poorly planned operation. Many of Kennedy's advisors lamented that they did not argue strongly with him not to do it. Secretary of State Dean Rusk blamed himself for not speaking out against it, as did Secretary of Defense Robert S. McNamara in their memoirs.

The Bay of Pigs pictured Kennedy as a neophyte on foreign affairs. And this may have encouraged Nikita Khrushchev to think that the new president, who was very young, only in his forties, was also inexperienced in foreign affairs. In any event, a summit meeting was planned in early June in Vienna to discuss a wide range of issues and Kennedy had agreed to this.

My first article in the Sunday review started as follows:

> President Kennedy made final preparations for his trip to Europe this week. He will meet President de Gaulle in Paris on Wednesday, Thursday and Friday, and then travel to Vienna for weekend talks with Soviet Premier Khrushchev. The President will fly to London to confer with Prime Minister Macmillan before returning to Washington.

I then discussed the various issues and I began with an anecdote saying:

> John F. Kennedy likes to tell about the time Samuel Adams confronted the British colonial governor after the Boston Massacre and warn him of the coming American Revolution. Adams later wrote in his diary, "It was then that I fancied that I saw his knees tremble." There is no reason to suppose Nikita S. Khrushchev's knees will tremble after his confrontation with the President next weekend, but the Communist leader should at least come away from the informal Vienna talks with no doubts about America's intentions. He should know in the President's words, "our patience at the bargaining table is nearly inexhaustible, though our credulity is limited — that our hopes for peace are unfailing, while our determination to protect our security is resolute."

In any event, after that meeting, we later found out that the talks were very rough, indeed. I later wrote in the *Star*:

> President Kennedy reported on his Vienna trip to the Nation and said it was, "as somber as it was immensely useful." No specific improvement was

seen, however, in the Berlin situation or in the Geneva talks.

The Geneva talks were on arms control where Kennedy was very interested in getting some cutback in nuclear weapons.

Premier Khrushchev has not spoken yet but the President reported without delay to the nation in a broadcast, a first of its kind, on what had happened. He spoke in a somber mood about two days of "sober, intensive conversation." The Berlin situation grew even darker with the Soviet Union protesting against the West German parliamentary meetings scheduled for Berlin.

How rough were the talks? Secretary of State Dean Rusk, who accompanied Kennedy to the talks with Khrushchev gave this blow by blow account: "At one point Khrushchev said to Kennedy, ' 'We are going to negotiate a new agreement with East Germany, and the access routes to Berlin will be under their control.' If there is any effort by the West to interfere, there will be war." Rusk added:

> "Diplomats almost never use the word 'war'; they
> always talk about 'gravest possible consequences'
> or something like that. But Kennedy went right

back at him, looked him in the eye, and said,
'Then there will be war, Mr. Chairman. It's going
to be a very cold winter.'"

"Clearly at he Vienna summit, held only two months
after the Bay of Pigs fiasco, Khrushchev set out to
intimidate this new, young president of the United States.
The experience sobered and shook Kennedy. He stood
head to head with Khrushchev in their verbal duel, but
for the first time he felt the full weight of Soviet pressure
and ideology. It was a brutal moment, and Kennedy was
clearly startled that Khrushchev would try to roll over an
American president. What bothered Kennedy even more
than the Berlin issue itself was that Khrushchev would
even make such an attempt to intimidate him."

The book, "Khrushchev's Cold War. The Inside Story
of an American Adversary" which is based on previously
secret documents from the Khrushchev period poses the
question: "how dangerous the Cold War really was."

"How close did we ever come to nuclear war? The
Central Committee documents of Nikita Khrushchev
reveal that starting with the Presidium meeting on May
26, 1961 [leading up to the Vienna summit with Kennedy]
the world moved closer to nuclear war than at any time
since the Soviets tested their first atomic bomb in August

1949. Even if Khrushchev's war talk was the product of a frustrated man, rather than a sign of a mental breakdown, the Soviet leader on that day deliberately set in motion the machine of war."

But on the eve of the Vienna summit, Walter Ulbricht, the East German leader, had told Khrushchev that his immediate objective was to close the border between the two Berlins through which so many East Germans were fleeing. "This was more important to the East Germans than a peace treaty," he was told.

On July 25, Kennedy gave a long-awaited speech to the American people in which he said: "I hear it said that West Berlin is militarily untenable. And so was Bastogne. And so, in fact was Stalingrad. Any dangerous spot is tenable if men—brave men—will make it so."

Basically, as the weeks went on that summer, Khrushchev made clear that he was threatening to sign a peace treaty with East Germany by himself by the end of 1961- that would freeze the western powers out of Berlin if the West doesn't sign separate peace treaties with East Germany and agree to West Berlin being an open city.

Secretary Rusk, a calm man by nature, gave the first official U.S. reaction. "We refuse to over-dramatize the

Berlin crisis. Mr. Khrushchev's 'military tone' was a 'keen disappointment' to those who wanted peace." He made it clear, however, that the West knew its rights in Berlin and "it is obvious that the U.S. cannot accept any validity to any claim to extinguish its position in Berlin by unilateral action."

The *Star*'s headline over my week in review article was "Berlin "Tension and Tactics"" the next week and the following week: "The Elements of a World Crisis." I must add that some of my colleagues who had joined the Army Reserves for 6 months in lieu of the draft like me, were called up for active duty. They were not sent to Europe for military action. They were just called because Kennedy wanted to mobilize some troops. I had a friend of mine named Adam Clymer and he was called up to work in a military post office in Maryland.

He wasted several months until he was discharged. In any event, the Berlin crisis went on and on the entire summer and finally it reached a crescendo in August when, without any warning, on August 13th the East Germans began putting up a wall in Berlin on orders from Moscow. This became known as The Berlin Wall, which stayed up until it was finally taken down in 1989. It came as a great shock to everyone in the West. A quote from Dean Rusk's memoirs, from his book *As I Saw It*:

I was at a baseball game on August 13th when I was informed the East Germans had begun to build a barricade and to spring barbed wire between East and West Berlin, the first step in what eventually became the Berlin Wall. This move caught us by surprise, but we soon determined that the East Germans aimed the Berlin wall at their own people, not the people of West Berlin. They were not trying to keep anyone out, but rather to keep their own people in. It was a startling demonstration of the nature of Communist society. We quickly decided that the wall was not an issue of war and peace between East and West. There was no way we would destroy the human race over it. By and large even though we thought their actions despicable, what Eastern Europeans did to their own people was not an issue of war between east and west.

So it was a strange summer! This wall going up – as long as the west could still get to West Berlin, it made it harder to get into East Berlin but it wasn't impossible. Westerners could still go in and out of East Berlin by showing your ID.

In fact I was invited two years later by the West German government to make a trip to Berlin to see the

Wall. I made a trip into East Berlin through the wall and out again. It was my first time there.

It was a strange time, a very strange time. All this attention on Berlin. The crisis began to weaken, however, and by September and October, the UN General Assembly was called into session and we had the usual speeches.

Kennedy himself spoke to the UN General Assembly. The lead of my story dated October 1st 1961:

> The Berlin crisis was the principal subject of discussion in and outside the General Assembly last week. President Kennedy and Foreign Minister Gromyko both addressed the General Assembly and Mr. Gromyko continued exploratory talks with Secretary of State Rusk and British Foreign Minister Lord Home. The Berlin crisis for four months has swung like a pendulum from darkness to light, from fear to confidence, and from bellicose threats to peaceful assurances. Last week it appeared to slow down held up by a brighter promise of a peaceful settlement. Whether it will remain in place or swing toward war ultimately will depend on the skill of the diplomats. But developments in New York indicated that a promising start had been

made. Undoubtedly a great deal of the optimism can be attributed to the re-convening of the General Assembly where "peace," "negotiation," and "settlement," are on everyone's lips. The optimism however had some substantive roots. These included a speech by President Kennedy on Monday in which he told the General Assembly that the West was willing to negotiate a treaty that would take into account the "interests of others" provided the freedom of West Berlin was protected.

An address the next day by Foreign Minister Gromyko, in which he hinted the Soviet Union might ask the United Nations, to take a hand in resolving the crisis and in which he again "guaranteed the freedom of West Berlin in return for Western cooperation in signing a peace treaty with East Germany."

In any event, there was a Soviet Communist Party Congress in Moscow, the 22nd in fact, and at that Congress Mr. Khrushchev addressed the group and apparently never mentioned any ultimatum on Berlin and that led observers to believe that the crisis was about over because as I wrote:

Premier Khrushchev announced last week that his government would not insist on a German peace treaty being signed by December 31st. World attention last week was focused on Moscow where top Communist officials gathered for the 22nd party conference. The main attraction was Tuesday's 6½ hour oration by the apparently inexhaustible Nikita S. Khrushchev. His day- long polemic covered the whole spectrum of international affairs. And it listed in detail all the problems facing the Communist movement as a whole. While casting a curious eye at the internal Red intrigues, Western officials paid particular attention to what Mr. Khrushchev had to say about Berlin, the most explosive issue presently dividing East and West. They felt that if Moscow were planning to reduce its demands, or to ease tension, the party congress would be the appropriate place to announce it. In his speech, Mr. Khrushchev, delivered a pro-forma attack on the West, blaming it for "creating a dangerous situation in the center of Europe, threatening to use arms in reply to our proposal to eliminate the remnants of World War II."

Mr. Khrushchev did not mention, however, that the whole crisis stems from the Soviet Union's desire to change the status quo in Germany. After his opening remarks, Mr. Khrushchev took the more conciliatory position and said that American and British leaders were "showing a certain amount of understanding of the situation and are inclined to seek a solution to the Germany problem and the question of West Berlin on a mutually acceptable basis."

Then he claimed the role of peace-maker. Mr. Khrushchev said that the Soviet Union had no intention of issuing an ultimatum about the peace treaty. In June he had said such a treaty had to be signed by the end of the year. "If the Western powers show readiness to settle the German problem then the question of the terms of signing a German peace treaty will not be of such importance," he said. "We shall then not insist that the peace treaty be signed without fail by December 31, 1961."

Western leaders had been told privately by Mr. Gromyko that the ultimatum would be dropped and were not surprised by the public announcement.

So by the end of October, the Berlin situation was no longer a real crisis and Western diplomats now had other crises on their hands and were looking toward what would then become their obsessions that would be Vietnam and the Middle East. And later in 1962 they would be stunned by Cuba.

CHAPTER 5

The Cuba Crisis

As 1962 began, President Kennedy was generally optimistic about the world's trouble spots. In his State of the Union address, he said that regarding the "brave city of Berlin," the United States is "prepared to talk when appropriate and to fight if necessary." But he hesitated to predict whether or not negotiations would be fruitful.

Kennedy said, "A resolution can be found and with it an improvement in our relations with the Soviet Union. If only the leaders in the Kremlin will recognize the basic rights and interests involved."

The other troubled areas he mentioned were in Southeast Asia where he reaffirmed the administration's desire for a neutral and independent Laos, where there was a cease-fire in effect but it was unstable. It was uncertain whether the Hanoi regime in neighboring North Vietnam would try to take over Laos, as it would do eventually.

In Latin America, where the fledgling U.S.-sponsored Alliance for Progress was just beginning to take off. And Cuba remained a problem area.

Looking at the world from the Kremlin's point of view, the world was unsettling to Khrushchev because he continued to look for ways to force Kennedy on the defensive throughout the year. In fact we now know that he sent word to his ambassador in Laos to inform the Pathet Lao that he no longer wanted to abide by the neutrality agreement that had been worked out the year before and to throw his support with the Pathet Lao, which was backed by North Vietnam. He encouraged the Pathet Lao to take over the capital of Laos, Vientiane, and to aid the Hanoi regime in its march southward, eventually to move into South Vietnam.

A note of caution marked the President's generally optimistic report on the major trouble spots. This caution was reflected before by him in comments on our responsibilities in these areas: Berlin: the situation in the "brave city of Berlin" has been virtually unchanged since Mr. Khrushchev's original June 4th demands, Mr. Kennedy said. The United

States, he said, is "prepared to talk when appropriate and to fight if necessary." The President hesitated to predict whether or not negotiations would be fruitful.

Mr. Kennedy said, "A resolution can be found and with it an improvement in our relations with the Soviet Union. If only the leaders in the Kremlin will recognize the basic rights and interests involved."

The other crisis areas he mentioned were in Southeast Asia, where he reaffirmed the administration's desire for a neutral and independent Laos, where there was a cease-fire in effect but it was unstable. It was unsettled whether the Hanoi regime would try to take over in Laos. As it would eventually. In Latin America, where the fledgling U.S-sponsored Alliance for Progress was just beginning to take off. Cuba remained a problem area.

Looked at from the Kremlin's point of view, the world was unsettling to Khrushchev because he kept looking for ways to force Kennedy on the defensive throughout the year. He encouraged the Pathet Lao to take over in the capital of Laos, Vientiane, and to aid the Hanoi regime in its march southward, eventually to move into South Vietnam. That move would lead eventually to, of course, what would become in later years, the battle for pre-eminence in Vietnam and the Vietnam War. Of course this would be thrust on Presidents Johnson and Nixon.

The year 1962 would be marked, however, by a very surprising development, which caught the Kennedy Administration by surprise toward the end of the year. In the summer of 1962, the Politburo decided with the enthusiastic urging of Khrushchev, to arm the Castro regime with nuclear weapons and anti-aircraft missiles, secretly.

The Soviet Union signed a defense treaty with the Castro regime secretly and began shipping in missiles and Soviet troops over a period of several weeks and months.

This was a long distance by boat. It was done really to put the Kennedy Administration on the defensive. All of this took place against a background of an American election for Congress that was to take place in November, 1962. It oddly coincided with many Congressmen reporting that Cuba's defenses were being built up by the Russians and this was being denied by the administration.

It was a strange situation where it was unclear whether the Congressmen knew more about what was going on than the administration for a while. You had a very odd situation. For instance, on October 14, 1962, the *Washington Star* had a front page story that said:

"Kennedy wraps critics of his Cuba policy."

President Kennedy denounced "self-appointed generals and admirals who want to send someone else's sons to war" in a blast at Republican critics of his policy on Cuba today. His fire was aimed particularly, aides said, at Indiana Republican Senator Capehart's calls during his reelection campaign for military action against Fidel Castro's communist regime in Cuba. Mr. Kennedy also asserted that America is stronger than ever now and better equipped to prevent a war and better equipped to win the peace in his speech to a cheering throng of more than fifteen thousand at an Indianapolis airport Democratic rally on his way here for another campaign speech tonight. Birch Evans Bayh Jr., a 36-year old attorney, fighting Senator Capehart for his Senate seat told his Indianapolis crowd just before he introduced the President, "We won't permit Mr. Capehart to blunder us into nuclear war in Cuba or anywhere else." With obvious reference to Cuba and such critics of his Cuban policy as Senator Capehart, the President urged voters to repudiate confused and intemperate talk that strengthened the claims of our adversaries. In discussing Cuba Mr. Kennedy said, "There is no time for talk which strengthens the claims of our adversaries. This is no time for confused and intemperate remarks on the part of those who have neither the facts nor the responsibility to determine this nation's course. This is a time for men to talk softly and carry a big stick. And that is the kind of man you have in Birch Bayh."

As it turns out, of course, the Russians were sending armaments and nuclear weapons to Cuba at this very moment. But it was not yet noticed by the Kennedy Administration. This would be very embarrassing. In my week in review peace on October 14th my lead article on the foreign policy section was,

"Cuban policy critics forcing the issue."

High administration officials indicated last week that despite American anger over Cuba, Berlin remains this country's major international concern. They warn that Soviet miscalculation in Berlin could lead to a nuclear war. Premier Khrushchev once described West Berlin as a "painful bone in his throat," thus his determination to force the allies out. Many Americans, including some members of Congress, feel the same way about Cuba. Just 90 miles from Florida, Cuba infuriates American pride. Thousands of Russian technicians, the construction of anti-aircraft rockets, and the belligerent tone of Cuban statements, have all tended to infuriate many Americans. The Kennedy Administration has said many times that Cuba poses no threat to the United States. Indeed, United States Navy planes patrol Cuban waters daily keeping a close watch on military developments in the island. So far, all installations there are reported to be defensive. Despite this reassurance, the cry continues to "do something about Cuba." The American Legion on Friday called for an armed invasion of Cuba. With the election less than a month away, politicians mostly on the Republican side have seized on Cuba as an emotional, political issue.

This became quite an issue because, as the weeks continued, we now had the strange situation that in that next week U2 spy planes actually detected some ominous signs in Cuba. And on the *Star*'s front page on Sunday, October 21st, that is a week after Kennedy had blasted Senator Capehart for raising false claims about Cuba, Kennedy announces that he was ending a six-day political tour because he had a bad cold. The next day, October 21st, a Monday, the *Star*'s headline was an ominous two-line banner headline:

Kennedy will speak tonight, "matter of highest urgency." Troop ship action hints Cuba move.

I can still remember listening. I was then doing the Sunday column so I wasn't writing the daily story, waiting to hear what he had to say. But clearly we were in a time of high crisis. He then, of course, announced that they had found this very serious situation in Cuba. We now know that the Soviet Politburo, when they got word from Washington, from their embassy that this speech was going to be given, called everyone into session and waited to hear whether in fact Kennedy was going to invade Cuba and whether they had found out about the missiles and everything else that was being poured into Cuba. They were relieved to hear that the Americans were going to give Ambassador Dobrynin an advance copy of the text of the speech one hour before it was to be delivered at 7 pm Washington time.

What I wrote on the Cuban crisis after it became clear we had one:

"A time of grave crisis in the Cold War."

A speech by President Kennedy on Monday night ordering a quarantine against offensive weapons sent to Cuba set off a series of dramatic events which strained Cold War tensions virtually to the breaking point. It all happened so quickly that even the President's top aides were surprised. On Sunday, October 7, one of them,

McGeorge Bundy, a White House advisor on security matters was saying on a television interview, "There is no present likelihood that the Cuban people and Soviet Government would in combination attempt to install a major offensive capability."

The very next day, a military reconnaissance airplane over Cuba, changed this evaluation and started a round of events, which culminated a week later in one of the most dramatic moments in United States history.

About 10 p.m. Monday October 15th, Defense Secretary Robert McNamara, received a set of aerial photographs which partially substantiated refugee and Congressional reports of intense missile activity in Cuba. Later, Mr. McNamara said, "That was the first time that we had any reason to believe that there were offensive weapons in Cuba."

President Kennedy was shown the evidence at 9am on Tuesday, October 16th. Mr. McNamara said, these pictures were not "definitive" but raised a strong suspicion that there was more than we saw in that particular instance." Orders were given to intensify the aerial surveillance and hundreds of photo interpreters worked on thousands of feet of film 24-hours a day. That week, however, the Cuban situation received comparatively little publicity.

High level talks on Berlin dominated the news and most public opinion was convinced that if an international crisis developed, it would occur over the Berlin question and not over Cuba.

On Thursday, October 18th, Mr. Kennedy had concrete evidence of the Soviet buildup in his hands. That afternoon he also had a meeting scheduled with Soviet Foreign Minister Gromyko to discuss the Berlin crisis. Apparently Mr. Kennedy chose to test the sincerity of the Soviet government rather than confront Gromyko with his new information. The Russians have insisted in private and in public that their aid to Cuba has been only "defensive." Mr. Gromyko did not change this line and this angered Mr. Kennedy.

Mr. Kennedy later charged Mr. Gromyko with deliberate falsification and told the world that the United States cannot "tolerate deliberate deception and offensive threats on the part of any nation large or small." What were the offensive weapons that were discovered on Cuban soil? As Mr. Kennedy explained to the public, the photographic evidence revealed two distinct types of installations. In the first category were medium-range ballistic missiles (MRBMs) and the type identified in Cuba are known as mobile MRBMs with a range of about 1200 miles. They can be put in place within a few days. As Mr. Kennedy pointed out, these MRBMs can carry a nuclear warhead as far north as Washington.

The second category includes intermediate-range ballistic missiles (IRBMs) with a range of about 2300 miles. These missiles require fixed position launching pads and these, according to Mr. Kennedy, are not yet completed. Since these missiles can reach every area of the United States, a full arsenal of IRBMs in combination with MRBMs would give Cuba and the Soviet Union the power to destroy much of this country. In addition, the air photographs revealed Ilyushin 28 medium bomber planes with a range of about 700 miles.

These bombers are, however, sub-sonic and can be defended against. This new offensive nuclear strike capability discovered only during the week of October 15th was something the administration had not counted on publicly or privately.

Previously, Washington thought that talk of missiles was either erroneous exile information inspired perhaps by a desire to prod the United States into an invasion or Republican campaign propaganda. But learning that these weapons existed, the administration had to act.

Top military and foreign policy officials met throughout the weekend of October 20 – 21st. The unusual evening activity in the State Department and at the Pentagon led to speculation that something big was going on.

And so, this crisis developed, and it lasted for much of the week. Until finally, on October 28, a Sunday morning, an exchange of notes between Khrushchev and Kennedy led to the end of the crisis.

Bobby Kennedy, the President's brother, played a part. He met with Soviet Ambassador Dobrynin. In an attempt to save face for Kennedy and Khrushchev, Kennedy agreed to pull out some American missiles that had been installed in Turkey in exchange for the Soviets pulling out their missiles. The crisis ended on a Sunday morning. The Russians in a hurry to make it clear that the crisis was over – in fact broadcast in English over all their radio stations that the crisis had ended. It was quite a relief for everyone.

I can still remember that day. I was then living in Washington, D.C., of course, and I remember how people were extremely nervous about the situation. I called up a friend who lived in Georgetown in Washington and telling her at about 9 in the morning: "Roberta, pack a bag and get ready to leave in about fifteen minutes. I'll pick you up and we'll leave immediately." Georgetown on a Sunday morning is virtually deserted. I pulled up in my car and she got in and I drove her across Key bridge which separates Washington from Virginia. She was nervous as hell. She assumed that some war was about to break out. Little did she know that the crisis had just ended. When we crossed the bridge, I told her what had happened and she was angry with me. But then we celebrated with a big breakfast in Georgetown.

CHAPTER 6

Kennedy's Assassination

In retrospect, it is hard to remember the amount of fear generated by the Cuban missile crisis in the United States when the possibility of nuclear war on our own shores was seen as a distinct possibility. But in the end, both sides "blinked." Even though the public had assumed that the crisis had ended in early November, it really was not over until November 20. On that day, I wrote, Khrushchev informed Kennedy that he would withdraw his "last offensive weapons" from Cuba, the Il-28 twin-jet bombers, and Kennedy quickly followed with an order to end the naval blockade of Cuba.

Kennedy announced all this in his first meeting with the press in nearly two months just before Thanksgiving. This all came out apparently when Fidel Castro refused to allow any U.N. inspectors and Khrushchev sought to calm the situation. Khrushchev also sent Anastas Mikoyan to

Cuba to calm down Castro and Mikoyan stopped off in Washington on his way back to Moscow.

As the New Year began in 1963, there was a clear sense of confidence in Washington that there was an upswing in world developments. In his State of he Union address, Kennedy, a lifelong sailor, drew upon seafaring language to suggest what may lie ahead: "My friends, I close on a note of hope. We are not lulled by the momentary calm of the sea, or the somewhat clearer skies above. We know the turbulence that lies below, and the storms beyond the horizon this year. Now the winds of change appear to be blowing more strongly than ever, in the world of communism as well as our own.

"For 175 years we have sailed with these winds at our back, and with the tides of human freedom in our favor. We steer our ship with hope. as Thomas Jefferson said, 'leaving fear astern.'"

Kennedy sensed that change was afoot in Khrushchev's thinking. "A moment of pause is a not a promise of peace," he said. "Dangerous problems remain from Cuba to the South China Sea. The world's prognosis prescribes not a year's vacation, but a year of obligation and opportunity."

About the same time that Kennedy was giving his State of the Union speech, Khrushchev was in East Berlin for the East German Communist Party Congress. I used an unusual top for my analysis of that meeting. I wrote that "Wu Hsiu-chuan is a lowly member of the Chinese Communist Central Committee. Probably because of his lack of rank, he has had the pleasureless job of representing Red China at several recent East European party congresses—and of hearing his country attacked for its "dogmatic" policies. Undoubtedly, Wu was prepared for his latest mission to the East German party congress in East Berlin. But it is doubtful that Wu anticipated the reaction his rather routine address received."

"On Friday, Wu got up to speak his part. All week, European Communists from Nikita S. Khrushchev down had criticized the 'dogmatic' Albanians 'and those that support them'—meaning the Chinese. Now it was to be Peking's chance to criticize the Tito 'revisionists' and 'those that support them'—meaning the Soviet Union and every other Communist Party in Europe."

I wrote that "as soon as he started to speak, the 2500 delegates, mostly East Germans, began shouting, jeering, and even shoe stomping. Nobody could have heard what Wu was saying, but they all knew it was similar to what the Chinese press has been saying for the past few months." I wrote that "Mr. Khrushchev's speech was his most moderate yet."

He noted the vast number of American nuclear warheads—he guessed 40,000—and said that a nuclear war would destroy almost all the civilized world—including China and Russia. He repeated his ideas on the futility of a policy based on nuclear war. As usual, Mr. Khrushchev implied that the Chinese want a nuclear war and he doesn't.

This simplifies the Chinese position. Actually, the Chinese say one should not fear a nuclear war but should act in spite of the threat of one. They say they do not want one—and so far have avoided a showdown with the West."

About this time, the editors of The Star decided to use their house Soviet "expert," namely me, in different ways. Newbold Noyes, the editor, and I. William Hill, who was the Managing Editor, who were always looking for ways to be unique and to add a bit of foreign coverage to the news report, liked the idea that I was a daily subscriber to Pravda and Izvestia, and also the U.S. Government translations of the Russian broadcasts. They encouraged me to write features and commentaries, and I was taken off the Week-in-Review, and just as U.S-Soviet relations began to improve, so did my responsibilities.

Eventually, the Star sent me on two-month trips to Eastern Europe to report on the countries there, and promoted my stories with my picture and the kicker "He's Now in the Soviet Orbit."

In the spring of 1963, Khrushchev brought back with him from his vacation retreat in Pitsunda on the Black Sea two new convictions: first that the Berlin issue should no longer be a roadblock to serious U.S.-Soviet agreements and second, that if a comprehensive nuclear test ban would be impossible to achieve with the West, Moscow would accept a partial test ban that outlawed tests in the atmosphere, in space and underwater. Only underground testing would continue. At the same time as the Russians were thinking of new initiatives, Kennedy and his advisers were doing the same.

Theodore (Ted) Sorensen, Kennedy's speechwriter had been in touch with Norman Cousins, who had met with Khrushchev, and put together a speech for a Commencement Day address at American University in Washington on June 10. Kennedy was at his most eloquent in that speech.

"Some say it is useless to speak of world peace, or world law, or world disarmament—and that it will be useless unless the leaders of the Soviet Union adopt a more enlightened attitude. I hope they do. I believe we can help them do it. But I also believe that we must re-examine our own attitude—as individuals and as a nation—for our attitude is as essential as theirs."

In the midst of the speech, Kennedy announced: "I am taking this opportunity therefore, to announce two important decisions in this regard:

"First, Chairman Khrushchev, Prime Minister Macmillan and I have agreed that high-level discussions will shortly begin in Moscow looking toward early agreement on a comprehensive test-ban treaty. Our hopes must be tempered with the caution of history—but with our hopes go all mankind,

"Second: To make clear our good faith and solemn conviction on the matter, I now declare that the United States does not propose to conduct nuclear tests in the atmosphere so long as other states do not do so."

The Russians reprinted the Kennedy speech in their press and allowed the Voice of America to broadcast it—unjammed— in Russian, demonstrating their backing for the Kennedy speech.

Kennedy shortly thereafter went on a trip to Europe, from June 23 to July 2. He stopped in England for only one day in Sussex, at the prime minister's country home, rather than in London where a sex scandal had put Macmillan's government in jeopardy and it was felt might tarnish Kennedy. Kennedy spent four days each in West Germany and Ireland and two days in Italy.

The biggest crowds, of course, were in Berlin, where it was estimated that three-fifths of the divided city turned out to greet him on June 26, "clapping, waving, crying as if it were the second coming," Arthur Schlesinger, Jr. recounted. Kennedy gave his most heartfelt statements of support. After visiting the Berlin Wall, which "shocked and appalled" him, he spoke to a million people gathered in front of the city hall, "a sea of human faces," Sorensen remembers, "chanting 'Kenne-dy', 'Kenne-dy.'"

The crowd's vigorous response troubled Chancellor Adenauer who reportedly said to Rusk, "Does this mean Germany can one day have another Hitler?" It also troubled Kennedy who said to his military aide, General McHugh "If I told them to go tear down the Berlin Wall, they would do it."

"Two thousand years ago," Kennedy proclaimed, "the proudest boast was 'civis Romanus sum.' Today, in the world of freedom, the proudest boast is 'Ich bin ein Berliner'. There are many people in the world who really don't understand, or say they don't, what is the great issue between the free world and the Communist world. Let them come to Berlin. There are some who say that Communism is the wave of the future. Let them come to Berlin. And there are some who say in Europe and elsewhere we can work with the Communists. Let them come to Berlin. And there are even a few who say that it is true that Communism is an evil system but it permits us to make economic progress. Lass' sie nach Berlin kommen. Let them come to Berlin."

About a month later, on July 25, in Moscow, the chief negotiator of the United States, W. Averell Harriman, British Science Minister Lord Halisham and Soviet Foreign Minister Andrei Gromyko initialed the partial nuclear text ban treaty in Moscow, which was formally signed in Moscow on August 5 by Secretary of State Dean Rusk, Foreign Secretary Lord Home and Foreign Minister Gromyko.

Rusk took with him to Moscow a distinguished delegation including Adlai Stevenson, who was then the U.S. Ambassador to the United Nations, and J. William Fulbright, the Chairman of the Senate Foreign Relations Committee. Rusk, in his memoir, "As I Saw It" recalled that "Khrushchev was immensely pleased with the treaty. He threw a huge reception in the Kremlin, where we met among other Russians all the members of the Politburo and high officials of the Russian Orthodox Church,

"Amid the festivities, my wife, Virginia, and I visited Leningrad....The entire trip was especially poignant for me: the beauty of Leningrad, a private visit for Virginia and me with Khrushchev at his Black Sea villa and of course the test ban signing, a source of elation to us all.

"One must live through dark times with the Russians to savor fully a moment like this. It was the first arms control treaty actually negotiated after 18 years of talks between Moscow and Washington."

I covered the Senate Foreign Relations Committee hearings on the treaty, including the sharp criticism of it by the scientist Edward Teller, and the strong support of it by other leading scientists. It was eventually approved by the Committee 16-1. This was not a surprise. I had earlier reported that General Maxwell D. Taylor, the chairman of the Joint Chiefs of Staff, had told the Committee that the Chiefs were in favor of ratifying the treaty, and that even Air Force Chairman General Curtis E. LeMay had said that on balance, he favored the treaty on political grounds. This was the first time a story by me led the paper.

"The Senate Foreign Relations Committee voted 16-1, today in favor of Senate ratification of the partial nuclear test ban treaty without any reservations." Fulbright said the only negative vote was cast by Senator Long of Louisiana. I got to know Senator Fulbright pretty well from covering his committee, and when Haynes Johnson, my colleague on the Star was asked by Doubleday to do a quick biography on the Arkansas senator, he asked me to be a co-author, and I agreed.

The book: "Fulbright: The Dissenter," was published in the summer of 1968, just as I was leaving the Star to join The New York Times. Fulbright was a gracious biographee. He opened his files to us, and only asked to read the final manuscript to have a chance to make any corrections.

The Non-Proliferation Treaty was formally signed by the United States, Britain and Russia in early August and ratified by the Senate in September. It was a bright spot in U.S.-Soviet relations. A minor footnote was that Yale professor, Frederick C. Barghoorn, an expert on Russian affairs, had been arrested as an American spy, as he was about to leave the Soviet Union, causing an uproar in Washington, leading President Kennedy to hold up plans to renew talks on a new cultural exchange agreement. But on November 16, after 16 days of confinement, Barghoorn was released and flown back to the United States. I covered that story extensively as well, having been a "cultural exchange veteran" myself. Everything was not going smoothly for American foreign policy, however. The United States government was growing increasingly concerned over the situation in Southeast Asia. Like most Americans, this was a part of the world with which I was quite unfamiliar. I knew that when President Kennedy took office he was concerned about keeping Laos neutral, and I had diligently memorized the names of the rival princes in Laos for my first week- in-review pieces for the Star.

But increasingly, attention was focused on South Vietnam, the country the United States supported since the Geneva conference of 1954 divided the country into two, with the Northern half dominated by Ho Chi Minh's Communists. President Kennedy had sent in U.S. military advisers as had President Eisenhower, but from all account, the situation on the ground was not going well.

A colleague of mine from the Harvard Crimson, David Halberstam, who had been Managing Editor of the Crimson in the Class of 1955 (I was 1957), was covering Vietnam for the New York Times, and was very critical of the ruling government headed by President Ngo Dinh Diem and his brother Ngo Dinh Nhu who were Roman Catholics and who seemed to be at war with the Buddhist Monks in the country.

On Friday, November 1, headlines reported that the brothers had been ousted in a coup, and the next day, the AP reported from Saigon that they had both been killed. The background for the assassination was made public years later, and it indicated that it began with a cable drafted by Roger A. Hilsman, assistant secretary of State for Far Eastern Affairs, on August 23, while all senior officials, President Kennedy, Secretary of State Rusk, Secretary of Defense McNamara were on vacation out of Washington.

The cable which was to be sent to the new U.S. Ambassador in Saigon, Henry Cabot Lodge, raised the possibility of urging the Vietnamese to overthrow the Diem brothers in a coup. The cable was read over the phone to Kennedy who reportedly gave his assent thinking his other advisers approved it. This was also the attitude of Rusk and McNamara. All these officials later regretted doing so. Despite Washington's hopes, no better government ever took office. Problems in Southeast Asia were to prove the most serious for future administrations until Saigon fell to Communists in 1975.

Because I was only 28 years old, and a bachelor, in 1963, the members of the Washington Evening Star's Newspaper Guild's chapter thought it fitting that I should be the Guild chairman and go to all the evening meetings. I agreed, thinking it might be an interesting experience.

But 1963 was also a contract year, and the Newspaper Guild contract with the Star was due for renewal in mid-December, and the "hot issue" on the table was the Guild's "demand" that experienced reporters be guaranteed a minimum salary of $200 a week after five years. Newspaper salaries were not very high in those years. The Guild had a professional manager who handled the daily negotiations, and advised us. He had an abrasive personality which rubbed management's sensibilities. We had a meeting with management scheduled that afternoon, and I was going over my notes at my desk in the Star's newsroom on the morning of November 22 when I saw a crowd swarming around the "ticker" machines—the teletypes that spewed forth the news from AP.

It said in bulletin form at first "Kennedy shot." The initial reports held out hope he was alive even though we later learned he was dead from the first. The Star's "Extra" said in its AP bulletin lead: "Dallas, Nov. 22—Two priests stepped out of Parkland Hospital's emergency ward today and said President Kennedy died of his bullet wounds. He died at 1 pm CST."

For someone like me, who had identified with Kennedy's Harvard connection and his relative youth, his assassination was a shock. It also seemed to me something of a personal loss. I looked to Kennedy as a different kind of president, more in tune with the world of today of the 1960s that I was familiar with.

My negotiating meeting obviously scrubbed, I was asked by the national desk to put together a biography of Lyndon Johnson to run in a late "extra" edition that would be sold on the streets at 6 pm. So, I went into the "morgue," the room where the Star kept clippings of stories and assembled as much biography as I could, and wrote a piece. I have no record of what I wrote that day.

After that was done, I was asked to go with Roberta Hornig, a colleague on the paper, to Lyndon Johnson's home in suburban Maryland—he was one of the last Vice Presidents to live in a private home. We were sent there, along with many TV people to mill around outside his fashionable home in suburban Maryland, on that unseasonably warm November night in the hope that LBJ would come out and chat, but he did not and about 2 a.m. we went home.

The next day, Saturday, I came into the Star's office early, and was asked to put together a profile on Lee Harvey Oswald, who, by then, had been arrested for shooting President Kennedy from the window of the Texas Book Depository Building. Luckily for me, there was a good article about Oswald that had been written several years earlier in Moscow by a reporter for the North American News Alliance who wanted to know why he wanted to live in the Soviet Union.

My lede said: ""Lee Harvey Oswald, the accused slayer of President Kennedy, is a moody young man who turned to Cuba for love after Russia spurned him." But I was as shocked as anyone the next day, while on Pennsylvania Avenue, watching the funeral procession heading toward the Capitol, I heard that Jack Ruby had just shot Oswald.

The next president was Vice President Lyndon B. Johnson, who had a reputation in Washington as a man who could get anything done on Capitol Hill, but who knew very little about foreign affairs. I was to spend a considerable amount of time covering this president in coming years.

This was a bad exaggeration. Johnson had a broader knowledge of foreign affairs than he was generally given credit for, and of course during World War Two, had been sent to Australia and New Zealand by President Roosevelt.

The negotiations with the Star for the Guild contract resumed, and went down to the deadline. In fact, we concluded them in the offices of the Federal Mediators' Office in D.C. The Guild was assigned one set of offices and The Star another set. The Star's Business Manager, Samuel Kauffmann was opposite me on the negotiating table at the end of the talks and I remember him saying "You went to Harvard? How can you put up with that guy?" meaning the Guild agent. I replied, "Well, it you could come up with the $200 a week, we would be in business." He finally agreed to it, after five years, provided I endorsed it personally to the membership meeting set for Sunday morning at the Hilton Hotel. Needless to say, I agreed. And on Sunday, I was a hero for a day.

The Star decided to send me on my first reporting trip to Eastern Europe in the first months of 1964, but I was around to cover the initial goodwill messages between

Johnson and Khrushchev talking about peace, a carryover from the nonproliferation treaty of the previous year. The two men had exchanged public letters talking about non-aggression pacts, which did not go very far, given that the tensions at this time were not between them but in other parts of the world.

CHAPTER 7

My First Overseas Trip for The Star And Vietnam Crisis

My first trip to Russia and Eastern Europe for The Star in early 1964 went smoothly. It was a time without any real obvious crisis in world affairs even though as we later found out, behind the scenes President Johnson and his top aides were becoming increasingly worried about the situation in Southeast Asia. On that trip, I visited the Soviet Union, Poland, Czechoslovakia, Hungary and Rumania. While in the Soviet Union, I even flew as far east as Alma-Ata, the capital of Kazakhstan, from where the Soviet space shots were launched, not that I was allowed to visit the space center.

On April 12, 1964, The Star ran the first of my series under the slug: "The Parting Curtain, Ties Breaking in Red Bloc." To those that followed the Soviet bloc, I don't think it told them much new, but to the average reader, perhaps it did. What I wrote was: "The ties between Russia and its satellites are breaking under the pressure of rising nationalism and depressed economic problems." I added that "throughout East Europe, long-time symbols of Russian domination are fast disappearing."

"What is remaining," I wrote, "is an alliance of Communist nations beset by national rivalries and ideological non- conformity." Ironically, the lead story in The Star that day was an AP article on a press conference held by President Johnson who said that Soviet Premier Khrushchev is "seeking to preserve peace in the world."

What I found in my travels around Russia, however, was that Khrushchev, who had just turned 79, was losing his popularity at home. I wrote that even though he was "applauded around the world as a man of peace," his popularity "at home, however, seems to have slipped and his leadership appears to have lost some of its luster." I said that "a 6,000 mile tour of the Soviet Union leaves a visitor with an impression, not so much of an anti-Khrushchev sentiment, as of an apathy toward the Russian leader" who by then had been in charge for more than a decade. When I wrote that article, I had no idea, of course, that Khrushchev himself would be ousted in what amounted to a 'palace coup' six months later in October 1964, that led to his replacement by a troika of Leonid I. Brezhnev as party secretary, Aleksei N. Kosygyn, as prime minister, and Dmitri Polyanski, as deputy prime minister.

The few Russian intellectuals I met on the trip all pointed me to what they considered the most important intellectual breakthrough in recent years, the publication of the novel, "One Day in the Life of Ivan Denisovich," by Aleksandr Solzhenitsyn which had been published in November 1962 in the literary journal Novy Nir with the personal blessing of Khrushchev himself. The intellectuals were telling me that the editor of Novy Mir, Aleksandr Tvardovsky, probably could not publish the same novel today. In fact, he had nominated the novel for the Lenin Prize but the Communist Party did not support it and the party paper Pravda lambasted the book for its rough language, which of course reflected the language used by the camp's prisoners. The novel had already been reprinted in dozens of foreign languages abroad and was a worldwide sensation, focusing on the barbarities of Stalin's prison camps.

In my circuit of the East European countries, I was struck by the intellectual independence of the Poles, who on their own had signed a contract with CBS to produce "My Fair Lady" in Polish in five Polish cities. And in my article, I noted that "My Fair Lady" will be the fourth American musical produced in the last two years. "Wonderful Town,"

"Can Can" and "Kiss Me Kate" had preceded it. I quoted a Polish official who admits he dislikes jazz as saying that he estimates that "80 percent of all jazz and popular music played on state-run Radio Warsaw is American."

In Budapest, I visited the American Legation (still no embassy there), hoping to meet Josef Cardinal Mindszenty, the famous Hungarian clergyman who was living in exile there, and who, it turned out, was unable to leave, until 1972, when he finally moved to Vienna, where he finished out his life. I was barred by the State Department from talking to him. Hungarian officials, however, were quite outspoken in wanting closer ties with Washington and were doing all they could to facilitate them. In fact, I had to admit that of the cities I visited then, Budapest was my favorite. In my article: "Budapest is a sophisticated city that seasons its Marxism-Leninism with a heavy dose of paprika. The result is a socialist society that is agreeable not only to Hungarians but to the visiting foreigner as well." I think I was taken by the fact that Hungarians had night spots that were open after midnight and created a Western atmosphere. Janos Kadar, the Hungarian Communist leader, called this process, "building socialism," I wrote. Westerners say it is "liberalization." The Hungarians "just enjoy themselves."

In Romania, I documented what had been reported elsewhere—that the Romanian party leadership was seeking to become independent of Moscow. The American embassy was quite helpful in documenting what was going on. My lead said it all: "Romania's quiet rebellion is the talk of East Europe. With few polemics but a good deal of shrewd diplomacy, Romania has convinced Western observers that it is now the most independent member of the Soviet alliance." But the relative independence of the countries of Eastern Europe, in the long run, had little to do with the growing crisis in Asia, which The Star at this point seemed relatively unfocused on.

After I returned to Washington, it was clear that I was now the Star's senior State Department correspondent. In the summer of 1964, it was becoming apparent that Vietnam, and with it, Laos, were going to be serious campaign issues in the presidential elections that fall. Lyndon Johnson was running against Senator Barry Goldwater, and Goldwater, an arch conservative, was publicly attacking the administration for not doing enough to support the South Vietnamese war effort.

The United States had seemingly danced around the situation in Laos for years, never certain how seriously to take the crisis. A deal had supposedly been hammered out by Khrushchev and Kennedy in 1962 to neutralize Laos around Souvanna Phouma. But by May, it was apparent in public that a crisis was unfolding in Laos and this was of grave concern to Secretary of State Rusk At the same time, on May 18, 1964, President Johnson asked Congress for an additional $125 million to help out the South Vietnamese, in the wake of continued attacks from the Viet Cong, who were aided by the North Vietnamese. One of the problems in writing about Southeast Asia from Washington was that virtually nobody had much experience there including me.

I wrote a story on May 18, saying "The United States today mapped diplomatic and military plans to counter the Communist drive in Laos." Quoting McCloskey, I wrote that the United States called the attacks by the Pathet Lao and North Vietnamese Viet Minh a "flagrant violation of the Geneva agreement" [of 1954]. We were also told that Rusk had asked several nations to "to exert diplomatic pressure on Red China which is considered a leading force behind Communist activity in Laos."

Meanwhile, top level meetings were held at the White House with military and civilian leaders and again at Pearl Harbor to seek an agreed policy, but there was no agreement reached on how far to go in using American military force. Henry Cabot Lodge, the envoy to Saigon, resigned, to help out the Republican Party in the presidential elections. Maxwell Taylor, replaced him.

Early in August 1964, the American public became rudely awakened about Vietnam. As McNamara wrote in his memoirs: "Before August 1964, the American people had followed developments in Vietnam sporadically and with limited concern. The war seemed far off. Tonkin Gulf changed that." According to McNamara, "What happened, in short, was that in January 1964, the National Security Council had approved CIA support for South Vietnamese covert operations against North Vietnam, code-named Plan 34A." On the night of July 30, 1964, a 34A mission carried out by South Vietnamese patrol Boats attacked two North Vietnamese islands in the Tonkin Gulf thought to support infiltration operations against the South. The next morning, a U.S. destroyer, Maddox, on patrol, steamed into the gulf, well away from the islands. But two and a half days later, on August 2, the Maddox reported it was being approached by high speed boats and was being attacked by torpedoes and automatic weapons fire. It reported no injuries or damage. According to McNamara, North Vietnam, in its official history of the war, confirms that it ordered the attack on the Maddox. At the time of the attack, the Maddox was in international waters, more than 25 miles from the North Vietnamese coast.

In response, Johnson met with his top advisers, and remembering that President Truman had run into criticism from Republican leaders in Congress for unilateral actions in the Korean War, Johnson decided to seek a Joint Resolution of Congress backing retaliation against North Vietnam.

He got it quickly, 88-2, in the Senate and 416-0 in the House. McNamara, who later soured on the Vietnam War, wrote that "no doubt exists that Congress did not intend to authorize without further, full consultation the expansion of U.S. troops in Vietnam, from 16,000 to 555,000 men, initiating large- scale combat operations with the risk of an expanded war with China and the Soviet Union and extending U.S. involvement in Vietnam for many years to come." But nothing was done immediately.

It turned out that I was to participate in covering the real start of serious U.S. participation in the Vietnam war, but I did not realize it at first. On Sunday, February 7, 1965, The Star had a banner headline that read: "Viet Cong Attack 2 U.S. Camps." The story by the Associated Press said that eight Americans were killed and at least 63 wounded when Viet Cong forces launched coordinated onslaughts on two big U.S. compounds at Pleiku, 240 miles north of Saigon. At least seven parked aircraft were destroyed. The attack took place at the same time as Soviet Premier Kosygin was arriving in Hanoi on an official visit. The story pointed out that this was "by far the worst attack directed against U.S. forces during this war."

As Richard Fryklund, The Star's veteran Pentagon correspondent noted, the attack occurred while McGeorge Bundy, the White House National Security Adviser, was on a fact-finding trip to South Vietnam. Fryklund said that "hasty meetings last night at the White House, State and Defense Departments indicated that a sharp American response—possibly an air strike against North Vietnam—was under preparation."

In his memoirs, McNamara wrote that Bundy "promptly recommended[by cable] a retaliatory air strikeagainst North Vietnam of the kind that had been under consideration in Washington for months. Pleiku and our reaction to it contributed significantly to the escalation that ensued."

The President immediately called a National Security Council meeting which was also attended by Congressional leaders in the Cabinet Room in the White House. Even though a strike against North Vietnam carried a risk because of Kosygin's presence in Hanoi, McNamara reported that almost everyone present, including Soviet specialist, former U.S. Ambassador to Moscow Llewellyn Thompson, warned that a reprisal attack meant that the United States would no longer be "in a penny ante game." President Johnson heard Senator Mansfield out, and then ordered the attack, basing his action on the authority of the Tonkin Gulf Resolution of the previous summer.

Bundy returned to Washington on February 8 with a pessimistic report that stated, according to McNamara: "The situation in Vietnam is deteriorating and without new U.S. action, defeat appears inevitable...The stakes in Vietnam are extremely high... The international prestige of the United States, and a substantial part of our influence, are directly at risk in Vietnam. There is no way of unloading the burden on the Vietnamese themselves, and there is no way of negotiating ourselves out of Vietnam which offers any serious promise at present...Any negotiated withdrawal today would mean surrender on the installment plan."

Ironically, Johnson approved the proposed bombing plan but described it—according to McNamara—as a step to defeat aggression "without escalating the war." McNamara said this was an understatement that ignored the magnitude of the change in U.S. military operations the program entailed. McNamara says Johnson knew this but feared the public's reaction, and chose to stilt his comments. McNamara says that Johnson finally decided on February 19 to begin regular air strikes against North Vietnam but he again refused Bundy's advice to announce the decision publicly.

As both Rusk and McNamara point out in their memoirs, Johnson did not want to talk publicly about enlarging the war, even though it was self-evident. For instance, on the front page of the Washington Star on February 11, there was a banner headline: "Big New Raids Blast N. Vietnam." And I had a story that said: "the latest air strikes against North Viet Nam indicated that President Johnson has decided to continue his 'strike for strike' policy even though it incurs the risk of a wider war," And this was followed two weeks later with an important press conference by Rusk, ruling out any peace talks with Hanoi until it ended its "systematic campaign" to overthrow the Saigon government.

On Sunday, February 28, the United States made public a 64-page document charging North Vietnam with carrying out aggression against South Vietnam "as real as that of an invading army." The 14,000 word document was to be made public and circulated worldwide. It was officially called "Aggression from the North: The Record of North Vietnam's Campaign to Conquer South Vietnam." I wrote the story about the report, and my lede said: "The United States charged North Vietnam yesterday with carrying out aggression against South Vietnam 'as real as that of an invading army.'" The bombing campaign against North Vietnam, called "Rolling Thunder," continued as did the fighting in South Vietnam. In March and April, as the bombing continued, U.S. Marines were landed to protect the air base at Da Nang. I wrote a story on April 14, 1965, under a headline: "Officials Expect Hot Fighting Before

Any Viet Nam Talk." President Johnson, in a speech at Johns Hopkins University, had offered unconditional negotiations, but had gotten no takers from the Communist side.

But with student and others beginning to protest the Vietnam war, Rusk in a speech to international lawyers on April 23, 1965, was clearly hot under the collar, as he lambasted his critics for "speaking nonsense and ignoring simple truths in Vietnam." Rusk said: "I sometimes wonder at the gullibility of educated men and the stubborn disregard of plain facts by men who are supposed to be helping our young to learn—especially to learn how to think." Rusk compared the situation in Vietnam with that in Europe on the eve of World War II. "We are told that Southeast Asia is far away—but so were Manchuria and Ethiopia."

This went on all summer. The rhetoric about Vietnam; the constant fighting in the South; the U.S. air attacks on the North.

By now, I had a set routine. I would leave my apartment which was located on the second floor of a townhouse on Washington Circle not far from the State Department and drive to The Star building in Southeast Washington, and check in with the desk to see what was going on and update any news for the first edition. Then I would drive to the

State Department and park in the department garage with my special pass, and go to the press room, where I had a typewriter and a phone with a direct line to The Star. All of my colleagues who also covered the State Department were similarly set up. Around noon, we would all go to the briefing room were Bob McCloskey or one of his deputies would hold forth. Afterwards, I would try to question him off the record on some aspect of policy.

In addition, covering the department was relatively hassle- free in the early 1960s. One needed only a State Department Correspondents Association card to gain admission to the building, and once in the building, a reporter was free to roam the halls. I used to drop in frequently on the offices of the Asian bureau, dealing with Vietnam, and the Intelligence and Research Bureau dealing with the Soviet Union. Paul Cook, who was in charge of the latter, became a good personal friend. He was extremely knowledgeable about Russian officials, and we enjoyed bantering with each other. Also, Bill Luers, in the Soviet office, who later became an ambassador to Venezuela, and president of the Metropolitan Museum of Art, was a friend in those days.

By the end of August, 1965, the Johnson administration was willing to try the United Nations in an effort to get something started in Vietnam. The U.S. ambassador, Adlai

Stevenson, had dropped dead in the streets of London in July, and President Johnson had persuaded Supreme Court Justice Arthur J. Goldberg to resign from the court and replace Stevenson as U.N. Ambassador. Washington was stunned by the move—at least I was. I could not understand why Goldberg would give up the Court seat. In his memoirs, Goldberg says he was promised by Johnson that he would be renominated for the Court, but that did not happen.

Pope Paul VI came to the United Nations, met with President Johnson and Goldberg in Johnson's presidential suite at the Waldorf- Astoria Hotel and then went to the General Assembly to make an elaborate appeal for peace, which I covered for The Star.

CHAPTER 8

Return to Russia

At the urging of Burt Hoffman, The Star's national editor, I made a second trip to Russia in less than 18 months. This was my first trip back to the Soviet Union since the ouster of Nikita S. Khrushchev in a Kremlin coup the preceding October, 1964.

I had, of course, been following events through the press but had been preoccupied with Vietnam, so going to Russia in the spring of 1965 was a good break for me. I went to Moscow, Tbilisi, the capital of Georgia; Sochi, the Black Sea summer and winter resort which in 2014 hosted the Winter Olympics, but in 1965 was just a popular getaway; and lastly, Kiev, the Ukrainian capital.

I won a Washington Newspaper Guild award for the series of articles which resulted from that trip, but reading them now, I can see that I was caught up in a misplaced assumption or hope that the new Brezhnev-Kosygin leadership was going to bring about some fundamental changes in Soviet life. The lead paragraph in the first article summed up this hope:

> "Russia after Khrushchev is undergoing a quiet revolution. If it succeeds, a new Soviet society could emerge, hardly resembling the inhibited, paranoic nation the West has come to know."

Unfortunately, what I detected as hopeful signs did not really pan out.

I wrote for instance: "Encouraged by the new leaders to find cures for Russia's sagging economy, dozens of top ranking economists have been engaged for several months in a free-wheeling debate on how to vitalize agriculture and industry,

One night in Moscow, I chose to dine by myself in a new hotel, the Minsk, and since I was alone, I was seated at a table with two Russian women who turned out to be psychiatrists. I asked them if there had been an increase in the number of their patients, They both exclaimed "Absolutely."

When I asked why, they said it was because life is becoming more complicated, more demanding for their people. They have more choices now, therefore more strains.

I wrote that "In the last few years there has been many improvements in Soviet life. There is a much greater variety of clothes, all sorts of clothes, now, therefore more strains."

I wrote that "there is a much greater variety of radios and TVs, housing has improved, even private cars are not completely out of reach."

But people keep complaining.

"It is sometimes amusing," one graduate student I quoted said in very good English. "I can buy a Soviet radio or electric razor and it will last forever, and I will tell all my friends about it."

"You will buy the same radio or the same razor and it will break down in a month. Then try to get it fixed."

"That is why we like to buy foreign-made goods," he said. "We think they are more dependable."

One of the articles from that trip that I enjoyed writing the most occurred when I went back to Sokolniki Park in Moscow, which houses the large pavilion lauding the "economic achievements of the USSR." It was in this park that the United States held its mammoth exhibition in 1959 that I witnessed when I was part of a "delegation of youth.". I went back to the park on a nostalgic walk, accompanied by a Russian guide. While we walked around, the guide said to me: "Pretty awful, these buildings aren't they? They're all Stalinist, unbelievable waste of money," she went on. "I often wonder why Stalin and probably Khrushchev also, deliberately created such ugliness. They could have just as easily, created something lasting and beautiful."

In that article, I credited Premier Kosygin with doing more than "any other man to foster this attitude." I wrote that "his public statements are models of frankness, and in comparison with the propagandistic tirades of the past, they sound refreshingly objective." The fourth article in my series dealt with the Russian poets, always a favorite topic of mine. Through the years, I had gotten to know Andrei Voznesensky (died in 2010 at age of 77) and Yevgeny Yevtushenko (died in 2017 at age of 83). I decided to devote a whole piece to the poets, I wrote:

"Such well-known American poets as Allen Ginsberg and Robert Lowell might have commanded a few thousand dedicated readers. But the leading Russian poets can sell 240,000 copies of a new book in 24 hours, and can fill a sports stadium for a reading, if the authorities will let them."

"A young theatre company in Moscow Taganka] is performing a stage version of Voznesensky's book of poems, "Antimiri" (Opposite Worlds). Even though the poetry is quite difficult to follow, every performance has been sold out."

"This is the best show I've ever seen," a young college student said at the end of the two-hour performance. I could come back every night."

Voznesensky, a slight and somewhat shy man, reads his poetry in a melodic voice. He loves the sounds of words, and the texture of his words is in the Pasternak tradition. "Androysha," as his friends call him, is now considered to be the No.1 poet in Russia slightly ahead of Yevtushenko, who at the end of his life married for the fourth time and moved to Tulsa, Oklahoma where he and his wife both taught at colleges there.

My fifth article in the series was an effort to explain Soviet nationality policy, with an emphasis on the Jewish question which had arisen as a political issue in the United States because of the immense difficulty Soviet Jews had in emigrating to the United States or Israel at that time.

Of course, as I am writing these words, there really is not much of a problem any more. Ever since the Gorbachev years, emigration has been much more open. There is a steady stream of Soviet Jews to and from Israel these days.

"The first lesson to learn when visiting the Soviet Union is that everyone is not a Russian, and those who are not, do not like to be called Russians," so I began the article,

"On the banks of the Tbilisi Sea, an artificial lake outside the Georgian capital, the American started a conversation.

"You know, we Americans are a good deal like you Russians." "I am a Georgian," was the prompt reply. "And we Georgians are a lot like you Americans."

A table conversation in a Soviet restaurant might begin like this:

"Where are you from?" "Washington, in the United States." "What's your nationality?" "American."

"No, what is your nationality? I know your citizenship is American."

After several such conversations, the American finally understands the difference in the Soviet Union between citizenship and nationality,

"I am Jewish," the American says, knowing that this will be a satisfactory answer for the Soviet Union.

As a Jew myself, I had some very personal experiences in the Soviet Union going back to my days during the summer of 1959 on my youth exchange program when as soon as a Russian Jew found out I was Jewish, I would hear the most intimate details of hardships that he would not have passed on to a gentile. And of course, Moscow's policies toward Jews inevitably got caught up in its broader

Middle East policies as we were about to see after the 1967 Six Day war.

What I wrote in 1965 was accurate. The Soviet leaders had decided to do nothing for the Jews—neither to let them assimilate freely into Russian society by abolishing the need to have a nationality designation in their passports nor to provide them with the facilities for allowing the Jewish religion and society to flourish.

Moreover, because of the anti-religious policy inherent in communism, it is very difficult for Jews to practice their religion. Synagogues are denied state funds for restoration and the normal religious materials of Jews—prayer books, shawls, torahs, etc. cannot be produced. The Jewish religion is more restricted than the Russian Orthodox which is a state religion.

Soviet authorities are very sensitive about the Jewish problem and stoutly deny there is any sort of discrimination. They say the reason synagogues close is that Jews do not use them. The same reason is given for the lack of a kosher market in Moscow and for the lack of Jewish schools.

I wrote in 1965 that "my impression as an American Jew was that Soviet Jews were extremely interested in learning about their kinsmen abroad. Many of them want to travel, if given the chance. But travel was very difficult in 1965 for Jews,

Now there seem to be no prohibitions. Thousands of Jews in recent years have settled in Israel and the United States.

The final part of my series dealt with the new Soviet leadership which of course I had no direct contact with during my trip to the Soviet Union. I wrote that "Nikita S. Khrushchev's face is gone from the Soviet scene (he died in 1972) and no one has replaced him.

That was true in 1965, but soon Brezhnev ascended to the top where he stayed until he died in 1982.

I pointed out that in 1965 there was very little information available in the Soviet press about policy making or foreign policy, I wrote that "Soviet leaders apparently have tried to keep differences below the surface, and they may not become apparent until the crucial decisions on a new five-year plan and on a new Party Congress are reached.

CHAPTER 9

Back to Vietnam

By the end of August 1965, the Johnson administration was willing to ask the United Nations to try and get something started on Vietnam. It told the United Nations that it was willing to consider reunification of Vietnam, a long-time objective of North Vietnam, but only as part of a total package. This was also, in effect, the new U.S. Ambassador Arthur J. Goldberg's maiden voyage to the United Nations General Assembly.

Goldberg, who had been a Supreme Court Justice, had been persuaded by Johnson to resign to take the U.N. job, which startled the press corps, including me. Adlai Stevenson had dropped dead in the streets of London in June. Goldberg, in his memoirs, implies he was promised by Johnson that he would be renominated to the court, but he never was.

I was invited to meet with Goldberg at his apartment in Washington one evening to chat about foreign affairs and I found him quite interested in pursuing the search for solutions. He, of course, would become deeply involved in 1967 in drafting Resolution 242, ending the Six Day war in the Middle East, but I am jumping ahead.

On October 4, 1965, Pope Paul VI came to the United Nations General Assembly and met first with President Johnson and Ambassador Goldberg at the presidential suite in the Waldorf- Astoria hotel. At the United Nations, the pope made an earnest appeal for disarmament and peace. I wrote an analysis the next day, quoting an American diplomat : "He would never forget the words of the Pope's declaration against war, spoken in French: "Jamais plus la guerre"—no more war, never again.

Later in October, The Star gave prominence to a report I wrote quoting a "leading Viet Cong official" saying that relations between the Viet Cong and Red China were "considerably strained" over the question of Vietnam peace talks with the United States. My report was quoting a broadcast over Radio Prague saying that Nguyen Van Dong, the official National Liberation Front representative in Moscow, telling a press conference in Helsinki, that the Viet Cong were not insisting that the United States pull out of South Vietnam before peace talks can start, in contradiction to the Red Chinese position. All the Viet Cong wants, the report said, was that the United States recognize them as a partner in the talks.

On Election Day, November 2, 1965, an off year for presidential races, the Washington area was startled when a young Quaker, Norman R. Morrison, a father of three, burned himself to death outside the Pentagon in protest against the Vietnam war. It was done in late afternoon in front of hundreds of startled homeward bound Department of Defense employees. He had been holding his 18-months old daughter, but she was unharmed because he had either put her down or dropped her from his arms. His wife, Anne, also a Quaker, issued a statement later, through a friend: "Norman Morrison has given his life today to express his concern over the great loss of life and human suffering caused by the involvement in this war. He felt that all citizens must speak their convictions about our country's actions." Morrison's death occurred too late for that day's Star, but it commanded a major place on the next day's front page. It also was on the front page of The New York Times.

There were no public statements about the Morrison death by any high official. In fact, Secretary Rusk gave his first press conference since August 27 three days later on November 5 and said the war in South Vietnam was "progressing well" despite an increase in the number of North Vietnam regulars in the fighting. He said the United States will not allow a Communist military victory in South Vietnam and said it was now "quite clear" the infiltration from the North won't succeed.

McNamara, in his memoirs, says: "Morrison's death was a tragedy not only for his family but also for me and the country. It was an outcry against the killing that was destroying the lives of so many Vietnamese and American youth."

He says that "I reacted to the horror of his action by bottling up my emotions and avoided talking about them with anyone—even my family."

If Rusk on November 5 said the war was "progressing well," two weeks later on November 27, his mood was decidedly different. On that day, some 20,000 protestors against the Vietnam War had clogged the streets around the White House in the biggest anti-war protest to date, Rusk held a late afternoon press conference, and in my front page story, I wrote that he was "openly pessimistic about chances for a negotiated Vietnam settlement."

Rusk suggested that the peace marchers "try to get North Vietnam to agree to unconditional discussions with the United States."

"If they addressed a letter to both sides saying, 'Will you agree to negotiations without preconditions?' We would say 'Yes..'" Rusk said, "and I would be interested in knowing what Hanoi would say." I wrote that Rusk strongly suggested that the peace marchers would find Hanoi just as adamant against talks as U.S. officials have discovered.

As Christmas approached, it was generally assumed that there would be a bombing halt for a couple of days over the holiday. What none of us journalists knew, nor did other high officials know, was that Secretary McNamara, who was with his family in Aspen, Colorado, over the holidays, telephoned the president who was at his ranch in Texas, outside Austin, and flew down to see him on December 27.

McNamara, in his memoirs, says that he and the president talked for three hours about an indefinite pause in the bombing. McNamara says, "I stressed my judgment that the possibility of sparking talks that might ultimately lead to peace outweighed the military disadvantages of deferring resumption of the bombing."

"He finally agreed to extend the pause for an indefinite period and to mount a massive diplomatic effort to move Hanoi toward negotiations," McNamara says. Johnson told him to tell Rusk and others in Washington what he wanted done, and although Rusk opposed extending the pause, he went along because he understood "I had already convinced the president," McNamara says.

McNamara says that when he returned to his family in Aspen, he was "very pleased" with the results of his talks, "yet I felt a strong sense of guilt for having gone around my colleagues to win my case. It was the only time I did so in my seven years as secretary."

At that time, it was, of course, a major story for us. At first, we wondered if the halt in the bombing was the result of some clear signal from Hanoi that it would agree finally to negotiations, but it was soon evident that that was not the case.

My sources at the State Department—and these were by and large desk officers with Asian experience—were extremely dubious anything positive would come of this effort. On the Sunday paper of January 2, 1966, The Star devoted most of the front page to the situation, with a banner headline that said: "Global Search for Peace." I wrote a news analysis of the diplomatic efforts that was extremely downbeat based on my conversations with diplomats in Washington and my own instincts:

"President Johnson is making a determined New Year's attempt to find a peaceful solution to the Vietnam war. This effort undoubtedly will continue in the weeks ahead, but there are only the slimmest of hopes that he will succeed.

"Hardened diplomats, while recognizing the sincerity of the president's well-intentioned and well-publicized peace offensive seem reconciled to the view that the Vietnam war probably will not be ended at a conference table but rather in the jungles and highlands of South Vietnam and in the skies over North Vietnam.

"As President Johnson and his special peace envoys keep insisting: a negotiated peace is possible. But the diplomats who must wrestle daily with the Vietnam question say a settlement is possible only at a political price unacceptable to either side. Neither contender can pay the price demanded by the other without enormous loss of prestige and great damage to its national interest."

My colleague, Richard Fryklund, who was a senior Pentagon correspondent, was much more optimistic than the diplomats about the likelihood of an American military victory in Vietnam. His analysis said:

"American professional soldiers expect the real war to start in Vietnam after the negotiations talk simmer down as they are sure they will."

He wrote: "The American fighting men in Vietnam are confident they will win. That is, they feel they will defeat the Communists regularly in the pitched battles, learn to handle guerrilla hit and run operations and slowly spread government power through the countryside until the Viet Cong quit or are pushed out of South Vietnam."

In any event, after a major diplomatic effort which included sending high-level diplomatic envoys around the world to meet with the Pope and various other important leaders, President Johnson's peace offensive came to an end without any success.

Johnson had indicated in advance that he would order the resumption of bombing if he did not receive a positive response from Hanoi and finally on January 29, 1965, Ho Chi Minh himself rejected, as I wrote, "with finality the Peace Offensive."

Ironically, the chill in diplomacy was more than matched by the weather in Washington which reached nine degrees on that very wintry day.

One of the major problems I had as a young reporter in Washington was in cultivating reliable sources. My most trusted source was Robert McCloskey, who, although being the official spokesman for Rusk, was also a good friend and was willing to share with me materials that were helpful in steering me in the right direction.

Rusk tried to have Friday afternoon background sessions with the regular State Department correspondents to give us the flavor of the news.

But nobody told us that McNamara had been responsible for the long bombing halt.

Rusk, in his memoirs, made it clear that Vietnam remained for him a tough issue to deal with. He felt that he had underestimated Hanoi's willingness to stick with its policy and overestimated the American public's willingness to support the war.

In any event we are ahead of ourselves. As 1966 proceeded, what had begun in 1965 continued with more anti-war protests in the United States and more efforts by President Johnson for support at home for his various policies.

But even though I spent most of my time on Vietnam, I still found time to pay attention to Russian affairs. This unusual story gripped me.

A young American named Newcomb Mott, who in a bizarre story, made his way from Norway to a tiny Russian village called Boris Gleb, 220 miles north of the Arctic Circle on September 4, 1965, hoping he could buy some trinkets and make his way back to Norway, and eventually to the United States,

Instead, Mott was arrested and put on trial in Murmansk, sentenced to prison, and who then, Soviet authorities claimed, committed suicide on a train. It was truly a bizarre story.

By May 1966 there was a bit of optimism in Washington because the Saigon government had smashed Buddhist control of the city of Da Nang and only faced opposition from dissident groups isolated in northern Hue. This was a far cry from the situation in 1963 when the Buddhists in effect caused the overthrow of the regime of the Diem brothers.

Against this upbeat mood, President Johnson undertook a 17-day Pacific trip, which included a meeting in Manila that was attended by the nations which had troops in Vietnam.

This was my maiden trip with the White House press corps— and the custom still prevails,. There was a charter aircraft for the press which accompanies Air Force One.

I had not asked the editors for the assignment. Perhaps they thought a 17-day trip might be too grueling for Jack Horner, the regular White House correspondent. I had filled in at the White House for Horner on his Saturday day off when Johnson often had press conferences walking around the White House gardens taking questions as he did so,

For me, who was 31, it was an exhilarating experience. We flew on a Pan American charter with attractive hostesses and great cuisine non-stop from Washington to Hawaii.

Johnson made it clear in his first speech at the airport in Honolulu that he did not expect a "strategy of war" to come out of the Manila conference or any "spectacular formulation for peace."

"We do not expect to pull any rabbits out of any hats in Manila," he said. "There are no surprises to spring on anyone. We know the most important weapon in Vietnam is patience and unity."

From Hawaii, Johnson stopped in Pago Pago, the capital of American Samoa on his way to New Zealand. From there, Johnson went to Australia, the Philippines, Thailand, Malaysia, and South Korea. Johnson also made a surprise visit to Cam Ranh Bay Vietnam, even though there had been speculation he might do so.

CHAPTER 10

Crossing the Pacific With LBJ

Not only was this my first overseas trip with the White House press corps but it was my introductions to filing overseas with the White House reporters. I soon found that at least in 1966, one had to rely on the big cable companies, ATT, ITT and Western Union. There were representatives from each on the press plane ready to serve you when necessary.

From Honolulu, you could telephone your home office and dictate your story, which I did, but once we got to foreign countries, you had to rely on the cable companies which had people manning telex machines wherever we went.

At the Honolulu airport, Johnson stressed that there would be no new "strategy of war" nor any "spectacular formulation for peace" worked out at the Manila conference.

In short order, on October 18, 1966, we made a refueling stop in Pago Pago, the capital of American Samoa, where the weather was over 100 degrees. Probably, as many as 7,000 people turned out to see the visiting presidential party. Johnson was the first and so far the only American president to visit the island. We all got a quick tour, were told how TV was used for educational use. And there was a tribal ceremony in which the chiefs paid homage to the "White Bird" as Johnson was called.

From there we flew on to New Zealand. Johnson's Air Force plane had to land at the Ohakea airport, 90 miles north of the Wellington airport because of its size and then fly on to Wellington, the capital. At the welcoming ceremony, in the rain, Johnson recalled his time as a wartime emissary for President Roosevelt in 1942. He said he had come down with a fever of 105 degrees in the Fijis and that New Zealand doctors "pulled me through a very rough and lonely time—and since then I have thought of New Zealand with the warmest gratitude" In a televised speech to the New Zealand parliament, Johnson again offered to include North Vietnam in a post war "Great Society," aid program for Southeast Asia. He said it was futile for North Vietnam to continue the war.

He called on North Vietnam's leaders to join in a noble war" on hunger, ignorance, and disease in Southeast Asia.

In New Zealand, Johnson's reception was cordial but cool and kept down in size by the cold spring day. But when we arrived in Canberra, the Australian capital, we were met with a shining sun, a gentle southerly breeze and cooperative businesses and schools which contributed to a mammoth crowd wherever Johnson went.

Along the way, there were hip-hip-hoorays and serenades of "for he's a jolly good fellow." There were no visible anti-war pickets along the route."

At one point, Prime Minister Harold Holt, who was with him, said: "I'm glad you're not running for prime minister, Mr. President." After warning against any miracles from the Manila meeting, Johnson said there is a new vision, "a new hope," in this vast area of the world.

But as far as crowd stories go, nothing topped Melbourne, the very "British" city in southern Australia. A wild, cheering crowd, estimated at some 500,000 people jammed the streets to the point that the security people worried about the safety of Johnson and his wife. At times the crowd was so pressing that as many as fifty American and Australian security agents had to push and shove to get the limousine moving.

I was in the White House pool that day—my first time to have that responsibility—and as such was being driven in a car right behind the officials. At one point, two youths, later said to be brothers, rushed from the throng as Johnson's car was stopped, and threw two plastic bags of paint on the glass bubble over Johnson's car.

One bag of green paint landed on the front windshield, covered about two-thirds of it, as well as part of the car. The other bag of red paint landed on the bubble part of the car. Three Secret Service men outside the car were splattered. As far as The Star was concerned, this was the big news of the trip so far. It gave my story a banner headline.

On the flight back to Canberra, I was still the pool reporter and was allowed to sit in the front compartment along with Johnson and Holt. His aides brought him back sheathes of wire service stories. I was fascinated by the interest Johnson was paying to reports of a speech by Senator Robert Kennedy, at that time already a potential candidate for the presidency in 1968. Johnson asked Holt on the plane if he had ever seen such a large crowd before. Holt said only once—when the Prince of Wales came. "But he was our Prince Charming," he said as if to reassure Johnson.

Johnson continued the next day to Sydney, Australia's other major city, where police were expecting more anti-war protestors, and they were not wrong.

My story reported, however, that "although there was great apprehension—and some incidents –the president got through the day with an easier time than he had yesterday in Melbourne." Later in the day, he returned to Canberra, changed into a Western outfit and went to a barbecue given by an old Texas friend and now ambassador to Australia, Edward Clark. And finally, he flew to Brisbane in the north, noting that a million American GIs had passed through Brisbane during World War II.

The actual six-nation conference began in Manila in the Philippine House of Representatives with a fiery speech by President Ferdinand Marcos. There were also similar speeches by the South Vietnamese leaders. President Johnson did not speak. In a closed door session, General Westmoreland briefed the group on how the war was going, He said the ratio of enemy killed was rising, but they still were continuing to come into the South.

While the speeches were going on, there were about 1000 protestors outside the U.S. Embassy against the war as well as outside the Manila Hotel where the U.S. delegation was staying. The press received briefings from U.S. military on the war situation.

On the last day of the conference, a final communique was delayed for several hours, but it was eventually issued. It said that U.S. and the forces from other allied countries can be withdrawn six months after North Vietnam "withdraws its forces, ceases infiltration, and the level of violence thus subsides"

I dutifully filed my story on the communique via the telex operators at the press center, then took advantage of the post- conference, partying but ended up in my hotel room around 10 pm. I knew I was supposed to get up early for a morning tour of Corregidor with LBJ, My phone rang at about 10:30 pm and it was the embassy calling. I was told that instead of Corregidor, I would be taken with others to the Embassy for a very important briefing at 10 am.

When we assembled in the embasy auditorium, Bill Moyers announced that we were all going to Vietnam with the President, that all communications were now cut from Manila. We were then bussed to Clark Air Force Base and got on our PanAm plane and flown to Cam Ranh Bay, the U.S. air base in Vietnam. It was a very smooth trip. Obviously, the servicemen at the base were surprised and delighted to see the commander-in-chief who mingled with them in a very hot mess hall. And Johnson also went to the officers' club to greet the airmen. He also walked through the base hospital wards, handing out purple hearts, signing autographs, and issuing medals.

In my story, I wrote: "Johnson, who got closer to an actual battlefield than any president since Lincoln, told Westmoreland and his top field commanders "to come home with that coonskin on the wall."

As we were flying back to Manila, I realized I had a serious filing problem. Since the only way to file from Manila required turning over a typed piece of copy to a telex operator I was frustrated because I did not have my portable with me. But luckily, Chuck Bailey of the Minneapolis Tribune, one of the best correspondents of his era, who was also a Crimson editor of an earlier generation than mine, generously lent me his portable to I could bang out my story.

When the press plane landed in Manila, I handed my copy to an RCA motorcycle messenger who zipped it to the press center for filing, And when I got home I was pleased –but not surprised—to see that the Star had a banner headline with my story: "President Johnson made a surprise 2 ½ hour to a U.S. base in South Vietnam today and vowed never to let down the American servicemen or the Vietnamese people."

I wrote that in his remarks, Johnson said, "I came here today for one good reason: simply because I could not come to this part of the world and not come to see you." I noted that there had been speculation for weeks that Johnson would visit Vietnam on this visit but nevertheless, the timing had caught many reporters off guard.

One of those caught "off guard" was my good friend Don Oberdorfer of the Washington Post who covered Asian affairs for The Post. He had gone ahead to Corregidor and badly needed a fill-in on the Vietnam visit which I gave him. Don and I were friendly competitors for many years until he retired a few years ahead of me. He passed away in 2015.

From Vietnam, we flew to Thailand for a rather subdued visit with the king and then on to Malaysia for a quick word of support for the government which was also fighting Communist insurgents. And then on to South Korea, where Johnson received an incredible public display of support in the streets of Seoul where an estimated million people thronged the streets to greet him.

Johnson took a special train to meet with U.S. troops along the border with North Korea. Mentioning the Manila conference, Johnson said, "We have talked to the statesmen and the soldiers of the Pacific-Asia area. If we can only ever learn to do our job as politicians as well as you do yours as soldiers, we'll eliminate yours— there won't be any need for soldiers."

"But until we do, you're going to have to carry on," he said.

From Seoul, we flew to Anchorage, Alaska, landing in frigid temperatures, and then flew on to Washington, landing about 6:30 p.m., met by a large Democratic Party greeting party given that Election Day was only a week away. Johnson said: "If our countrymen will stand with us—if we travel the difficult road together—-we will come out well in the end. Where there is deep division in a land, there is danger. But where there is unity, there is strength."

To symbolize the division, about fifty demonstrators from the Women's Strike for Peace bore signs stating, "Make Love Not War" and other signs of protest.

In short, the long trip did nothing to reduce the widespread opposition to the war in the United States and only hastened Johnson's decision to find a diplomatic way to end the conflict—an effort which would frustrate him to the end of his term.

CHAPTER 11

A Most Eventful Year

As 1967 began, I pressed Newbie Noyes and Burt Hoffman for an opportunity to visit South Vietnam, a country I had written about so regularly, but had never set foot in. In mid- March, even though most of his advisers thought the trip a waste of their time, President Johnson decided he wanted to fly some 8,000 miles across the United States to Hawaii, and then on to the farthest American possession in the Pacific, Guam, to meet with the South Vietnamese leaders. The Star agreed to let me go on the press plane to Guam.

The occasion was a meeting on March 20-2, 1967 between the top American officials, including President Johnson, Secretary Rusk, Secretary McNamara, presidential advisers, Averell Harriman, Maxwell D. Taylor, the outgoing Saigon ambassador Henry Cabot Lodge, the new one, Ellsworth Bunker, and the CIA Director, Richard

Helms, and the top South Vietnamese, Nguyen Cao Ky and Nguyen Van Thieu.

It was an interesting meeting for me. Guam today is a tourist mecca in the western Pacific. But then it was a military outpost. It was where the B-52 bombers took off to attack North Vietnam. It was populated by military families and natives. It was the rainy season and it did rain. And It was a most unusual meeting. The Vietnamese had just promulgated their first constitution, under considerable American pressure, but what was on their mind was not to boast of the new document, but to press Johnson for stepped up U.S. military support, in particular stronger military action against the North Vietnamese.

In this they seemed to echo, the U.S. Joint Chiefs of Staff. Ky said in his arrival statement that the North Vietnamese will only negotiate when they "feel they are losing." Therefore, he said, it was necessary to step up the military pressure. "How long can Hanoi enjoy the advantage of restricted bombing of military targets?" Ky asked. "How long can the Viet Cong be permitted to take sanctuary in Cambodia, be allowed to regroup and come back at their will?"

"How long can supply through Laos be permitted to operate? How long can war materiel be permitted to come into Haiphong harbor? How long can the North be permitted to infiltrate soldiers and weapons across the demilitarized line?" he asked passionately.

Johnson, on the other hand, focused almost exclusively in public on the new Vietnamese constitution.

"Now, your great task is to conduct a national election for a new government," he said at the start of the working session. "The success of that election is as important as any of the military operations we shall conduct in the months ahead."

Johnson added later: "All those who have thoughtfully studied the modern history of Vietnam know that military power alone cannot secure the peace and ensure the progress of that nation — nor of any other. Free political institutions are indispensable to the success of South Vietnam's long struggle against terror—and those who support her in that struggle rejoice in the success of this past week."

The two-day Guam meeting ended without any major news. Johnson, in farewell remarks at the airport, said "We did not adopt any spectacular new programs at this meeting. The nature of this war is not amenable to spectacular programs or easy solutions. It requires courage, perseverance, and dedication. Yet we leave Guam refreshed by the conviction that on every front— military, political and social—we and our allies are making substantial progress,"

In a way, the two-day conference was a strange one. It seemed upstaged by the Vietnamese strong statements calling for more military action, and Johnson's denial that there was much discussion of military policy during the talks. One could only sympathize with his advisers who thought it a waste of time to come all that way for the trip.

While, the Guam meeting was winding down, Ho Chi Minh replied publicly to a secret letter that Johnson had sent him on February 8 via the North Vietnam embassy in Moscow, offering to stop bombing North Vietnam and freeze troop levels if North Vietnam stopped infiltration of South Vietnam. The message from Ho said the United States must stop all acts of war against North Vietnam first. It was just the latest in Hanoi's rejections of LBJ's offers to talk.

Richard Critchfield, The Star's Saigon correspondent was in Guam with me and we both flew to Saigon together. I stayed at the Caravelle Hotel, where correspondents had stayed for years. It was a quiet time in South Vietnam. The fighting was not heavy, and I had a chance to visit different parts of Saigon including Cholon, the Chinese section, for some very good Chinese food. And at the American embassy, some of the analysts were old friends from the State Department who shared some of their reporting with me. Dick introduced me to some Vietnamese officials he knew, and I wrote a few stories for The Star. The most fruitful story I wrote came from some captured Viet Cong documents attributed to Le Duan, who was the General Secretary of the North Vietnamese Communist Party.

One said that even if he North Vietnamese agree to negotiations with outside parties, such as the United Nations, or the United States, the Viet Cong were told to continue their guerrilla war against the South Vietnamese.

"We must foresee this so that we have a correct understanding and should not depend upon negotiations," the document said. "The reason why we advocate negotiations is that we want to prove that we are always concerned about peace on a correct basis," Duan was quoted as saying. At another point, Duan discusses the visit to Hanoi in January 1966 by Aleksandr N. Shelepin, a high-ranking Soviet Politburo member, during the prolonged halt in U.S. bombing when the United States was seeking the start of negotiations. Duan said that there are "a number of revisionists" in the Soviet Communist Party and that Hanoi's leadership "struggles to correct them." Duan said that Shelepin "seems to have suggested negotiations." Duan added, however, that "because we have foreseen this, we issued a communique containing our determination to fight the U.S. aggressors. Therefore the revisionists' scheme has failed, and they have acquired our opinion." This turned out to be accurate because in subsequent years, Soviet leaders continuously talked about negotiations but never seemed to do anything about producing anyone at the table.

From Saigon, I flew to Hong Kong for my first visit to that then British outpost, which was a citadel for China watchers. The United States then had a well-staffed consulate in Hong Kong and no embassy yet in Beijing (it was still called "Peiping" in official Washington). From talking to officials there I got a good briefing on the on-going Cultural Revolution then sweeping China under Mao Tse-tung's personal auspices. I guess I was one of the first to write about the downfall of Liu Shao-chi, on April 3, 1967. He had been chief of state, whose treatment and eventual death is one of the genuine stains of the Cultural Revolution. I also wrote correctly that Prime Minister Chou En-lai had survived the purge.

Back in Washington, I was startled by the news of the "defection" to the United States of Stalin's only daughter, Svetlana Alliuyeva Stalin, who arrived in New York suddenly on April 22, 1967, from Switzerland to seek asylum. She said that religion was a major reason for her decision. It was the start of a long journey for the woman, who was highly-educated, but who had problems in her life settling down. She had fallen in love in Russia with an Indian citizen, who had died there and she had carried his ashes to India, but the Indian government would not allow her to remain in India. Eventually, the United States agreed to allow her into the United States hoping to avoid a big splash, since President Johnson was hoping for

Soviet cooperation on Vietnam. But it was clearly a major news story, and The Star encouraged me to cover it to the fullest. We ran her full statement that was issued to the press upon her arrival at JFK airport in New York. She was quite excited about coming to America.

She was helped out by George F. Kennan, the former U.S. ambassador to the Soviet Union, who was then the leading Soviet specialist in the country, and who had read her manuscript, "Twenty Letters to a Friend" and helped her get it published later in the year. Svetlana eventually married an American architect, in Wisconsin, had a child with him, went back to Russia, lived for a while in England, and died in Wisconsin at the age of 85. In the end, I am afraid she never had a happy life.

At this time in my life, I guess I was known primarily as a Soviet expert, since The Star had sent me on trips there and I had written extensively on the Communist world, and on Vietnam since you couldn't write on world affairs without writing about that part of the world. But suddenly, I was to be introduced to the Middle East.

The June 1967 Six-Day war in the Middle East still reverberates today.

CHAPTER 12

The 1967 Middle East War
And Its Aftermath

The outbreak of what would become known as the Six Day War in June 1967 came as a surprise to many of us, so focused as we were at The Star on Vietnam at that time. It had been a given that ever since the 1956 Middle East war that the U.N. peace keepers had ensured the borders and that there was little likelihood of an eruption of fighting across them.

But for reasons that are still unclear to me today, Gamal Abdel Nasser, the Egyptian leader, reported to Syrian leaders that Soviet intelligence was reporting that Israel was about to attack Syria. Israel denied this, and in fact, there was no indication that this was true, but the rapid mobilization of Egyptian and Syrian troops led to a corresponding mobilization by Israel in May 1967.

What led to the war, of course, was Nasser's very public demand that U.N. peacekeepers who were sent to the area after the 1956 war had to leave the Sinai, and more importantly, from the Israeli point of view, from the Gulf of Aqaba, which was Israel's waterway south to the Red Sea.

Meanwhile, Israel's Foreign Minister Abba Eban arrived in Washington for talks on May 26 and conferred at the White House with Johnson, Rusk and McNamara.

What ensued over the next week was a hectic effort by the United States and Britain to line up an international flotilla to go through the Gulf of Aqaba to demonstrate Israel's right to passage through the waterway.

But the effort could not get Security Council support. And for some reason, the Syrians kept claiming that Israel was massing for an attack on its borders, when it was not.

This led to a mobilization by Egypt and then by Syria. And then by Israel. And the Israelis—despite pleas from the White House to hold their fire, decided on a preemptive attack against Egypt and Syria.

Jordan then was persuaded to join the war on the Arab side and the ensuing war was a total disaster for the Arab side. In six days, Israel occupied the entire Suez peninsula, the West Bank of the Jordan River, East Jerusalem, and the entire Golan Heights in Syria Since that war, only the Sinai has been returned to Egypt under the terms of the Egyptian-Israeli peace agreement signed by Anwar Sadat, Menachem Begin and President Jimmy Carter at the White House in March 1979, finalizing the accords reached at Camp David in September 1978.

Ever since that Six-Day war, the United States has tried to reconcile the parties and restore some of the occupied lands to the Arabs. So far, these efforts have failed, with the exception of the peace treaty between Egypt and Israel which led to Israel returning the Sinai to Egypt.

But the June 5 war was also a signal moment in U.S.-Soviet relations, It was the first time the "hot line" had been used in a real situation. On June 5, according to Robert McNamara's memoirs, a general on duty at the Pentagon called him and said "Premier Kosygin is on the 'hot line' and wants to talk to the president. What should I tell him?" McNamara was furious that there was not a direct line to the White House but that was quickly worked out and eventually Kosygin was put through to Johnson.

It was a message, not a conversation.

In Johnson's memoirs, he says: "Kosygin said that the message 'expressed Soviet concern over the fighting.' Kosygin said the Russians intended to work for a cease-fire and that they hoped we would exert influence on Israel and use our influence to bring hostilities to an end, and

Johnson said that we were pleased the Soviets planned to do the same."

Johnson and McNamara, in their memoirs, remember June 10 as being very tense with Kosygin threatening over the hot line to use force if Israel did not stop its advance in Syria. But Johnson was able to assure Kosygin that the Israelis would accept a cease fire once the Golan Heights had been secured.

By June 11, there was a cease fire. This, of course, was a signal moment for Israel. It will always be remembered as the high water moment in its military achievements in the Middle East.

Israel's air force had carried out a spectacular series of raids against the Egyptian planes on the ground and had destroyed the Sinai army of Egypt. With complete dominance of the air, the Israelis also moved to within striking distance of Damascus.

And of course to King Hussein's lasting regret, he felt as an Arab leader he had to join the war and lost East Jerusalem and the West Bank to Israel.

In the aftermath of the Six-Day War there was considerable diplomacy. I was sent to New York to cover Kosygin's appearance before the special General Assembly session which he had called. I also wanted to be on hand in case there would be a Soviet-American summit. There had not been one since Khrushchev and Kennedy had met in Vienna in the summer of 1961.

Kosygin's four-engine Ilyushin 18 turbo-prop landed at JFK airport at 5:05 a.m. on Saturday, June 17, 1967. There was an unusually large number of journalists at the airport on this very sunny late spring day.

His motorcade sped toward Manhattan but instead of driving directly to the Soviet U.N. Mission on East 67th street, it stopped on Third Avenue and 53d street. Kosygin, Ambassador Anatoly Dobrynin. U.N. Ambassador Nikolai Fedorenko, and an interpreter, accompanied by a swarm of security agents got out and started walking briskly up largely deserted Third Avenue.

They were followed by reporters and photographers, including me, someone who had just turned 32 a month earlier, and was in pretty good shape, trying to keep up with the Russians, as best as they could.

I wrote that Kosygin, who had been agitating at home for better consumer facilities, seemed fascinated at looking in the window of Clark's Coffee House at 66th street and Third Avenue and by the high rises along the street.

There was no action over that first weekend, but on Monday, Kosygin addressed the special session and lambasted Israel and the United States and demanded a return to the status quo ante which everyone knew would not happen.

In Washington, Johnson, who had snubbed the special U.N. session, spoke about the Middle East from the State

Department calling for sharp limits on arms shipments to the Middle East and free passage through international waters.

There then ensued about a day and a half of diplomatic bickering to try and arrange a venue for a Kosygin-Johnson meeting. Kosygin did not want to come to Washington and Johnson did not want to go to New York.

Rusk came to New York to serve as an intermediary with Gromyko. Eventually, the governor of New Jersey, Richard Hughes, suggested to Johnson that Glassboro State College, serve as a compromise since it is about half way between Washington and New York. His proposal was accepted by both sides

The first meeting was held on Friday, June 23, in the house of he college president which was called "Hollybush Mansion"

There was a major effort by both sides to demonstrate good will during the talks. My front page story in The Star on June 24 has as its lead: "President Johnson and Soviet Premier Aleksei N. Kosygin return to this college town tomorrow to follow up on their extraordinarily smooth initial get-together yesterday."

"Not since the time when former Premier Nikita S. Khrushchev came away from his meeting with President Eisenhower at Camp David in 1959 has there been such an apparently successful summit meeting between U.S. and Soviet leaders. Kosygin said that there were so many issues yet to be discussed that they decided to extend the talks another day." And that, I wrote. "has created an unusual sense of euphoria here."

But experts again warned that there had been so far no breakthroughs on any major issues and they did not expect any before Kosygin went home.

On their day off on Saturday, Kosygin flew on Air Force One with several East European allies to Niagra Falls where he was greeted warmly by other tourists as he enjoyed himself on a tour boat under the falls. Johnson flew to Texas to see his newly-born grandson.

The talks then resumed at Glassboro on Sunday afternoon, but apparently broke no new ground.

Kosygin held a press conference at the United Nations in which he said that any improvement in Soviet- American relations "could best be served by one first step—and that is, an end to the American aggression in Vietnam."

He said that war "leaves an impression on all relations between Russia and America." In my front page article, I wrote that Kosygin said Johnson would be welcomed in Russia "only after the aggression is halted and a truly peaceful policy is followed." Actually Johnson was invited to Russia to start talks on limiting missile deployment later in his term, but those talks were cancelled after the Soviet Union invaded Czechoslovakia in August 1968. But we are ahead of ourselves here.

While little progress was being reported on the broad Middle East and Vietnam issues, Rusk and Gromyko privately were working on an agreement on non-proliferation of nuclear weapons.

I had a front page article on June 28, 1967 that said Rusk and Gromyko "have followed up last weekend's summit conferences" with the draft of a non- proliferation treaty that probably will be submitted to the Geneva disarmament conference within a few days. The article said that "Although sources say that total agreement—and a treaty—is still quite a distance down the road, there is satisfaction that something rather concrete has emerged in the aftermath of the Glassboro sessions."

The treaty actually went into effect in 1968.

Meanwhile, we learned from his memoirs that McNamara submitted to the president on May 19, 1967, a long memorandum "that raised the possibility of a compromise: restricting the bombing to interdiction of the infiltration 'funnel' below the twentieth parallel; limiting additional deployments to thirty thousand after which a firm ceiling should be imposed and adopting a more flexible bargaining position while actively seeking a political settlement."

McNamara says his memo to the president "unleashed a storm of controversy." He says "it intensified already sharp debate within the administration. It led to tense and acrimonious Senate hearings that pitted me against the joint chiefs of staff and generated rumors they intended to resign en masse.

"It accelerated the process that ultimately drove President Johnson and me apart. And it hastened my departure from the Pentagon." In November, he assumed the presidency of the World Bank.

CHAPTER 13

Celebrations in Moscow

After the excitement over the Middle East had died down at the end of June 1967, with Ambassador Goldberg succeeding in getting Resolution 242 passed which to this day is the ambiguous resolution on how much territory Israel is obliged to give up in the Middle East. Goldberg resigned his post in 1968, frustrated in not being able to get Johnson to stop the bombing in Vietnam, He was replaced by George W. Ball, who had been Rusk's Under Secretary of State. Meanwhile, the elections in South Vietnam went pretty much as planned with Nguyen Van Thieu being elected president and Nguyen Cao Ky premier. At that time, the warfare in South Vietnam had slackened a bit at least publicly and there was another burst of optimism in Washington hoping for possible peace talks that of course did not occur.

And in September, I wrote a front page piece on Sunday, September 10, 1967 that said the United States was warning Russians that unless they agree to set a time and place soon for arms control talks, the United States was going to go ahead with an anti- ballistic missile system (ABM).

The Soviet Union meanwhile was making plans to celebrate the 50th anniversary of the Bolshevik Revolution on November 7. The Star seemed pleased to send me out one more time to Eastern Europe and Russia for what was becoming a regular pilgrimage. This time I started again in Warsaw. The first time I had visited the Polish capital was in the summer of 1959 on my way to Russia in my summer in the USSR as part of the exchange of youth.

At that time, there was still rubble in the street, and it was evident that 14 years after the end of World War II, things were still tough. Now, in the summer of 1967, things looked a lot better. There was a very discernable middle class in Warsaw, living in cooperative apartment houses.

I wrote: "One long time resident says the most significant change he has noticed in the last two years is that people now seem to finally feel at home and are taking better care of their neighborhoods. Undoubtedly, the fact that most people now have to buy their apartments from cooperatives, rather than getting them free from the state, has contributed to this sense of responsibility."

On my first trip to Poland for The Star, I had written with some excitement that the Poles had signed a contract with CBS for having productions of My Fair Lady staged around the country in Polish, one of several Broadway musicals, so favored.

By 1967, foreign plays were old hat, and the problem was a shortage of Polish playwrights. In the movie field, I wrote that Poland had gained acclaim in the 1950s due to Wajda's "Ashes and Diamonds" and Polansky's "Knife in the Water." I wrote that currently, the Polish film industry was suffering. Little did I realize that as I was wandering around Warsaw in those warm October days in 1967 that 13 years later Poland would be engulfed in serious tension over labor unrest in the shipyards of Gdansk that would spread nationwide, and produce the Solidarity trade union, the first Polish Pope, and eventually lead to the downfall of all the Communist regimes in Eastern Europe.

From Poland, I moved on to Bucharest, Romania, where I again reported on the separatist movement in the Communist Party there which has tried for several years to limit the influence of the Soviet Union. Not much had changed from my last visit. Once again, I found the U.S. Embassy boosting the Romanians for their independent line. Then. I went to Prague where there was considerable excitement in the air. As I had noted in my series of articles a year ago, Prague was the closest to Greenwich Village as existed in Europe, I thought. They loved the beatnik poets, and on this trip, I began a story this way:

"She was young, pretty, and wearing a miniskirt. Her English was comprehensible. 'Will you give me something, five or six dollars? I have a passport and I want very much to go to Paris.' Most of the foreigners in the Alcron Hotel's coffee shop were taken aback by the unexpected request from the young woman. But one must expect anything these days in Prague for there is a clear desire for freedom here and this quest takes many forms." I personally was clearly infected with the Czech spirit. The first time I had visited Prague was on my way out of the Soviet Union in the same summer of 1959.

I had several Czech journalist friends in Washington who told me about the ferment in Prague and I had lunch with a couple of their editors who told me about what was going on internally. I wrote somewhat philosophically: "It is now Czechoslovakia's turn to seek the definition of freedom and as might be expected, there is little agreement here about freedom, the meaning, its value and its allocation."

"Walking along Prague's streets gives some indication of what is going on," I wrote. "Over the past few years, young generations have gone beat. Blue jeans and long hair are everywhere. It is not a hippie revolt, but rather the young stating an intention to dictate their style of dress, even though President Antonin Novotny has lashed out at the Western mode."

I kept in touch with my Czech friends in Washington after I returned, and of course, as 1968 progressed, I could feel the tensions in the air, which led eventually to the Soviet invasion in August 1968.

Meanwhile, I moved from Prague to Moscow to cover the anniversary celebrations. I stayed at the National Hotel, which was my favorite in Moscow. It sits on the edge of Red Square, and no sooner had I gotten into my room than I was visited by two Novosti representatives who, I presumed, were also KGB operatives,. They offered me their best services, and any help they could provide. I took a cab to Ed Stevens house. Ed, who died in 1992, was the longest living Western correspondent in Moscow. At that time, he was a stringer for The Star and believe it or not he and his wife had a private house in Moscow. I wrote my stories from his house and filed them by telex from there. While in Moscow, I made two side trips. On one, I went to Riga, the capital of Latvia, because I had never been to the Baltic area. But it was not very interesting to me. And I went to Leningrad, where the Bolshevik Revolution, of course, had started, in what was then called Petrograd, the name having changed from St. Petersburg [what it is now called again]. It was quite cold in late October in Leningrad, and like a good tourist, I went to the Lenin "sights" which included the Finland Station, the train station where Lenin entered Russia from Finland and launched his campaign to start a second revolution, to replace the February revolution which was dominated by wealthy classes. After that revolution the Czar and his family went into exile in the Russian east.

Eventually, I took the train to Moscow and back to the National Hotel. I was able to report, based on briefings from the American embassy, that the Russians would resume talks on curbing missiles once the holiday celebrations were over. From the briefings, I reported that "in general, despite the Vietnam war, the United States and Russia are on fairly good terms. Relations are not as cordial as they were in 1964, but are better than they were last year."

For instance. I wrote that I also found in conversation with Russians not only in Moscow and Leningrad but also in Riga that despite Moscow's major involvement in the Vietnam war, "the public in Russia and the rest of Eastern Europe show a surprising lack of interest in the war."

"This conclusion is held by veteran Western diplomats in the Communist world and is borne out in conversations with Soviet citizens...At first it seems as if the people here are merely being polite, but after talking with them, it becomes clear they simply do not regard the war as important to them or their country."

The anniversary ceremonies began in the newly-built glass and marble Palace of the Congresses inside the Kremlin walls with Leonid I. Brezhnev, the party leader, giving a long, four hour speech that called for a world summit meeting of Communist leaders and sharply attacked the "Mao Tse-tung group.". He did not mention Stalin or Khrushchev by name and there was no discussion of any peace talks on Vietnam. He mentioned the United States twice as a World War Two ally, and once for bombing Vietnam. In the next day's session, only two Eastern European leaders, Wladislaw Gomulka of Poland and Todor Zhivkov of Bulgaria endorsed the call for the world meeting.

Finally, November 7 dawned and the official celebrations of the Anniversary came to an end with the annual parade through Red Square which in those days was a working seminar for the defense attaches of the various foreign embassies. It had become customary for the Kremlin to show off its newest missiles by rolling them out on parade in the midst of the other hardware shown in the military parades. The huge crowd, allowed into the square with special passes, loved the parade which went on for several hours, and included civilians of all stripes after the military had their time in the sun. My lead said: "The Soviet Union marked its 50th birthday today with a bit of nostalgia and a parade of armed might including several new missiles." I added that although the new weaponry received major attention, "the atmosphere created on the day was not particularly martial and Defense Minister Andrei A. Grechko's speech was restrained." After the festivities were over, reporters were briefed by defense attaches. They said the most significant new missile was a 160-foot ICBM, which Tass said was powered by a "new, highly efficient type of propellant." The attaches said this indicated the new missile may be similar to the solid-fueled Minuteman missiles.

The large crowd in the square, of course, did not come particularly to see the new military hardware. They loved the "historic" marchers. I wrote: "To the delight of the crowd, several companies of young men, dressed in 1917 style uniforms, began marching through Red Square — the famous Red Guards, the Red Cossacks, the Bolshevik Commissars, and several ranks of horse cavalry, some of them pulling machine guns and light artillery pieces of World War I vintage." I noted that "Following the military show, the festivities were turned over to sportsmen groups and scores of work brigades, young Communist leagues and delegations from everything from Intourist to Writers Unions—all of whom marched through in good spirits, even if their ranks became a little disorganized."

And so my trip to Russia to cover the 50th anniversary celebrations was about over. My article summing up the festivities may have reflected the gray skies that take over Moscow in November, in advance of the cold winters ahead. I wrote that "The 50th anniversary celebrations of the Bolshevik Revolution have ended with no major surprises and more than a few stifled yawns by political observers here." I suppose I should have added that a positive note was that nothing was done to rule out an eventual rapprochement with Washington. Summing it up, I noted that Brezhnev's place as Number One in the hierarchy was further cemented, and it would stay that way until he died in 1982. There was no sign during the celebrations of any peace plan for Vietnam, and no new peace offering to China. The Russian consumer was promised a better future, indicating that the leadership knows the public is still not happy with the situation in the stores.

CHAPTER 14

1968—A Pivotal Year for Me

The sobering fact upon returning to Washington at the beginning of December 1967—-I had visited Bulgaria and Yugoslavia also, places I hadn't been before, and wrote short pieces about both of them— was that Vietnam now more than ever still dominated everything.

There was a twinkle of hope at the New Year that maybe, just maybe, Hanoi was willing to negotiate. I wrote a front page story on January 2 saying that "Top US officials are giving close study today to a Hanoi statement promising talks with the United States in return for a halt in U.S. bombing raids." The story, of course, noted that this was the first time that North Vietnam had said "will" instead of "could" hold talks. As a result, I wrote, the new statement was being scrutinized "at the White House, State Department, and Central Intelligence Agency."

It had been made on Dec. 30 by North Vietnam's Foreign Minister Nguyen Duy Trinh at a reception for a visiting Mongolian delegation and it had been carried by the Vietnamese News Agency. The key sentence said: "After the United States has ended unconditionally the bombing and all other acts of war against the DRV [North Vietnam], the DRV will hold talks with the United States on questions concerned."

On January 5, I followed it up with another front page story saying Secretary of State Rusk says the United States "is taking seriously North Vietnam's proposal to hold talks in return for a bombing halt but wants to know whether it is 'a peace feeler…or purely a propaganda move.'" Rusk held a press conference to raise questions about the sincerity of the offer by Hanoi to talk. And President Johnson, in his State of the Union address on January 16, 1968, repeated what he called his "San Antonio Formula," for peace talks, again calling on the North Vietnamese to begin talks "promptly and with reasonable hopes they would be productive" and that Hanoi not try to take military advantage of a bombing halt. The whole issue of "talks" became irrelevant in a matter of days, of course, when the North Vietnamese and the Viet Cong launched what became known as the Tet offensive toward the end of January.

The annual Tet holiday that year began on January 29, a time of holiday-making for Vietnamese, but the Viet Cong and North Vietnamese chose to make a strong statement on this holiday.

The offensive began in the north near Khe Sanh, where there was a U.S. Marine outpost, and it picked up steam, as Viet Cong hit almost every populated place in the South, including Saigon. And to garner the most publicity for the effort, the Viet Cong were able to send guerrillas into the U.S. Embassy compound on January 31. The Star had a banner headline, "Day-Long Saigon Battle Subsides." The story by the excellent AP Correspondent in Saigon, Peter Arnett was headlined: "It Was a Fight for Survival For Americans in Embassy"

There was an additional story about an embassy officer having to defend himself in his bedroom by shooting an intruding Viet Cong to death. The next day, The Star, along with other newspapers ran on the front page, the gripping photograph by AP photographer Eddie Adams of South Vietnam's police chief executing a Viet Cong captive by shooting him in the head. That was probably one of the most anti-war photos of the conflict.

My analysis of the Saigon fighting was stated simply that day: "North Vietnam and the Viet Cong have launched their 'winter- spring offensive' whose goal, as stated in captured documents, is "an extraordinary victory in a relatively short period of time." The article quoted my government sources as saying that Viet Cong agents, "carried away with enthusiasm, have even told village meetings that the war will be over by February—with a "coalition government" set up in Saigon that would fall under Communist sway."

Adding to the woes in Washington was the unexpected seizure by North Korea early in the morning of January 23 of the U.S. Navy Intelligence ship the USS Pueblo with 83 men aboard. This became a major international incident and alarmed Washington for several weeks but it was eventually determined that the North Koreans were not working in unison with the North Vietnamese. In fact, I wrote on February 3 that "the sense of urgency that prevailed in Washington after the seizure of the Pueblo on January 23 has now largely dissipated."

As the days went on, there were also signs of ferment anew in Czechoslovakia which had attracted my attention during my visit there in October. Not only had President Novotny been pressured to resign, but an outsider, Aleksandr Dubcek, whom virtually no one in Washington had ever heard of, was the new leader, and was becoming a hero to the liberal intelligentsia in Prague and elsewhere in that country. I made a mental note to visit Prague again soon.

Meanwhile, Haynes Johnson and I had finished our biography of J. William Fulbright, "The Dissenter," and it was due to be published in October. My contribution to the book was mainly research, during my few weeks of vacation, sitting in Fulbright's office, and going through his files, and writing memos. Haynes traveled to Arkansas.

Fulbright was very much in the news in the spring of 1968 because he was quite unhappy with the Vietnam war, and really wanted to grill Secretary Rusk. I had done a "take out" on Rusk that ran on the front page of The Star on January 21, 1968, just before the Tet offensive. It was headlined: "Cool, Sure Dean Rusk: Turmoil Over Vietnam War Leaves Him Unshaken." Of course, I wrote that piece without knowing, as I do now, having read his memoir, about his personal anguishes over Vietnam, and his own son's psychological stresses over it.

In any event, on March 11 and 12, Rusk agreed to testify in open televised testimony before Fulbright's Foreign Relations Committee. There had been clear tension previously between the two southerners, and during the hearing, Rusk said that he regretted very much that differences between him and the committee had led to a virtual freeze in communication between them and he thought it would be useful for the two sides to meet more often but he thought televised hearings were of minimal value. Fulbright was pressing for advance consultation before there would be any escalation in the U.S. involvement in Vietnam, and Rusk put him off on that issue.

For much of the first months of 1968, the issue for the Johnson administration was in persuading Hanoi to agree to sit at a negotiating table without having to stop bombing North Vietnam completely. President Johnson met with his "wise men" regularly for advice, and by this time, I was becoming a regular second-string White House correspondent, filling in for Horner, particularly on Saturdays. I can still remember Saturday, March 30, 1968 well. Johnson liked to walk along the Rose Garden outside the White House Oval Office and have an impromptu press conference. He announced at one of those impromptus that he would give a nationally televised speech Sunday night on Vitenam, the culmination of his several weeks of talks with advisers and "wise men" about what future actions to take. Johnson told us that the speech would deal with moderate troops increases as well as the need to appropriate an additional "few billion" for the war effort. About the same time, Secretary Rusk had departed Washington for a meeting of Asian allies in New Zealand.

So, The Star's headline on my front page story in Saturday afternoon's paper was "Johnson Bars Major Change in Viet Policy." On Sunday morning, The Star had a banner headline on a similar story by me saying much the same thing. In other words, I had no idea of what was about to happen that night. In fact, as far as I knew, Johnson was the leading Democratic Party candidate for re-election at that time. Being a bachelor and living at Washington Circle in DC, which was only about six blocks from the White House, I decided to go to the White House on Sunday night and hang around. Because The Star was an afternoon newspaper, our deadline was not until about 6 a.m. Monday morning for our first edition on Monday.

Our only morning newspaper was on Sunday. So, I got to the White House press room around 6 pm and picked up my advance copy of LBJ's speech, which was interesting in itself. He said that he was offering a drastic cutback in the bombing so that 90 percent of the population of North Vietnam and most of its territory would be spared bombing. This was to be the main incentive to get the Hanoi regime to agree to begin negotiations. As correspondents were rushing off to their offices with the advance copies, George Christian told them that LBJ would have some additional personal notes at the end. When I heard that, I decided to stick around the White House.

And like, I suppose, everybody watching the speech, I was shocked by the President's concluding words:

"I have concluded that I should not permit the presidency to become involved in the partisan divisions that are developing in this political year. With America's sons in the field far away, with America's future under challenge here at home, with our hopes and the world's hopes for peace in the balance every day I do not believe that I should devote an hour or a day of my time to any personal partisan causes or to any duties other than the awesome duties of this office, the presidency of your country.

"Accordingly, I shall not seek and I will not accept the nomination of my party for another term as your President. But let men everywhere know, however, that a strong and a confident, a vigilant America stands ready tonight to defend an honored cause, whatever the price, whatever the burden, whatever the sacrifice that duty may require.

"Thank you for listening. Goodnight and God bless all of you."

At about 11 pm, after dozens of reporters had reassembled in the press room downstairs, Johnson agreed to meet with us in the Mansion to discuss his surprise decision. This produced a feature article by me for Monday's Star, with a headline above the nameplate of The Star "Only Family and Close Friends Knew of Year-long Decision"

Johnson was wearing a light blue turtle neck shirt and eating a cup of tapioca pudding when he met with us. The way Johnson put it, he says that about a year ago, Johnson who was 59 when he was speaking with us that night began talking to Mrs. Johnson about the possibility that he would not run again because of the growing dissension in the country. The polls were beginning to show drops in his popularity and the anti-Vietnam demonstrations were getting uglier, he said. Mrs. Johnson encouraged him to call it quits when his term expired in January 1969.

Last August, Johnson told the then Secretary of Defense Robert S. McNamara that he was thinking of not running. He said he also told Dean Rusk ahead of time as well as the current Defense Secretary Clark Clifford, and George Christian.

Suddenly, on Wednesday, April 5, Hanoi, which until now had insisted on a complete halt to U.S. bombing raids said it was agreeable to talks with the United States even in the absence of a complete cessation of aerial attacks. This shocked most people in Washington. North Vietnam said, though, that the discussions should "be about the unconditional cessation of bombing and all other acts of war against the DRV (North Vietnam)." There was no agreement on where to hold the talks—-that would take days of back and forth negotiations later on during the month.

But first, Johnson wanted to fly to Honolulu to confer with the South Vietnamese allies, as well as with South Korean President Chung Hee Park, and dozens of senior aides from Saigon and Washington. We were all to leave on Friday, April 5, but on the evening of April 4, in Memphis, Martin Luther King Jr. was assassinated, and this touched off massive riots in the District of Columbia that spread to the center of the city. Our press plane as well as LBJ's did not take off. Instead, Washington was thrown into chaos.

Riots broke out throughout the black neighborhoods of Washington, which included much of Capitol Hill. A curfew was imposed, although I could drive around with my press credentials. After a couple of weeks, the rioting stopped and the curfew was lifted.

Meanwhile, as the rioting eased and the curfews were lifted in Washington, a kind of game was being played on where to hold the talks with Hanoi. The United States balked at Hanoi's suggestion of Warsaw. And Secretary of Defense Clifford said that President Johnson wanted to keep the U.S. troop level in South Vietnam at 549,000. By April 25, there still was an impasse on where to hold the negotiations. Both sides had turned down suggestions made by the other. As my story indicated, the one city, not mentioned was Paris. My article that day said "there is little disagreement that Paris is by far the most logical choice as as a site."

And finally, on May 3, Hanoi proposed Paris in a message to the United States and it was accepted and Johnson announced it in a press conference. The talks were to begin on May 10, with Averell Harriman and Cyrus R. Vance as the chief U.S. negotiators, and Xuyyan Thuy, the Vietnamese negotiator. On May 10, however, instead of substantive talks, there were preliminary discussions. More ominous, as it turns out, was an item I wrote that day on the front page, headlined: "Soviet Military Threat To Czechs Discounted". There were rumors in Eastern Europe about preparations in the Warsaw Pact for "another Hungary" to quash the growing liberalization in Czechoslovakia, but U.S. officials could not believe the Russians would be so stupid as to do that again. They would, however, three months later.

On May 12, I wrote an interpretive article in The Star that again showed the Soviet anxiety about Czechoslovakia but again, I was wrong in saying that "Russia Seems Able Only to Fret Over Liberalism In Bloc".

When the Vietnam negotiations finally began on May 14, there was as expected, no give on either side. The North Vietnamese wanted the United States to stop all bombing and the United States wants North Vietnam to deescalate its military activity. My article on the first round of talks said that experts were not surprised because they expected the talks to be tedious without much change in position. In fact, after the first week of talks, American officials were saying privately that until Hanoi lifted its "veil of fantasy" about the Vietnam war, no progress was possible.

Then suddenly, on June 20, 1968, Secretary Clifford, at a Pentagon news conference, expressed unexpected optimism about the Paris talks. He said "there are signs indicating slight movement toward agreement in the Paris negotiations." He said that instead of just the usual diatribes hurled at each other the two sides are now discussing matters during "longer and longer recesses" which he described in a positive manner. But Rusk, the next day, without publicly disagreeing with Clifford, said at his own press conference that the only changes in the Paris talks are "bits and straws." Harriman, himself, when he came back to Washington for consultations, said there had been no progress whatsoever in the talks.

On June 27, Soviet Foreign Minister Andrei A. Gromyko stunned Washington when he announced from the Kremlin that Russia was ready to open talks on mutual cutbacks in both offensive and defensive missiles—an arms control project, I noted, "long advocated by the Johnson administration." Since Johnson had just been to Glassboro, N.J. to give a commencement address two weeks earlier, marking the anniversary of his summit meeting with Prime Minister Kosygin, I was sure that Gromyko's speech would get Johnson eager to have his long-awaited summit in Russia. Then on July 1, Johnson announced that the two governments had agreed to hold talks at some future date to discuss the reductions that Gromyko had mentioned.

But this would prove to be impossible because of Czechoslovakia later that summer. He made the announcement as he signed the treaty banning the spread of nuclear weapons which had been negotiated sometime earlier.

CHAPTER 15

Czechoslovakia is Invaded And I Join The New York Times

Increasingly, as the summer of 1968 wore on, I was convinced the Soviet Union was going to repeat the mistakes of 1956 and invade Czechoslovakia, just as it had invaded Hungary in 1956. That would, of course, in effect repudiate all the praise I had levied about the new leadership in my articles that had won me an award in 1967 from the Washington Newspaper Guild.

On July 23, I wrote in The Star that the entire Soviet Politburo was about to descend on Czechoslovakia. I wrote that "this is unparalleled in the history of the Communist movement and dramatizes the importance that Moscow attaches to halting the accelerating liberalism in Czechoslovakia.

At the end of July, I wrote, based on reports from Prague, that the Czech nation was solidly backing the

Dubcek reforms in the face of Soviet threats. The Russians meanwhile had gotten support from East Germans, Poles, Hungarians, Bulgarians and Hungarians, which was particularly striking since both the Poles and Hungarians had suffered badly at the hands of the Russians in 1956.

The Soviet leaders finally came to the border town of Cierna Nad Tira on July 29 for two days of talks with the Czechs. There was no communique and there were varying reports in the press. A week later, on August 4, a statement was signed in Bratislava by Czechoslovakia, the Soviet Union, Poland, East Germany, Hungary and Bulgaria that was meant to show "unity" but really was meant to ratify the compromise hammered out when the Soviet and Czech leaders met alone at the end of July.

I became dubious at this point about the future of the Prague leadership and wrote a news analysis, with a headline—"What Price Did Czechs Pay." I wasn't sure the Russians would invade, but wasn't ready to bet against it at this point. I was hoping The Star would fly me to Prague but I couldn't persuade the editors to do so.

We later learned from LBJ's memoirs that an agreement had been worked out with Soviet leaders for a press release to be issued on the morning of August 21 saying that Johnson would visit Leningrad in the first ten days of October 1968 to discuss "questions of mutual interest." The idea would be to talk about a reduction in strategic missiles.

But at 7 p.m. p.m. on August 20 Ambassador Dobrynin was told to deliver a personal note to Johnson informing him of the intervention of the Warsaw Pact forces into Czechoslovakia.

At about that time, I was covering a meeting of the platform committee of the Democratic Party in advance of the next week's party convention in Chicago that was taking place at the State Department on the ground floor. Rusk was speaking on foreign policy, and just before he was to take questions, his assistant, Benjamin Read, handed him a note. Rusk turned white and said he had to return immediately to his office. That's when we all learned that the intervention in Czechoslovakia was underway.

Rusk says that when he returned to his office on the seventh floor of the department he telephoned Dobrynin "to protest the invasion, telling him that the Soviet action was like throwing a dead fish in the president's face. I insisted that Dobrynin telephone Moscow immediately and tell Moscow not to announce Johnson's scheduled visit the next morning [as was planned] because that would have been interpreted worldwide as the United States' condoning the Soviet march into Czechoslovakia."

On August 28, I did a news analysis saying that "administration officials would like to see the Czechoslovakian crisis disappear as soon as possible so President Johnson could hold his planned summit meeting with Kosygin." But I added that before that could happen, the arrangements worked out between Russia and Czechoslovakia must look like "a workable compromise and there are strong doubts that it will."

Of course, the summit did not take place, and the negotiations on reducing missiles did not begin until November 1969 in Helsinki and not at the summit level either.

Meanwhile, the Democratic Party convention in Chicago, wracked with dissension by anti-war activists, chose Vice President Hubert Humphrey as the standard-bearer for the 1968 presidential election. He would lose to Richard N. Nixon.

A personal note here. In July 1968 just before the July 4 holiday, I was invited to New York by Seymour Topping, the foreign editor of The New York Times, for an interview. Raymond Anderson, the No. 2 in the Moscow bureau, had been expelled, and the Times wanted a replacement quickly. I had been recommended to Topping by Peter Grose, a former Moscow bureau chief for The Times, whom I had met on one of my trips to Moscow, and had gotten to know in Washington quite well when he began to cover the State Department.

The Times was looking for someone who knew Russian and who could move quickly into the bureau and help out Henry Kamm, who was the bureau chief, and due to depart in the summer of 1969. I had the interview with Topping and met with other Times executives but did not hear back. I assumed after a while that I was not getting the job and put it out of my mind.

But on Friday night, August 30, the start of the Labor Day weekend, I got a telephone call from Topping telling me that The Times wanted to offer me a job as a Moscow correspondent but would want me to work for a few months in Washington for The Times to get used to how the Times operated. I told him I would get back to him in a few days.

My girl friend and future wife, Marie-Jeanne Marcouyeux, who was a French and Italian interpreter at the State Department, was having dinner with me at my apartment when Topping called.

I talked over The Times offer with Burt Hoffman and Crosby Noyes, Newbold's brother, who had been the chief European correspondent for The Star. They both said I would be crazy not to accept the offer. And I did. Charlie Seib, the managing editor, told me to leave as soon as possible. He did not believe in people hanging around after they had given notice.

So in early September, I started work for The Times, initially sitting on the foreign desk to meet the various editors. While in New York, the Fulbright book came out and was featured prominently in some book stores. I then moved back to Washington and finished my apprenticeship with The Times in the bureau there, finally departing for Moscow in February 1969.

A postscript about Czechoslovakia: A conservative Communist Gustav Husak took over in 1969, and he was in charge until the dramatic days of 1989 when Communism was purged from Eastern Europe.

CHAPTER 16

My First Days With The New York Times, Washington and Moscow

Joining the Washington bureau of The Times was like old home week for me, since I knew many of the people in the bureau including the bureau chief, Max Frankel, who himself had been a Moscow correspondent from 1957 to 1960. The Times agreed to pay me $325 a week, promising to raise it to $400 when I became Moscow buro chief in the summer of 1969. I was then earning $270 a week for The Star.

I started covering the Washington end of the Vietnam diplomacy just as I had for The Star. My first front page story for The Times, however, had nothing to do with foreign policy. I was in the Times bureau on a Saturday morning, September 28, 1968, when the White House press office called and said President Johnson was flying down to Kentucky to give a speech and did The Times want to be on the press plane? Whoever was in charge of the bureau that day said yes, and when it was ascertained that my Washington Star White House pass was still valid, I volunteered. And so, there it is: "Johnson Decries Politics of Fear", dateline, Fort Mitchell, Ky, Sept. 28—By Bernard Gwertzman, Special to The New York Times."

The major story in Washington at that time besides who would win the presidential election, was whether the United States would stop the bombing of North Vietnam to encourage the peace talks in Paris to proceed, as demanded by Hanoi. There were clearly diplomatic efforts going on to invigorate the peace talks. On October 16, I had a front page story twinned with one from Saigon written by Gene Roberts, both talking about a reduction in fighting in South Vietnam. My piece said "the fighting in South Vietnam has dropped off again in recent weeks, with American casualties approaching the low point in the summer's 'lull'"

"This has raised once more the question whether North Vietnam has ordered a slowdown in military operations as a political signal to Washington or is simply building up its forces for another offensive," I wrote.

Then the next day, On October 17, I led the paper with a story that said: "There were indications today that the United States was making a new diplomatic proposal on Vietnam that would include a halt in the bombing of the North." I noted that in Saigon the U.S. Ambassador

Ellsworth Bunker met twice with President Nguyen Van Thieu to discuss the possibility of a cessation. There was speculation that a new proposal for a halt in the raids was being formulated."

Two weeks later, I wrote on October 31 that "authoritative sources said today that Gen. Creighton W. Abrams, the United States commander in South Vietnam, told President Johnson yesterday that he could accept the military consequences of a complete halt in the bombing of North Vietnam under present battlefield conditions." The story added that "Washington was alive with anticipation today that [Johnson] was on the verge of stopping the bombing as part of a package agreement arranged secretly with North Vietnam and South Vietnam to move the Paris talks to a more meaningful, substantive stage."

Johnson finally spoke to the nation on the evening of October 31 to announce a bombing halt on that day and negotiations to begin on November 6. I wrote a sidebar saying: "Caution is Voiced." "U.S. Officials Expect the Negotiations to Be Long and Difficult." But of course, the real story was that South Vietnam did not show up for the negotiations and that killed the chances for any real progress, There were strong indications then that the Saigon government was persuaded by the Richard Nixon campaign, namely Anna Chenault, to believe that once Nixon was elected—he was the favorite—he would be better for Saigon. Johnson himself suggests this in his memoirs. And there are FBI tapes that substantiate this. Nixon actually won the elections by a very narrow margin.

Just before Christmas, word came that the crew of the USS Pueblo, the intelligence ship that had been captured in January 1968 by North Korea, were being released and flown to San Diego. New York was looking for Jewish volunteers to cover the story at Christmas time, and I was "volunteered." I had actually covered for The Star the capture of the Pueblo in January at a time when it was uncertain whether that would trigger a major confrontation. But apparently, that crisis was self-contained. My story on the return was straight-forward, and just barely made the first edition deadline: "San Diego, Dec. 24—The crew of the intelligence ship Pueblo returned to the United States today in time for Christmas with many of their families. Led by Comdr. Lloyd M. Butcher, the 82 survivors arrived at the Miramar Naval Air Station outside this city and were met immediately by emotional, sometimes hysterical greetings and embraces of wives, mothers, fathers and children."

And as the year neared its end, the United States lifted its suspension of official cultural exchanges that had been imposed after the Soviet-led invasion of Czechoslovakia in August. On December 29, the State Department announced that the Moscow State Symphony would be allowed to make a tour of the United States starting in February 1969.

And at the end of November, China surprised the United States by proposing a resumption of ambassadorial level talks in Warsaw on Feb. 28, 1969 with Nixon administration representatives and for the first time publicly called on the United States to join "an agreement on the five principles of peaceful coexistence."

We had no idea at that time, of course, but in coming months, first Henry Kissinger and then Nixon himself would visit China and open the way to recognition of "Red China." I would find when I arrived in Moscow that one of the most important stories would be the rising tensions between Moscow and Beijing.

A few days before the turnover in administrations, I was handed over a deliberate "leak" as a sort of farewell present by the outgoing Rusk/Katzenbach administration at State Department. Jack Rosenthal, who was an old friend of mine from Harvard Crimson days and still was a good friend, (Jack died in August 2017) was then Katzenbach's special assistant and they had a good story to tell. I was invited to the department, and Katzenbach revealed that the State Department had issued a security clearance to John Paton Davies Jr. who during the McCarthy era in the 1950s had been dismissed from the Foreign Service as a security risk. Davies was one of the old so-called "China hands" who had served in pre- Communist China and who had advocated that the United States make an effort to prevent the alliance between Communist China and the Soviet Union.

The story was put on the front page on January 15, 1969. It was my last Washington by-line until I returned from Moscow in the fall of 1962.

I then turned to the business of packing and getting ready for my flight to Moscow. On January 26, the 24th birthday of Marie-Jeanne Marcouyeux, I surprised her by proposing marriage and she accepted. We agreed to get married sometime in April. Everything became hectic. Max and Toby Frankel gave me a send off party at their house in Washington. Marie-Jeanne and I drove up to New York for a farewell party at my parents' house in New Rochelle, N.Y. and to celebrate our engagement. We even had time to pick out an engagement ring in NYC.

I left New York for London on February 13 and spent a few days at the bureau learning the communications ropes. At that time the bureau was located in the London Times building and was open 24 hours a day, and handled worldwide communications for New York. You could file by cable to London (particularly attractive to correspondents in British outposts like India or Hong Kong who got empire rates) or by phone or telex which was just beginning to show its face. The London bureau had a direct high speed cable connection to The New York Times office in New York. So, as I was to learn, and use often, from the Moscow bureau of the New York Times. On a news story, in 1969-

70, the way we usually filed was to pick up the phone, dial the operator, and say in Russian: "Ya Ka-Choo (I want) Pa-zvonite (to call) Londonoo (London) and then give the number, which by now I have forgotten. By the time we had left, the Russians had installed a telex machine in our office. Upon arriving in Moscow, I was met at the airport by Henry Kamm, who was to guide me through the daily routine of the Moscow correspondent. Henry was one of the best correspondents on The Times, and later won a Pulitzer Prize for his coverage of the boat people escaping from Vietnam. He did not like it much in Moscow, but had good contacts with the growing number of dissidents. In the aftermath of the invasion of Czechoslovakia in August 1968, there was a simultaneous crackdown on liberalization in Russia and that produced a number of Russians who produced a steady number of documents actually typed and copied via carbon paper and distributed to correspondents. Henry was one of the correspondents who had good contacts with this group.

The Times had its living quarters and office at 12/24 Sadovo/ Samotechnaya, known in short as 12/24 Sad/Sam. This is one of the ring roads around the Kremlin. It is close in so one can actually walk to downtown Moscow from that building fairly easily. In fact as of this writing Times people still live and work there. In 1968 my apartment was Apt. No. 1 on the ground floor in Entry No. 1. The apartment was fairly spacious. It had a large bedroom, another bedroom we used for storage, a room we used for dining, a large living room, a kitchen and a bathroom, and a long hallway. The fixtures were rather old-fashioned.

The apartment came with a fulltime maid/cook named Shura, who spoke no English, whom we privately called "Col." Shura, assuming she had to report everything to the KGB. We had a driver named Ivan who lovingly took care of our Chevrolet Impala and Soviet Chaika. In the office, were two long-time assistants, Boris and Sara. More about them later. I arrived, of course, in the dead of winter but the apartment house, which reportedly was built by German POWs at the end of World War II, was well insulated and comfortable. At the suggestion of Peter Grose, I had bought an Abercrombie and Fitch winter coat which looked strange on Moscow streets but did keep me warm, and of course a Russian fur Shapka hat.

Henry had a wonderful wife, Barbara and a son and daughter, and they all were very helpful to me and later to Marie-Jeanne when she moved to Moscow in April after our wedding in D.C,.

In those days, our building, like other such buildings which housed Westerners, was segregated. They had full-time police- guards who checked the ID of anyone trying to enter the building they did not know. This was good for preventing theft but was a deterrent to inviting Soviet guests to your apartment. As a result, we did very little entertaining except with the foreign community while we lived in Moscow.

[I recently spoke by phone with Neil MacFarqhar, the current Moscow correspondent. He told me he still lives in "Sad Sam" but he is the only foreign correspondent there now. Others live elsewhere around the city].

Across the street from our apartment house was an ordinary bread store, and I have to confess that it had a very good rye bread that one could buy every morning freshly sliced. It was one of the few "treats" in Soviet stores. As a result, I became an early customer of the so-called "valutni" store, the Russian word for hard-currency. It was a supermarket built by an Italian company with a contract to build several more around the country for Russians. But this one was reserved for customers using only hard currency certificates which you got at the Soviet bank. You could buy in that store the best of what was available in Soviet markets at amazingly low prices. But variety was sadly lacking. For instance, I love Bloody Marys. Obviously Soviet vodka was not in short supply. But tomato juice was. The only tomato juice was a Bulgarian import at the dollar store and I remember opening my first bottle and the juice shot up to the ceiling—it was so fermented. Of course the main alternative for special items like that was to import goods directly from stores in Denmark or Finland that dealt regularly with the diplomatic community. Our driver Ivan was familiar with dealing with Soviet customs agents. For instance, in those days I was a pipe smoker, and I regularly imported my pipe tobacco from Denmark. Likewise, we imported Pizza mix from there as well.

The winter of 1969 was a very combative one in Soviet-Chinese terms. There, of course, had been a steady drumbeat in ideological warfare between the onetime Communist allies for many years, but suddenly on March 2, each side announced there had been shootings and deaths by military units along the Ussuri River in the Far East near Damansky Island in Soviet Siberia. This led to a considerable amount of patriotic fervor in both Moscow and Beijing.

In Moscow, on March 7 and 8, thousands of Russians marched in protests past the Chinese embassy despite the cold. On March 7, as I recall, a plainclothes Soviet agent came up to me and in excellent English, asked "What do you think of all this Mr. Gwertzman?". I replied "Very impressive." I guess he was showing off how well the KGB kept us under surveillance.

The Sunday Week in Review section on March 23 asked me to write about the situation. My lead said: "On March 7, while thousands of Russians were marching past the Chinese embassy, an elderly peasant woman kept talking to herself, but loud enough for everyone around to hear: 'We fed them, we clothed them, and they kill our boys.'"

"Later that night, at a lecture hall filled with intellectuals, a man got up to ask the speaker how Russia could possibly defend its borders against the 'hordes of Chinese' on the other side.' That kind of attitude dramatized in a sense the mixture of anger and fear that most Russians feel about China. This is not to say that Moscow today is totally absorbed with the frontier question on the Ussuri River. It isn't. People are much more concerned, for instance, with whether the Soviet team will win the world ice hockey championship for the seventh straight year[it did]. But the China border crisis has for the first time in many years given the leadership a genuine popular issue."

The Ussuri crisis led the poet Yevgeny Yevtushenko [who died in 2017 while living in Tulsa, Okla., where he and his Russian wife were teaching at the university] to write a long poem in which he said that Mao Tse-tung and his followers "in their dreams see our homeland as a place/where in the fields grow not wheat/but quotations and more quotations/where beastly jaws chew up art as if it were seaweed."

On March 30, I wrote "the Soviet Union mobilized its newspapers and radio today behind its note to Communist China yesterday proposing negotiations to settle border differences." Every newspaper carried the 3,000 word statement in full on its front page. A week later on April 7, I wrote a news analysis in the paper that said "the Soviet Union and Communist China have apparently signaled each other in the last few weeks that neither wants the dispute over the Ussuri River to lead to a wider conflict. Both sides have shown military restraint along the banks of the river, the border between Manchuria and the Soviet Union's Maritime Territory and have, for the present, reduced the scale of polemics to normal levels."

In anticipation of my marriage to Marie-Jeanne, I had, of course, made sure the press office had no problem with issuing the proper visa papers ahead of time to the Soviet Embassy in Washington. And as soon as I got back to Washington, the first thing I did was invite the press attache to lunch to double check that when we brought her passport into the embassy the Monday morning after the wedding the proper visa would be stamped. And it was. Our wedding was held on April 19, 1969, in St. Thomas Apostle, her neighborhood church. My brother Steve was best man. My father held a dinner the night before at the International Club for the wedding guests and the wedding reception was held there afterwards,

We had a whirlwind honeymoon at the Savoy Hotel in London and the Crillion in Paris. We flew to Moscow where Henry Kamm met us.

On July 4, the new American Ambassador to Russia, Jacob Beam, gave the annual holiday reception on the grounds of Spasso House, the official U.S. residence. And there I was able to introduce myself and Marie-Jeanne to Andrei Voznesensky [who died in 2010 in Moscow] and pass on a request from Harrison Salisbury, who had sent me copies of his new book, "The 900 Days: The Siege of Leningrad" to give him a copy and ask him to write a poem for the OP-ED page which he now edited, in case the U.S. landed a man on the moon later that month.

Andrei, then pulled out a piece of paper, and wrote out a palindrom in Russian, "A Luna Kanula," which literally means "The Moon Has Sunk" and it means the same thing backwards and forwards. He and I struck up a modest friendship during our stay in Moscow. He and his wife invited us over to his apartment once and he came over to ours once.

Meanwhile, of course, the actual space launch of the manned moon probe, Apollo 11, scheduled for later that month was to be the dominating story that summer. James Clarity had joined the bureau as my No. 2, along with his wife and son and daughter, Jim was an excellent writer and reporter but he did not know how to drive so we signed him up for driving lessons with a Russian driving instructor who came over to the bureau with all sorts of charts etc. It seemed to take months to get him to get his license. Marie-Jeanne at the same time was taking Russian lessons at home with an excellent woman tutor as well as piano lessons. She was also going to ballet classes with the wives of diplomats to stay in shape. I must add that my wife, who spoke no Russian upon arrival was speaking beautiful Russian upon our departure in September 1992.

There had been some concern in the American press that the Soviet Union might try to upstage Apollo 11 with an unmanned spaceship that might land on the moon, pick up some fragments of the moon and return home, and thereby steal some propaganda thunder from the Americans.

And sure enough, on July 14, I led the paper with the following dispatch:: "The Soviet Union launched an unmanned spaceship toward the moon today (July 13) just three days before the scheduled blastoff of America's Apollo 11 on a planned lunar landing mission."

"The launching of the Luna 15 mission appeared to observers here as a deliberate effort by the Soviet Union to steal some of the moon publicity away from the United States and demonstrate that it is still very much in the space business. As usual, few details were released on the latest Soviet space venture."

On July 17, I reported that the Soviet Union "reported promptly" to the Russian people "about the successful launching of Apollo 11, but maintained silence for the third consecutive day on its own unmanned spacecraft Luna 15 which also is heading for the moon."

The main Soviet TV news show at 8:30 p.m, Moscow time, four hours after the actual launching "showed about five minutes of tape of the lift-off at Cape Kennedy," I always felt cheated missing the actual live coverage of the Apollo mission myself.

In the paper of July 18, I reported that "the Soviet Union broke its silence on Luna 15 today and said the unmanned spaceship had become the moon's latest artificial satellite. "Soviet radio, TV and newspapers continued to give heavy coverage to Apollo 11, surpassing the news given any previous American space effort. Pravda, for instance, carried a dispatch from New York on its front page, and a background article and picture of the three man crew on an inside page. The newspaper wished "the courageous crew a happy journey.;"

Finally, on July 21, on the historic front page which announced that "Men Walk on Moon" I reported at the bottom of column one in the first edition of the paper that Moscow had announced that Luna 15, its unmanned spacecraft had reached the moon's surface and ended its operations, meaning it had failed. My pride of authorship was lost, however, in the second edition, when the paper substituted a long poem by Archibald MacLeish.

Sometime later that summer, I got a phone call at the office from Andrei Amalrik, a prominent Soviet dissident writer, who was a close friend of Tony Shub, who had been the Washington Post correspondent and who had been expelled for his articles, many of which featured Amalrik. Amalrik was also a friend of Kamm, who had already departed for his next assignment in Asia.

Amalrik invited me and Marie-Jeanne to dinner the next Saturday night at his apartment in the Arbat section of Moscow. I accepted the invitation but in hindsight I was naive. Knowing my phone was being tapped, I should have been wary.

In any event we showed up at his apartment, and were greeted by a middle aged gentleman wearing a tweed jacket. I thought for a moment that perhaps this was a communal apartment, with several families sharing the space. But Amalrik quickly came up to me and whispered: "Obisk, obisk," At first I did not understand the word, but it finally dawned on me that he was saying there was "a search" going on in the apartment.

And sure enough, we were interrogated, and we watched the agents go through Amalrik's book shelves and papers. I had brought Amalrik a bottle of Scotch as a present, and that was confiscated. After about two hours, the chief inspector read aloud his summary of events and wanted me to sign. I said I wanted an American consular officer present. At that point, two rather nervous Russians who had been brought into the apartment earlier as witnesses, signed the document.

Afterwards, I asked Clarity to write a profile on Amalrik, which was published on December 23, 1969. Sometime later, Amalrik wrote an article in The New York Review of Books in which I was criticized for not writing about the search, and he also singled out for attack, Henry Shapiro of UPI, the dean of the foreign correspondents. Amalrik was later arrested, sentenced to a labor camp, released and exiled to Spain where he tragically died in a car crash.

The Times allowed its Moscow correspondent two breathers a year and we took our first in September by flying to Copenhagen and exploring the city in early fall, seeing some good movies, and seeing a Danish production of "Hair," which was terrific. On a whim, Marie-Jeanne bought herself a Persian Lamb coat there, and we also have great pictures of us sitting on the rocks near the coast.

Later in November, we went to Helsinki for the first round of the Strategic Arms Limitation Talks.

CHAPTER 17

Helsinki Talks and Start of U.S,-Soviet Diplomacy in the Nixon Era

The Helsinki talks were, in a sense, an aberration in U.S.-Soviet relations at the time. Begun in mid-November 1969 at a time when relations between the two superpowers were not exactly warm, these talks were ostentatiously cordial, and to a point, almost festive, despite the fact that Helsinki, at that time of year, was bathed in about 20 hours of darkness a day. For the journalists assembled, including those who brought their wives, as I had, it was a great working vacation.

We stayed at the Hotel Marski, in the center of Helsinki where the press center was located. We had time to visit Helsinki's many enticements. There were the examples of Finland's modern architecture everywhere. My wife loved shopping at Marimekko for clothing and modern glassware. some of which we still own. The restaurants were fun. In short, it was a great break from the Moscow doldrums.

And when Thanksgiving rolled around, the Finnish press office even invited the Soviet and American press who were still around, to a Thanksgiving dinner in the Hotel's restaurant. What I remember was that the invitation to dinner was well- intentioned, but there was not much turkey to eat.

The main trouble of course was that there was a complete press blackout. As a result, a great number of Washington correspondents who had flown out for this important round of talks, including my great friend and colleague from the Washington bureau, John Finney, who was covering the Pentagon and later was deputy chief of the Washington bureau and Chalmers Roberts, the Washington Post's senior correspondent. They both went back to Washington within two weeks.

The talks adjourned on December 22 and resumed the next year in Vienna. Another seven rounds of negotiations were held over a period of thirty months, alternating between Vienna and Helsinki, until an agreement was finally hammered out in time for the U.S. Soviet summit conference in May 1972 in Moscow between President Richard Nixon and Soviet Premier Leonid Brezhnev.

As Henry Kissinger, who at that time was national security advisor, and in fact ran Nixon's foreign policy, and not Secretary of State William P. Rogers, and Soviet

Ambassador to Washington, Anatoli Dobrynin point out in their respective memoirs, much of the negotiations for the treaty were actually worked out by Kissinger and Dobrynin in Washington in utmost secrecy.

Dobrynin wrote: "Our exchanges through the channel made it possible for the leadership of both countries to override the negotiations, to interfere and untie the knots of many principal and delicate disputes."

"On the other hand, negotiating simultaneously at two levels at times produced some confusion and occasional misunderstandings in the process," Dobrynin wrote, adding that it was more difficult for Kissinger to control than for his side. Dobrynin notes that Gerard Smith, the head of the U.S. Arms Control and Disarmament Agency, wrote in his memoirs that he had discovered the Kissinger-Dobrynin channel by accident. Smith and Raymond Garthoff, a member of the U.S. delegation to the talks, "were certainly unhappy, if not outraged at times by this parallel negotiation."

Dobrynin adds that "neither did anyone in the Soviet Foreign Ministry or other ministries represented by the formal talks, such as Defense, particularly like the idea that the channel was the main avenue of negotiations between the two powers. But while the highly centralized and confidential way of handling the talks was a Nixon-Kissinger idea, it was accepted and prevailed in Moscow too."

What was most interesting to me about this period was the scarcity of big time diplomacy on the scene in Moscow. Kissinger did not visit once during my time there, not did Secretary Rogers. Behind the scenes in Washington, Nixon was spending a great deal of time worrying about Vietnam. He had committed his administration fo following the lead of the Johnson administration's last days and trying to make progress at the Paris negotiating table. And he was also following the lead of the Johnson administration and starting to reduce the size of the U.S. force levels in Vietnam, all in an effort to assuage public opinion in the United States which was largely opposed on college campuses and among the intelligentsia.

Nixon himself delivered a major televised speech on November 3, 1969, in which he pleaded for domestic support "as he persisted in his effort to find peace in Vietnam and as he unfolded what he said was a plan to bring home all United States ground forces on an orderly but secret timetable," as reported by Max Frankel in The Times.

That speech, however, only spurred on the anti-war protestors who poured into Washington the following week. The Times fronted a story I wrote in advance of Nixon's speech that said Pravda had "belittled in advance President Nixon's speech on Vietnam tomorrow night and charged the United States with prolonging the war by not accepting North Vietnamese and Viet Cong terms for a settlement."

I added in my story that "the level of anti-American polemics has seemed to rise in the Soviet press, with the United States attacked for virtually every aspect of its foreign and domestic policies." Soviet television carried a 45-minute documentary on the United States that focused on the recent moratorium from bombing to demonstrate that President Nixon had lost the confidence of the American people. Mr. Nixon was accused of following the policies of Lyndon B. Johnson and the American people were said to be in a troubled mood.

Of course, besides the start of the Strategic Arms Limitation talks in Helsinki in November 1961, the Apollo 12 Moon mission also had a successful landing and return from the Moon, following up on the highly publicized Apollo 11 mission in April.

Working in Moscow, we noticed from afar how the State Department did not seem to have much power or influence in the Nixon administration. The word was getting through that Kissinger had much more influence and importance. Secretary Rogers was taking charge of Middle East policy and drawing up plans for peace that were being rejected by all sides—such as having Israel give up all the occupied lands from the 1967 war in return for peace.

A more active diplomacy toward the end of 1969 was taken by the West German government of Willy Brandt which forged ahead with relations toward the East European countries including Moscow, which eventually led to a big powers agreement on Berlin in 1971.

Meanwhile, as the year 1969 was coming to an end, Boris, my office manager, who was a ballet afficionado, told me that there was to be a change in the Bolshoi Ballet's Swan Lake. At that time, I was a complete neophyte in the world of ballet. Now, I consider myself, something of an expert. But I did know that Swan Lake was a classic ballet written by Tchaikovsky in 1871-2. In the original ballet, The Prince meets the Swan, Odette, originally a young woman turned into a swan by the evil sorcerer, Rothbart. In the original ballet, at the end, both Odette and the prince die by jumping in the waters near by and are seen pictured happily in heaven.

In the Soviet era, a happy ending was added, and Rothbart is killed and the couple live happily afterwards. I think Boris thought that the new Bolshoi director, Yuri Grigorovich, was going to restore the original ending in which the prince and Odette, commit suicide and are seen flying off to the heavens.

But he did not make the change. My story was put on the front page on the day after Christmas, and I was most pleased.

CHAPTER 18

Inside Our Moscow Bureau
And the Moscow Routine

As I was writing this book of memoirs, I thought it would be interesting for readers to describe what our Moscow office was like in the years I served there from February 1969 until we left in September 1971. It was located in the first entry of 12-24 Sadovo- Samotechnaya on the second floor.

The building itself, reportedly built by German POWs at the end of World War II, was deliberately populated with Westerners. No Soviet citizens lived in "Sad-Sam" then. And one had to pass a Soviet militia man at the entrance.

My personal apartment was in the last entry, on the first floor. It was large, and comfortable, and big enough to handle a large family which we did not have at that time.

Things have now changed. The building rents to everyone, and The New York Times is the only Western newspaper to have an office there now. When we lived there, besides The Times, Reuters, the Chicago Tribune, the Baltimore Sun, the Los Angeles Times and AFP had their offices there. And Western diplomats took up other apartments. There also was a Roman Catholic priest, Father Dion, who was the chaplain to the American Embassy, in a top floor apartment.

As bureau chief, I had a private office. The others all sat in a bull pen outside my office. Beyond them was a closed off area which housed the Tass tickers. We had two Russian language wires and one in English. Our office had bookshelves where we sorted the large number of Soviet periodicals we subscribed to. And we subscribed to almost everything.

We looked at every journal that arrived, seeking something interesting to write about. We also had the Moscow newspapers delivered to the office. Important statements from the government or Communist Party were usually carried not only in print, but the night before on Tass. In my office was a small safe and soon after she arrived after our wedding in April 1969, Marie- Jeanne became our office bookkeeper.

Boris Zakharov, my chief assistant, who sat in the front of the bull pen, had usually read Pravda on his way to work and would tell me when I walked in if there was something I needed to know from that. Sara Shaikevich, our other employee, who knew several languages, usually came to work in the afternoon and she translated for me in interviews. Even though I had studied Russian at Harvard, I was never fluent.

Marie-Jeanne, a native French speaker, who had been an interpreter at the State Department, began studying Russian with a tutor and soon began speaking much better than I did.

Our driver was Ivan, who took very good care of our office Chevrolet Impala, which I had purchased in Helsinki, as well as our locally purchased Russian Chaika sedan. Of course, I arrived in Moscow at the worst of times, in a way. Only a few months earlier, the invasion of Czechoslovakia had taken place in August 1968, and as a result there was an internal crackdown on dissidents and dissident thought.

Moreover, there was tension because of the deepening split in the Communist world between China and Russia, heightened briefly by the clashes along the Ussuri River in the Soviet Far East.

The 100th anniversary of Lenin's birth occurred in 1970. As a result, Moscow's book stores were inundated with Lenin portraits, and his books filled the stores. I wrote a piece summing it all up, saying: "What was significant was the apparent lack of impact the whole Lenin drive had on the average Russian. It seemed to neither raise nor to diminish his or her view of Lenin. There are no Soviet style Red Guards running around the streets of Moscow, waving Lenin posters. Nor are there anti-Lenin jokes making the rounds"

For the ruling Communist Party, the major event was the convening at the end of March 1971 of the 24th party Congress and a six hour report delivered by the Party Secretary Leonid I. Brezhnev. In my summary paragraph about his speech, I wrote: "there were few major surprises in the report, which was evidently meant to convey an impression of stability and continuity. On such controversial issues as Stalin's role in Soviet history, Mr. Brezhnev maintained the party's middle-of-the-road position that while it is wrong to dwell on Stalin's crimes, it is equally wrong to 'whitewash the past.'"

But on April 15, just two weeks after the party Congress had ended, Brezhnev went on national television to in effect talk openly about the country's poor economic record. He said "new methods and new solutions" were needed to solve the country's economic problems. He told the nation that he was speaking candidly about the country's economic problems because the party's leaders had decided that the people should know the problems as well as the successes that stand before us.

He said part of the problem was due to the stresses with China and with the invasion of Czechoslovakia, although he did not mention them by name, but he also said there were also "poor administration and a lack of work discipline."

In 1971, the Middle East continued to be a major foreign policy issue between Washington and Moscow. The Soviet Union ironically had been the first nation to recognize the U.N. Proposal to make Israel independent in 1948 (the United States was second) but after 1967, it was firmly in the Arab camp after the war which had been disastrous for Egypt, Syria and Jordan. In fact, some ten thousand Soviet military had been sent to Egypt to bolster Gamal Abdel Nasser's forces secretly. Israel believed they were flying Egyptian fighter planes against Israel. At the end of May 1971, Egypt and the Soviet Union announced a 15-year Soviet-Egyptian friendship treaty in Cairo.

This came as the American Secretary of State Rodgers was trying to work out an American- sponsored peace treaty for the region. But Rodgers had no takers. It was rejected by Israel because it called on the Israelis to return all the lands it had captured in the 1967 war, in return for peace.

On June 3, I had a front page story based on strong editorials in both Pravda and Izvestia sharply attacking efforts by the United States to promote a Middle East settlement and in particular to improve relations with Egypt.

At about the same time as the friendship treaty with Egypt was signed, the Soviet media began what seemed to me an unusual campaign against Jews It may have been touched off by the campaign in the United States started by Senator Henry Jackson, Democrat of Washington to make any most favored nation (MFN) treaty status with Moscow conditional on allowing Soviet Jews to emigrate freely to Israel.

This led to a most unusual press event. We foreign correspondents were all invited by the Foreign Ministry to the ornate "House of Friendship" in March 1971.

Under glaring lights, forty Soviet Jews, including Deputy Prime Minister Veniamin Dymshits, the highest ranking Jew in government, were sitting on a raised platform in front of us. One by one, with varying degrees of enthusiasm, they pledged their loyalty to the Soviet Union and asserted their hostility to Israel, Zionism and the United States.

What I wrote in a news analysis was "What they said was not new. This has been the propaganda line of the Soviet Union for years. What has made it interesting was that the "press conference" came at the end of a two week long vitriolic campaign against Israel, Zionism and the United States waged throughout the Soviet Union. And this was the first time that a group that Moscow chose to speak for all Soviet Jews had been assembled before the eyes of the world press to condemn Israel.

It was of course ironic to the extreme since so many Jews wanted to emigrate to Israel and were being turned away. It, of course, became a major political issue in the United States when the Nixon administration and subsequent administrations tried to extend Most Favored trade status to the Soviet Union and it was held up by an amendment co-sponsored by Jackson and Representative Charles Vanik, Democrat of Ohio. (Now of course, in 2018, Russian Jews can travel freely and now make up a significant proportion of Israel's population after restrictions were lifted on emigration during the Gorbachev years.)

The Chinese Communists boycotted the Soviet Party Congress but made other news late in the year with some adroit diplomacy of their own. After much to and fro diplomacy initiated by Washington secretly, they invited President Nixon to send his own private envoy to Beijing and Nixon sent Henry Kissinger who arrived secretly in the Chinese capital on July 9, 1971. Following Kissinger's return to Washington on July 15, Nixon announced on TV that he would visit Beijing to normalize relations sometime before May 1972. He actually made a three-city visit starting Feb. 21, 1972.

The news was reported on Soviet TV, but more importantly, on August 2, Moscow called a one-day meeting of all the Soviet-bloc countries and denounced any deviation from Moscow's line, The only country staying away was Romania, which strongly supported the U.S.-China moves to improve relations.

And on Aug. 10 Pravda ran a 2500 word article by Georgi A. Arbatov, the head of the USA Institute which was reprinted in full by Tass. My article, which the Times put on Page 1, said "The Soviet Union expressed the hope today that American efforts to reach an understanding with China would not lead to a reduction of interest in solving long- standing problems with Moscow. It affirmed Soviet concern that an anti-Soviet coalition might develop from Chinese- American contacts."

More directly concerning the summit with the Chinese, Nixon ever since he took office, had been privately trying to arrange a meeting with Brezhnev. He had been using Kissinger as his agent in private talks with Dobrynin in Washington or in San Clemente. But the Russians, while agreeable in principle, kept putting a summit off until a Berlin agreement could be worked out.

But now, having seen the Chinese beat them to the punch, the Russians moved quickly to make up for lost time. On August 5, Nixon sent a letter to Brezhnev, delivered by Kissinger to Dobrynin, suggesting a meeting. And on August 10, Brezhnev replied favorably. They agreed on a summit in Moscow in May, 1972, and an announcement was made in both capitals on October 12—in Washington by Nixon personally at a press conference.

An agreement on Berlin was reached on September 3 when the ambassadors of the United States, the Soviet Union, Britain and France signed a treaty governing the status of West Berlin. Of course, who would have known that by 1989, he Berlin Wall would come down and in 1990, Germany would no longer be divided.

One of my final achievements in Russia came about fortuitously through my friendship with Anthony Astrachan, the Washington Post correspondent in Moscow. He and his wife, Susan, had invited me and Marie-Jeanne for dinner at their apartment. They had a surprise guest, Zhores Medvedev, the Soviet biologist who had become a dissident. We had met Zhores a few times, and I had supplied him with detective novels, in English, which he loved. This time, he surprised us all by emptying his pockets of dozens of 35 mm. developed film cartridges. He explained that on these films are the typed publications called "Political Diaries" that he and his brother Roy had written in recent years. They wanted us to smuggle them out of the Soviet Union and to publish them in the West. We agreed on a system and Marie-Jeanne and I secretly translated some films at home under flashlight and published some documents in The Times. This was MJ's first byline in The Times.

My last stories from Moscow on this assignment came at the end of September 1971. just as we were preparing to leave Moscow, when word reached us that Nikita S. Khrushchev had died. I wrote the news story and the follow-up, his burial at Novodevichy Cemetery in Moscow. The Soviet press only had a one paragraph announcement.

CHAPTER 19

Back in Washington

In 1971, The New York Times had a rule for returning foreign correspondents. You could come home by air, or first class ship. Marie-Jeanne and I chose to return to New York on the SS France. Because of her father's ties to the French embassy, she had been on those French Line ships as a child; this was my first such voyage, and it was a great change of pace; black tie dinner every night., great food. Entertainment.

Upon returning to New York, we stayed for a couple of nights at the Algonquin Hotel near the Times, where I could drop in on the editors for a couple of days and then we rented a car and drove down to Washington where I would switch jobs with Rick Smith in the Washington bureau working for Max Frankel.

The bureau was then located on L Street in downtown Washington, and it put us up in a motel a couple of blocks away. We looked for a permanent dwelling in our off hours, finally settling on a comfortable house in Foxhall Village, a group of houses built after World War I, in English-style architecture.

In 1971, we were able to buy the house for only $59,000, helped out by a modest mortgage from Riggs Bank. House prices were still relatively low. We had saved quite a bit of money in Moscow, since most of our expenses were paid for by The Times. I was thrown into work almost immediately. And having covered State Department for the Washington Star, and briefly for the Times, it was fun seeing my old colleagues again, and sharing with them some of my Moscow "war stories."

In the Washington Bureau, Max Frankel was not only the Bureau chief, but also the senior diplomatic correspondent, in effect. Others who wrote about foreign affairs included: Tad Szulc, a veteran correspondent who broke the Bay of Pigs fiasco, Benjamin Welles, a son of former American diplomat Sumner Welles, and a Latin specialist, and Terry Smith, a son of Red Smith, a noted sports columnist, who later went on to cover Israel.

The State Department had not changed much. Most of the correspondents who were there when I covered it last were still there, with a few new faces added.

I soon confirmed what I had already surmised from afar, that Secretary of State William Rogers was only a figure head, that foreign policy was controlled by the White House, and in particular by President Nixon and his national security adviser, Henry Kissinger. And I was told by my colleagues in the bureau that Kissinger had an arrangement with Frankel that any queries from the bureau went through Max. Happily for me, at the end of 1971, when Max was getting ready to move to New York to become Sunday Editor of the New York Times, he arranged a lunch with Kissinger and handed the mantle of responsibility of calling HAK to me.

One of the first stories I covered was Washington's reaction to the expulsion of Nationalist China from the United Nations and Beijing's taking over its seat. China of course is one of the five permanent, veto-carrying members of the Security Council, but once the United States made it clear through the secret diplomacy conducted by Kissinger in the summer of 1971, setting up the visit of Nixon to China in February of 1972, the die was in a sense cast.

The Nixon Administration had hoped to keep Taiwan in the United Nations as a separate nation, but Beijing with its One China policy was adamant against that and was able to prevail in the voting. Nevertheless, Secretary of State Rogers, in a press conference I covered on October 26, said the decision to expel Nationalist China was "a mistake of major proportion." I wrote that "the mood within the Administration was described by a key official as one of disappointment, but not of anger or resentment. He said that "the Administration's main problem would be to combat erosion in American support for the United Nations."

Plans were going ahead, he said, for Nixon's trip to Beijing in February. The U.N. vote, he added, "improves the climate for that trip."

Meanwhile, a problem that arose while I was stationed in Moscow during the summer of 1971—the tensions between India and Pakistan—began to grow. In April, 1971, a crisis had arisen in East Pakistan with separatists urging more autonomy for the Bengalists, who of course, later formed the separate state of Bangladesh with the help of India.

At that time, in August, the Soviet Union signed a 20-year treaty of peace, friendship and cooperation in Moscow with India, signed by foreign ministers Andrei A. Gromyko and Swaren Singh. At that time, it was felt Moscow did this to match China's support for Pakistan during the current crisis over East Pakistan.

The situation seriously worsened in November and December when Pakistani troops moved in force into East Pakistan and cracked down in force on the people there.

This led the Indians to enter the fighting against the Pakistanis and to movements of American ships and statements by the Nixon administration accusing India of "aggression" and attacks from members of Congress saying that the Pakistani government was more at fault. By the end of the year, the crisis had seemed to calm down, with the creation of a new independent state, Bangladesh.

I tried to sum up the situation in an analysis on December 12, 1971, called : "The Big Powers: They Didn't Want This Tragic War": "For American officials, the war between India and Pakistan has underscored a sad fact about today's world: The big powers, in their effort to avoid a nuclear confrontation, seem

unable to prevent minor powers from engaging in tragic, bloody conventional conflicts.

"Neither the United States, nor the Soviet Union, nor Communist China wanted the Indo-Pakistani war, the third on the subcontinent in 24 years."

Nixon had always claimed that he felt compelled to come to Pakistan's defense in this conflict, not because he looked with favor on the repression in East Pakistan, but because he feared that India otherwise would attack and destroy West Pakistan.

Nixon's long-planned trip to Beijing was a great success. There was wall-to-wall television coverage in the United States. Frankel won a Pulitzer Prize for his coverage. It did open the way for an opening up of that vast country to tourism and newspaper offices and business trips. I finally made my own trip to Beijing with Kissinger a year later when he visited as secretary of state. Since then I have been back many times, as a journalist and also as a father visiting my son when James was working in Shanghai for a game company.

Meanwhile, no sooner had Nixon returned to the United States from China than a new crisis arose, this time over Vietnam. On Easter Sunday, April 2, 1972, North Vietnamese troops launched an attack across the demilitarized zone which I wrote was a "a clear violation of the 1968 understanding agreed to by the Johnson administration that produced an end to the systematic American bombing of North Vietnam and the start of substantive talks in Paris on concluding the Vietnam war."

These talks, of course, had gotten nowhere. But Nixon had systematically been pulling troops out of Vietnam.

Early in May, I and a few other news people accompanied Secretary of State Rogers on a trip to Western Europe to brief allied leaders in advance on Nixon's plans for his Moscow visit later that month. In London, Rogers vowed that the United States would not allow North Vietnam to conquer South Vietnam.

He spoke to newsmen a few hours after the allied side broke off the Paris talks indefinitely.

Rogers said on May 4 that "strong military action" would have to be taken to counter Hanoi's offensive. He vowed that "President Nixon will take whatever military action necessary to prevent a military takeover by force" in South Vietnam.

On May 7, in the morning, after we had arrived in Bonn, word came from Washington that the White House wanted Rodgers back in the United States for high-level consultations, so we all were rounded up for a sudden flight back home. I wrote in a story datelined "Aboard Air Force 86971 over the At;antic, May 7—" that Rogers believed that "Nixon was ready to risk his career and his reputation to stem the North Vietnamese invasion of South Vietnam, and was ready to use everything short of nuclear weapons to do so."

It turned out that Nixon had sent Kissinger on a "secret" trip to Moscow in late April to meet with Brezhnev and Gromyko on the situation in Vietnam. The Russians wanted the trip to discuss the May summit meeting and agree ahead of time on the various agreements that could be signed in Moscow. Nixon, however, was boiling over the situation in Vietnam and threatening in private to Kissinger to scrap the summit, if the Russians did not do something to curb the North Vietnamese advance.

He ordered Kissinger in his talks with Brezhnev to stress the importance of Vietnam. Kissinger came away from his talks in Moscow with the firm impression that Moscow had no love lost for Hanoi but could do little to influence North Vietnam. On the other hand, he felt that it would be a major mistake to cancel the summit since that was what Hanoi wanted.

Even before Rogers was summoned home, Nixon had met at length with Kissinger and other top aides to plot his strategy and had decided on mining Haiphong harbor and taking the risk that this would not jeopardize the forthcoming summit meeting in Moscow.

As it turned out, Moscow apparently wanted the summit very much, perhaps because Brezhnev wanted to visit the United States, which he was able to do in June 1973, a year later. In fact, the summits of 1972-73 can be regarded as high water marks for Soviet-American relations in the post-war years prior to the Gorbachev years.

The Moscow summit in fact was notable for the number of agreements reached. They ranged all over the lot, from health and science to disarmament and the United Nations and arms control. But they did not bring an end to the fighting in Vietnam. Nevertheless, upon his return to Washington, Nixon wasted no time to go on television to speak to the nation on June 1, 1972 and to tell a joint session of Congress, that was poorly attended because most members were away campaigning, that his summit meeting in Moscow had laid the basis for "a new relationship between the two most powerful nations on earth."

He also suggested that he might have made some progress on ending the Vietnam war during the Moscow talks. But he declined to reveal any details.

By mid-June, I was writing that American officials were expressing "considerable interest" in Soviet President Podgorny's assertion that there would be an early resumption of the Paris talks on Vietnam. Podgorny made the statement in Calcutta, India on his way home from a visit to Hanoi. Meanwhile, Nixon held his first televised press conference in more than a year on June 29 to announce that the Paris talks on Vietnam would resume on July 13 with Le Duc Tho and Kissinger there.

Kissinger meanwhile went again to Beijing in mid-June for consultations but there seemed no sign of any softening from Hanoi there.

I wrote in an analysis on June 25 that "what the United States has sought, in Moscow and in Peking, is help in making it known to Hanoi that Washington wants genuine negotiations, not just polemics."

Kissinger, in his memoirs, says that he sent his deputy Al Haig to Saigon to consult with President Thieu in early July. Haig and Thieu met on July 3, and Haig found a different Thieu than he had met before. In the recent round of fighting, Thieu felt that his army had done well enough that Hanoi would "no longer be able to defeat him, certainly so long as our airpower was avaialable to back him." Thieu calculated, Kissinger said, that he could make the U.S, election work for him. Thieu "smelled compromise even before most Americans did,"

Kissinger wrote. "Like me, he seemed convinced that a serious negotiation was imminent." But the problem, as Kissinger outlined it, was that Hanoi would still want eventually to conquer the South; while the United States, once the fighting stopped, would probably not be able to get back into it.

When Kissinger met Le Duc Tho in Paris on July 19, according to Kissinger's memoirs, the Hanoi leader was extremely conciliatory. He said Hanoi "was eager to settle the war during Nixon's first term." The North Vietnamese then proceeded to make a series of proposals that were in fact quite conciliatory. They dropped the demand for Thieu's resignation. Both sides then broke for travel.

Kissinger went back to Saigon; Le Duc Tho to Hanoi.

When the Kissinger team got to Saigon, he remembers being greeted "with unvarying dignity and courtesy,:" He says Le Duc Tho's "sparkling eyes gave no clue to his inner thoughts, which could not have been free of contempt for a superpower eager to settle for compromise when total victory seemed to him attainable." After they met on Aug. 14, Kissinger planned to visit Thieu again in Saigon. after first spending a day in Switzerland to celebrate his parents' 5oth wedding celebration. Kissinger notes that Saigon was teeming with rumors that he had come to impose peace. Ambassador Bunker told Kissinger that he thought Thieu believed he had the upper hand and would be more recalcitrant than ever. Bunker thought that Thieu was genuinely afraid of peace. "A world in which the South Vietnamese would have to stand entirely on their own was full of terrors that his pride would not let him admit."

Kissinger said that "The root fact was that Thieu and his government were simply not ready for a negotiated peace. They had a few vague ideas that amounted to an unconditional surrender by Hanoi," he said. "They were not satisfied with survival; they wanted a guarantee that they would prevail. They preferred to continue the military contest rather than face a political struggle."

So there was the final irony. After years of seeking a negotiated settlement, Kissinger realized that President Thieu did not want one, After presenting Hanoi's terms to Saigon in August, which Kissinger felt met his requirements, he wrote in his memoirs "Only gradually did it dawn on us that we faced not a drafting difficulty but a fundamental philosophical division. The root fact was that Thieu and his government were simply not ready for a negotiated peace."

"They had a few vague ideas that amounted to an unconditional surrender by Hanoi," Kissinger wrote. "They were not satisfied with survival; they wanted a guarantee that they would prevail. They preferred to continue the military contest rather than face a political struggle."

But all Washington was seeking was an honorable way to withdraw from Vietnam. Therefore if Hanoi were to accept the U.S. offer for a cease-fire, "we would not be able to respond with an open- ended commitment to continue the war in pursuit of unconditional victory." In other words, Washington found itself at odds with its long-time ally.

That September, Marie-Jeanne and I decided to take a longish vacation in France, to drive from Paris to Cannes, and to fly back to Washington from Nice. We were in Paris having coffee at the start of the vacation when we heard of the shooting of the Israeli athletes at the Munich Olympics. A sobering start to an otherwise terrific vacation.

It was off-season, so we avoided the crowds, and we were able to sample some very good restaurants along the way. We also created our first born, James. We followed the news the best we could. We got back to Washington to find the talks still going on.

The negotiations with North Vietnam reached a denoument on October 8, 1972 in Paris. Again, according to Kissinger's memoirs, Le Duc Tho said to Kissinger: "In order to show our good will and to ensure a rapid end to the war, rapid restoration of peace in Vietnam, as all of us wish for, today we put forward a new proposal regarding the content as well as the way to conduct negotiations, a very realistic and very simple proposal," Its essence was a cease-fire, withdrawal of U.S. forces, release of prisoners, plus no further infiltration—the basic program we had offered and insisted was essential since May 1971, Kissinger said.

He added: "I have often been asked for my most thrilling moment in public service. I have participated in many spectacular events: I have lived with power. I have seen pomp and ceremony. But the moment that moved me most deeply has to be that cool autumn Sunday afternoon while the shadows were falling over the serene French landscape and that large quiet room, hung with abstract paintings, was illuminated at the green baize table across which the two delegations were facing each other. At last we thought, there would be an end to the blood letting in Indochina.

"We stood on the threshold of what we had so long sought, a peace compatible with our honor and our international responsibilities. And we would be able to begin healing the wounds that the war had inflicted on our own society."

Of course, newsmen could not fathom what was going on exactly. The Nixon administration strongly believed in utmost secrecy in the conduct of foreign affairs. But on October 26, Hanoi Radio broadcast in many languages a long text in effect accepting all the major points put forward over the years by the United States, This came as a shock to Washington officials and reporters, all of whom knew that Kissinger had been meeting with Le Duc Tho, but had no idea of the progress seemingly being made.

I was one of a few hundred reporters crowded into the White House briefing room to hear Kissinger confirm that a breakthrough indeed had occurred. Kissinger said "peace is at hand" in Indochina and that a final agreement on a ceasefire and political arrangement could be reached in one more negotiating session with the North Vietnam "lasting no more than three or four days." He said that the remaining details would not halt the rapid movement toward an end to the war.

What he did not disclose at the press conference was the strong opposition from the South Vietnamese side to the terms offered by Hanoi. And in fact he treated Saigon as just an interested participant in the negotiations. But as the days dragged on, the early optimism faded, and on Dec. 16, Kissinger gave another press conference saying that the latest round of negotiations in Paris with Le Duc Tho had failed to reach "a just and fair agreement" to end the Vietitnam war. He also acknowledged that Saigon's objections to the accord were serious but said that the United States had not signed an accord because Hanoi's proposals were often "frivolous." He said that "we have an agreement that is 99 percent completed" but on the other hand," he said, "solution of the remaining 1percent requires a major decision by Hanoi."

This was followed by a brutal Christmas bombing of Hanoi and its environs by B-52s, the first bombings in months by the United States. At the same time, President Nixon made secret assurances to President Thieu of South Vietnam that the United States would come to his aid against North Vietnam if it attacked again. This was not made public until after the U.S. Congress ruled out any further U.S. military aid to South Vietnam in 1973.

It was regarded later as a stab in the back to the South Vietnamese.

But by then, Nixon was beginning to feel Watergate pressures. The Vietnamese peace accord was reached on January 27, 1973 finally.

CHAPTER 20

Nixon Falls, Kissinger Rises

On June 17, !972, a Saturday, I wandered into the Times' L Street bureau as I usually did on Saturdays, even though I had no pressing story to cover. I already had written a lengthy piece on the background to the Strategic Arms Limitation Treaty which President Nixon and Soviet Party leader Leonid I. Brezhnev had signed the previous month in Moscow. Henry Kissinger was en route to Peking for another round of talks, and Le Duc Tho, his Hanoi counterpart was reported there as well. The hope in the air was for progress toward winding down the Vietnam war by the end of 1972.

As was my habit, I wandered over to the wire "tickers" in the bureau to read what was coming over the wires that day, and I was struck that Saturday by a police story from Washington reporting that five men had been arrested at 2:30 am on charges of breaking into the offices of the Democratic National Committee in the Watergate

Apartment complex which was located near the Kennedy Center.

The news ticker did not give the story big play but I thought it quite interesting. The bureau on a Saturday morning was quite deserted. I urged whoever was in charge to "cover" the story somehow. Of course, the Washington bureau of The New York Times in those days had no police reporter. I had covered the police for the Washington Star in the early 1960s. Eventually, the acting head of he office sent a young trainee down to police headquarters for an arraignment later Saturday afternoon. One of the problems was that in those days, the first edition for the Sunday New York Times came out about 3 pm on Saturday afternoon, and the story of the break-in was put in the "caboose" section, where all the weddings were also put in those days.

Meanwhile, the Washington Post, under the byline of Alfred Lewis, its police reporter, of many years, played the story big on the front page, mentioning that one of those arrested was a former employee of the CIA, that three of them were native born Cubans, and that they were trying to tap into the contents of the Democratic headquarters.

The odd thing about Watergate is how long it took to become part of the country's consciousness. Even though I was a Washington correspondent for The Times, I was really not aware of what was happening behind the scenes. In part this was because I primarily covered foreign affairs, and my contacts with the White House at that juncture in

1972 were still limited. I could call Kissinger and I did, But I was not an intimate of his.

And frankly, I was more concerned in early 1973 on how the Vietnam agreement was playing out. It was not playing out well. The administration was complaining about North Vietnam's violations, and the failure of the Laotian and Cambodian Communists to accept the cease-fires. I was also trying to prepare for Brezhnev's arrival in the United States for his summit meeting. I remember Marie-Jeanne being told that our first child was going to be born at the end of June, and I called Kissinger to find out ahead of time when Brezhnev was to arrive and he told me off-the-record that it would be on June 16 or so. That made me feel less stressed.

Originally, Brezhnev had planned to take his wife and family with him to the United States, and to visit more than Washington and San Clemente, but Kissinger believes that when the Kremlin began to see how Watergate began to weaken Nixon, it sought to limit Brezhnev's travels. So in the end, he traveled alone, without his family. He was due to arrive at Andrews Air Force Base in the afternoon of Saturday, June 16. Again, because of The Times' early first edition deadline, I stayed in the Washington bureau, and sent a clerk with instructions to call me when the Soviet plane landed.

The phone rang about the time I expected, but it was Marie-Jeanne reporting that she believed she was feeling the first signs of "labor." I told her I would be home as soon as possible.

Since no business was to be conducted the first day of Brezhnev's visit, I was able to write my story, and file it, quickly. My lede said: "Leonid I. Brezhnev arrived in a heavy downpour today for the unofficial start of a nine day visit intended to spur arms control talks and to promote cooperation and commerce between the United States and the Soviet Union."

Secretary of State William D. Rogers, who led a small American welcoming party at heavily guarded Andrews Air Force Base just outside Washington, greeted the burly Communist Party leader by saying that "this is a wheat rain, which in America is a very good omen."

We got to the hospital around midnight, but James, our first born, was a bit stubborn. He wasn't born until about 5 am on June 17.

I was able to cover most of the Brezhnev visit but I did not go to California with Brezhnev. The two men signed a number of agreements in different fields, including oceanography, transportation, agriculture, research, and cultural exchange. They also agreed on income taxes, and atomic energy research and priorities on the current round of strategic arms limitation talks. The trade agreement was still hampered by the demands of Congress for unimpeded emigration of Soviet Jews.

As the weeks progressed, however, Nixon began to focus less and less on foreign affairs because Watergate began to overtake him. He was forced to demand the ouster of his closest aides Ehrlichman and Haldeman; and to face the prospect of being accused himself of masterminding the illegal activities. Kissinger clearly felt alienated from Nixon but also felt he could not resign as he had once planned to do. Al Haig, who Nixon had made his personal aide, had recommended to Nixon that he make Kissinger Secretary of State to replace Rogers. But Nixon, kept procrastinating. It was only in August, at a swimming pool in San Clemente, did Nixon offer the Cabinet job to Kissinger and even then in almost grudging words.

Kissinger, of course, was well known to the Senate Foreign Relations Committee, but his confirmation hearing was unusually long because in the Watergate atmosphere, he had to be grilled over the security wiretaps that were placed on some of his aides and newsmen early in his career as Nixon's security adviser.

In the end he was confirmed easily. Soon after his confirmation, Kissinger had an off-the-record dinner with the State Department regulars, who covered the department, including me. I don't remember all the details, including who was present. But I am sure that the chief network correspondents were there: Marvin Kalb of CBS, Richard Valeriani of NBC, Ted Koppel of ABC, Barry

Schweid of AP, but we did ask that he include us in his frequent travels abroad, and he promised to take us on his next trip to Peking.

He went up to the United Nations and on Sept. 24, addressed the General Assembly and gave a decidedly uninspiring speech. He gave a press conference and talked a bit about the "Year of Europe" which was pushed by Nixon and him but evoked not much interest in Europe. And on September 25, when he did meet with Arab ambassadors, he told them that the United States recognized their unhappiness with the Middle East stalemate and was ready to help find a solution but warned them against expecting Washington "to bring forth miracles." The Israelis were waiting for their own elections to take place at the end of October before doing anything.

Even though everyone knew that the Middle East was likely to be the next big crisis area, no one—and that meant no one— expected the Egyptians and Syrians to jointly launch a surprise attack against Israel on Yom Kippur, October 5-6, 1973, which became known as the October War.

And then suddenly, the Israelis, confident that they would not be attacked by the Egyptians and Syrians, found themselves under attack, and after the first week, I wrote: "Although Israeli forces have taken the offensive against Syria, they face a difficult and a long struggle if they try to crush the 60,000 man Egyptian force that has crossed the

Suez Canal. Is Israel—or Egypt—willing to avoid such a battle and agree to a diplomatic formula, including a cease-fire, that could open the way to a dialogue and, conceivably, to a more durable peace in the Middle East?"

I added that "the assumption that Israel could easily repulse a two-front offensive no longer seems valid." "Nearly 2,000 Israelis have been killed, double the number of those who died during the Six-Day War of 1967. That would be proportionate to 140,000 Americans dying. Some 500 Israeli tanks were destroyed and 75 planes shot down. But the Arabs have not made serious inroads into Israel and have suffered higher casualties."

I soon found myself focused almost entirely on the Middle East, I had covered the Six Day War in 1967 while working for The Star, but that war was completely different. It was over so quickly, and President Johnson wanted to adopt a posture of neutrality to keep the Russians from intervening on the Arab side.

That surprised me at the time since most Americans were clearly pro-Israeli and sympathized with the Israelis who argued that they had been forced into their pre-emptive attacks on Egypt and Syria, and later Jordan.

The October War was quite different. The United States and Israel were so confident that the Israelis were militarily superior to the Arabs that the Egyptian attack on the morning of October 6 caught them by surprise and cost the Israelis dearly in men and materiel. wThe Israelis were warned about the impending attacks from Egypt and Syria by many sources, including King Hussein of Jordan, but Prime Minister Golda Meir and her top aides discounted them until it was too late.

At first the U.S. defense establishment was wary of rushing to Israel's aid, thinking the Israelis did not need as much as they were seeking. But Kissinger prevailed upon them. And eventually planes and tanks were being shipped at a rapid rate.

Before the October war broke out, Kissinger had scheduled another trip to China and had promised to take correspondents along. To that end, the Chinese Mission to the United States, which was then located at the Mayflower Hotel in downtown Washington, arranged a big send-off dinner at the hotel for the Kissinger party, including the correspondents and their wives.

But at the end of the dinner, Kissinger and his aides slipped away and drove to Andrews Air Force Base for what was an unannounced visit to Moscow to discuss an end to the fighting which by then had lasted almost a month. A cease-fire was achieved but it took months for the actual boundaries to be worked out between Egypt and Israel and between Syria and Israel, and many more trips.

Finally, on November 5, Kissinger, his aides, including the State Department doctor, and a dozen or so correspondents, including me, left on our "China trip," but it would turn out to be much more than that. It began with a landing in Rabat, Morocco, where Kissinger had to deal, somewhat awkwardly, with Royal mounted guards, and then to Tunisia.

And then we got to Egypt where Kissinger had his first face to face meeting with Anwar el-Sadat, with whom he developed a close relationship through many negotiations.

I did not think that when we set out that this trip would actually be critical for both Egypt and Israel in bringing about a lasting cease- fire. But I was wrong. After Kissinger's initial meeting with Sadat in Cairo, Joseph Sisco, Kissinger's right hand man in the negotiations, flew to Israel and got the Israeli Cabinet's approval of the details. So while we in the Kissinger party flew on to Beijing (it was still being called Peking), Henry Tanner, the Times' Cairo correspondent was writing that Egypt and Israel were going to sign a cease-fire on the Cairo-Suez road, the first time the two sides had signed a joint document since the armistice agreement was negotiated in Rhodes in 1949 following the fighting that followed the birth of Israel in 1948.

My colleague in Israel, Terry Smith, reporting the Israeli attitude, said many Israeli officials were wary of Kissinger, not sure they were getting the full story of his talks with Sadat, but nevertheless felt they had no alternative but to sign the cease-fire agreement he had worked out with Sadat.

I wrote in a "Reporter's Notebook" that occasionally relations with the 17 reporters on the plene "became strained." Before reaching Cairo, Kissinger and McCloskey had both cautioned the press from speculating that anything "spectacular" might emerge from Kissinger's talks with Sadat. But when it was learned that the talks had led to a restoration of diplomatic relations with the United States and the basis for the cease-fire with Israel, "some newsmen felt badly deceived."

I wrote in my "Reporter's Notebook," from Peking later, that:

> "They complained and Mr. Kissinger replied that by "spectacular," he had meant a major breakthrough for a final political settlement. That, he said, had not come and so there was no cause for criticism."

> "The quarreling did not quickly abate. Mr. Kissinger came to the rear of the plane again and said that he would recommend that the press be assigned to the next Skylab mission so that McCloskey and I can get 90 days of peace."

Kissinger went from Cairo to Jordan to meet King Hussein, the most pro-Western of the Arab leaders, but who constantly frustrated Kissinger by his inability to make any deals with Israel. From Jordan, we flew on to Riyadh, the capital of Saudi Arabia, which in 1973 was very sparsely inhabited, compared with Jiddah, the port city. What I still remember is that after we landed, Kissinger jokingly said to me, and Murray Marder of the Washington Post, and Barry Schweid of the Associated Press, that since we were Jewish, we could not disembark. I replied in the same joking way that "if they let you off, we'll come too."

In his memoirs, Kissinger related how virulently anti-Zionist the king was in his diatribes, although later on, he tried to separate that from being anti-Jewish. Kissinger says he did get support from the Saudis for his efforts, although later on, there were problems with an oil embargo which lasted for several months.

On subsequent trips to Riyadh over the years, hotels were built with modern phones and telexes. But on this 1973 trip, the U.S. Embassy had provided two outside phone lines for the use of correspondents that went through Jiddah. I remember Marder waiting for a very long time to get a connection and screaming into the phone and finally getting through and thinking he was talking to the Post, and finding out he was connected to a drug store in D.C. Then we went to Iran where I was struck by the heavy auto traffic and the crowds in downtown Tehran. Several of us sampled the cuisine and of course enjoyed the caviar. We did not meet the Shah on this trip, but I had met him on an earlier trip to Washington, where he briefed the press himself. I had considered him a very worldly diplomat and was genuinely surprised when he was overthrown six years later.

We then flew on to Peking. As for as the China portion of the trip, Kissinger spent a good deal of it trying to reassure the Chinese that Nixon's problems with Watergate would not affect U.S. relations with China. He also privately learned that Prime Minister Chou En-lai, whom Kissinger highly respected, was on his way out, due to health reasons but also Mao's desire for complete control [Chou died in 1975], The Chinese were also wary of Nixon's seeming détente with the Russians. Kissinger had to reassure the Chinese that better U.S. relations with Moscow did not mean a lessening of American interest in Peking.

I personally was struck by the fact that in 1973, things were still pretty primitive in China. The Mindzu Hotel, where we all stayed, was a second-rate hotel. In a few more years, foreign companies would start building five-star hotels in Peking.

After a relaxing stop over in Tokyo, and a chance to raid the American PX in Alaska, we all returned home, somewhat weary but with some Christmas presents. I had bought a portable TV.

Reflecting the exhaustion of everyone once we got to the Chinese capital, I wrote in my "Reporter's Notebook" from Peking that Kissinger's spokesman, Bob McCloskey, had met with reporters today on the tenth floor of the Mindzu Hotel, where the official party was staying.

"It was one of the few times in the last week that he has been able to meet with newsmen at less than 30,000 feet."

CHAPTER 21

Kissinger's First Shuttle Accord

No sooner had we returned from our round the world journey in Kissinger's 707 jet at the beginning of December 1973 than it looked as if we were about to embark again to the Middle East. President Nixon was coming under increasing heat for his involvement in the Watergate break-in and was desperate for an agreement between Egypt and Israel that he could announce. Also, the Arab oil embargo was taking a toll in the United States. There were long lines at gas stations and there was considerable pressure at home to find a way to persuade Saudi Arabia to end its embargo.

Kissinger, from his initial visit to Saudi Arabia, knew that the Saudis were looking for some give from Israel and a go-ahead from Egypt before it would agree to an end to the embargo. Meanwhile, the Soviet Union, looking for part of the diplomatic action, had pressured for a Geneva peace conference at the end of December 1973.

The so-called peace conference was indeed convened and I attended along with Henry Tanner, The Times' Cairo correspondent. The conference was attended by the United States, the Soviet Union, Israel, Egypt, and Jordan. Syria declined to attend.

The conference, however, lasted only a few days, and before I knew it, I was back on Kissinger's plane flying home. But it had been agreed that after the Israeli elections at the end of the year, Kissinger would fly to Egypt and Israel to see if he could help resolve the problem of disengaging the two sides' troops that were in a dangerous cease-fire on both sides of the Suez Canal. The Egyptian Third Army was encircled by Israeli forces on the eastern side of the Canal and there were Israeli forces on the western side, Moreover, the Egyptians wanted some progress toward restoring their territory originally captured in the 1967 war.

Kissinger originally had planned to go out to the area for about a week at the most, make some suggestions and then have the details hashed out by negotiators in Geneva but he met with Sadat, who was at that time staying in Aswan, in southern Egypt, We checked into the New Cataract Hotel, which was connected to the Old Cataract Hotel, made famous by Agatha Christie in her mystery "Death on the Nile."

What we later found out after the accord was finally reached on January 17, about a week after Kissinger first started out on his mission, was that when he first discussed his ideas with Sadat, the Egyptian leader made it clear that he preferred Kissinger to try and work out a total accord with Israel and not have it go back to Geneva for further haggling.

Kissinger, before setting out on his trip, had met for three days in Washington with Moshe Dayan, Israel's veteran defense minister, who had encouraged him to press ahead. The Labor Government of Golda Meir was reelected and it was amenable to the initial accord, which was also favored by Sadat.

Of all Kissinger negotiations, this one in the end probably was the easiest, but for those flying in the Boeing 707, back and forth between Aswan and Ben Gurion Airport in Israel, it became something of a chore. I tried to have some fun with this in a "Reporter's Notebook" I wrote for the paper of January 16, 1974:

"JERUSALEML Jan. 15—A few minutes before takeoff from Aswan last night, Joseph J. Sisco stood in the aisle of the Air Force jet and said to no one in particular, 'Welcome aboard the Egyptian- Israeli shuttle.'"

I have always liked thinking that this article helped launch the term, "shuttle diplomacy;" But who knows.

In any event, the initial accord got the Israelis to pull their forces back to near what are known as the Mitla and Gidi Passes in the Sinai. And rules were put into effect on how many Egyptian forces could come over to the eastern side of the Sinai.

Sadat was quite joyous at this accord. The Israelis were pleased, although the right wing was not.

In Syria, where Hafez al-Assad [father of the current Syrian ruler, Bashar el-Assad] had been dubious about negotiating with Israel and had stayed away from Geneva, he received Kissinger for some four hours on his way home, gave him some negotiating ideas, which Kissinger passed on to the Israelis before flying home, and assured the Israelis that Israeli prisoners of war were being given good treatment.

The Israeli-Syrian negotiations, a few months later, would be the toughest of all Kissinger negotiations.

CHAPTER 22

Kissinger's Amazing Syrian Shuttle

Following the quick disengagement agreement between Egypt and Israel, Kissinger set out with his plane load of newsmen and women for what everyone assumed would be a more difficult effort—a similar deal between Israel and Syria. These two countries had virtually no communication between each other, and Israel already had occupied a good part of Syria's Golan Heights from the 1967 War.

Now the question was how much Syrian territory could Israel be persuaded to give up. Even before these talks began, Israel had refused to negotiate until Syria turned over the names of the Israeli POWs it held, and this was done earlier in the year during another Kissinger trip to the region, a moment which led to a somewhat theatrical scene when Prime Minister Golda Meir burst into tears upon receiving the list in Arabic from Kissinger in her office.

At the start of this round of "shuttle diplomacy" fighting was still going on when Kissinger's Air Force jet made its first landing at Ben Gurion Airport on May 2, 1974. Kissinger had recently gotten married to Nancy and this was her first trip on a "shuttle"—-she was to fall ill during the trip with some stomach trouble.

Originally, Kissinger was planning on a 17-day trip, but this "shuttle" turned out to be the longest of his diplomatic adventures, some 33 days. It was one that nearly collapsed several times. The newsmen were taken by both sides to visit the front lines to see why the area around El-Quneitra was considered so important and more importantly, the hills around it.

Before the 1967 war, some 17,000 Syrians lived there, but it was now a ghost town, and nearby some Israeli settlements were established.

The Kissinger party stayed at the New Omayad Hotel, which was walking distance to the shopping center of old Damascus, and where I bought my wife a beautiful gold Aleppo necklace from a local jeweler and a kaftan that she once wore to a black tie affair at the State Department. But after staying overnight once, Kissinger decided not to do it again because he was awakened at 5 a.m. by the cries of the Mosque nearby.

Thus, we fell into the habit of starting each day in Jerusalem at the King David Hotel, where Kissinger would meet with Israelis or at the Foreign Ministry. Then later in the afternoon we would drive to Ben Gurion Airport and fly to Damascus and go to the hotel and sit and write our stories.

We might then be bused to Hafez al-Assad's modest headquarters where Kissinger would have been meeting him and then be bussed back to the airport and flown back to Ben Gurion Airport, usually arriving around midnight.

I would then file my story by phone to the foreign desk in New York. In those days, The Times had an excellent recording room, men and women who took your calls over the phone and could handle the dictation at fairly rapid speed, and the phone connection from the airport was excellent. We also had good connections from the King David Hotel. At that time, the Israelis had some kind of censorship but they waived it for us.

This diplomatic "shuttle" lasted 33 days, longer than anyone had predicted, and it had its ups and downs. For a journalist who in effect was a "prisoner" on Kissinger's plane whose information was pretty much limited to what he dished out on the flights back to Tel Aviv after his late night meetings with Assad, it was at times frustrating. I did my best to roll with the punches. Here is a sampling of my stories from that historic "shuttle."

"KISSINGER BELIEVES SYRIAN-ISRAELI DECISION IS NEAR

Jerusalem, May 10—Secretary of State Kissinger told Israeli officials tonight that he might know by next Tuesday whether he could bring about an agreement by Syria and Israel to separate their troops on the Golan Heights during his current Middle East trip, now in its 13th day.... He told his aides and the Israelis tonight that he should know by Tuesday or perhaps Wednesday whether an agreement was possible. If it is, he plans to try to work it out by the end of next week. If he concludes it does not seem likely, he probably will return to Washington late in the week, perhaps Thursday or Friday."

"KISSINGER TALKS SHOW NO PROGRESS,"

Jerusalem, May 14—Secretary of State Kissinger shuttled between Syria and Israel today without making any significant progress toward a troop separation agreement between the two countries. He had set tonight as his deadline for deciding whether he could achieve the accord during the current mission, now in its 17th day. But newsmen were told on the way from Damascus that Mr. Kissinger still wanted 24 to 36 hours to try to extract a compromise from the two sides.

A senior official on the Air Force 707 jet said the situation was 'essentially in a holding pattern.' He thought the chances for an agreement by the end of this week, when Mr. Kissinger must return to Washington were slightly less promising than a few days ago."

"KISSINGER MAKES 'GOOD PROGRESS' IN MIDEAST TALKS

"Tel Aviv, May 20—Secretary of State Kissinger said today in Damascus that "good progress" had been made in his talks with President Hafez al-Assad of Syria toward concluding an agreement to separate Syrian and Israeli troops on the Golan Heights."

And finally:

"ISRAEL AND SYRIA ACCEPT ACCORD FOR DISENGAGING ON GOLAN FRONT, LONG KISSINGER EFFORT SUCCEEDS"

"Jerusalem, May 29—Israel and Syria agreed today on an accord to separate their forces on the Golan Heights. The agreement, which was worked out by Secretary of State Kissinger in a month of intensive personal diplomacy will be signed by Syrian and Israeli military officers in Geneva on Friday."

It was a truly exhausting trip. Some of my colleagues, particularly those working for TV networks on short deadlines made judgment errors, going on air saying the mission had failed when it had not. I was pleased with my work, but I was lucky in that I was able to just report the situation without making any judgment calls. On our way home from Israel, Kissinger stopped in Cairo and he filled us in on some important details. The most interesting was that three times during the trip, Kissinger was very close to giving up and returning to Washington without an accord. In Kissinger's rundown President Assad of Syria is a "central figure," I wrote, "a man of split attitudes, fascinated with the prospects of ending Syria's virtual isolation, but also deeply troubled as a result of the Syrians' traditional refusal to deal with Israel."

"The Israelis, in turn, regarded the Syrians with enormous suspicion and distrust and were extremely reluctant to give back any of the land on the Golan Heights that Israel captured in the June, 1967 war.

The first "crisis" was over control of the three hills and the land in and around the town of El Quneitra, the former Syrian administrative center for the Golan Heights that was seized by Israel in 1967. The Israelis were willing to return the two to Syrian administration, but they insisted that it be placed in the U.N. buffer zone. The Syrians, in turn, opposed having Israeli troops close to the town because that would inhibit Syrian refugees from coming back to the area, which is now virtually uninhabited."

The problem was resolved when Kissinger offered a compromise by which the Israelis withdrew some 300 yards beyond El Quneitra and agreed as well to a zone nearly a mile wide in which they would not be permitted to have troops. Both sides accepted the compromise. Kissinger was so sure the Syrians would not accept that when his plane arrived in Damascus on May 18 that afternoon, he and everyone else had their bags aboard for a flight to Cairo and to Washington. Instead the plane went back to Israel and the King David Hotel had to cancel the reservations of incoming tourists. On May 23, another problem arose over zones in which each side would thin out their forces, This was finally resolved that day, On the last day, May 29, with many details still not settled, Kissinger went to see Assad alone and the two men agreed that it was now necessary to end the negotiations peacefully in a way that did not precipitate a crisis.

Kissinger and Assad were drafting a statement for Kissinger's departure without an accord. I wrote: "When in the last five minutes, Assad told Kissinger that breaking off the talks [was] painful for him and really a pity considering how far they had moved toward an agreement. Kissinger then suggested that instead of finishing the departure statement they make one more effort to overcome the remaining differences. These talks lasted all day. The next day, the Israelis made the last concession, giving back another village in the northern part of the Golan area. And Tuesday night Kissinger went back to Damascus to wrap it up and celebrated with a midnight buffet.

During that lengthy shuttle, Kissinger celebrated—marked would be a better verb—his 50th birthday on May 27. The correspondents had chipped in ahead of time on a poster mimicking a Braniff Airlines poster of the time which featured a pretty airline hostess standing in front of a plane waving, and saying something likeL "I'm Jackie. Fly Me to Miami." We had a smiling Henry, waving, saying "I'm Henry, Fly Me to Damascus." I recently unearthed my copy of the poster, and it included Henry's signature saying, "Dear Bernie Gwertzman. Sorry I couldn't live up to all your Predictions."

CHAPTER 23

Nixon's Resignation and Kissinger's Farewell

Of course, Kissinger's diplomatic triumphs in the Middle East in 1974 in Egypt and in Syria came as President Nixon was being slowly crushed by Watergate. His closest White House advisers had all been arrested and subject to questioning and more to the point, his secret White House tapes had been subpoenaed by the Watergate counsel and pressure was rising for an impeachment of Nixon.

Nixon, himself, in what seemed like an act of folly, decided that he, too, wanted to share in some of Kissinger's Middle East glory and insisted on arranging a quick Middle East trip with Kissinger almost as soon as Kissinger returned from Syria and Israel in June 1974.

It was during this Middle East trip that Kissinger blew up at a press conference in Vienna and threatened to resign as Secretary of State if accusations were not withdrawn that he had lied about ordering wiretaps on subordinates—something that had been raised years earlier during his confirmation hearings.

Nixon also had a second trip to Moscow that summer before coming home and finally deciding to resign as president in August rather than face an almost certain impeachment trial.

The advent of Gerald Ford as president unfortunately came at a low water mark for American foreign policy. The Congress was implacable in its refusal to support military aid to South Vietnam or Cambodia which faced dire peril from its Communist foes in 1975.

Despite continuous pleading from Kissinger and Ford, Congress refused to vote support for saving the Saigon government which had signed on to the Vietnam agreement because of a promise from Nixon that the United States would come to its aid if Hanoi invaded.

In early 1975, Kissinger set out on another Middle East shuttle between Egypt and Israel to bring about a more important agreement than the one negotiated in early 1974. Yitzhak Rabin had replaced Golda Meir as Israel's prime minister, and although Rabin later on would prove to be a major force for diplomacy, in March 1975, he turned out to be a difficult roadblock to Kissinger. The issue was over Sadat's desire to gain control of the Mitla and Gidi passes in the Sinai and control of the oil wells there. That would also require peacekeepers, presumably U.N. or American.

As a passenger on Kissinger's plane, I wrote on March 19, 1975, "reporters aboard the plane were given an appraisal of the overall world situation that was the most pessimistic they had heard in some time."

"Some of the comments were clearly self-serving and underlined Mr. Kissinger's well-known concerns about Congress and the erosion of United States influence abroad. But reporters were inclined to take most of them seriously as at least reflecting what Mr. Kissinger and his closest aides were thinking."

"All around the world, American diplomatic influence is on the decline," the newsmen were told. "Portugal, Turkey, Cambodia, Vietnam, the Middle East—all are problems that no longer respond to American pressure and influence."

Finally, Kissinger returned to Washington in an extremely agitated mood. He failed for the first time to achieve an agreement between the two sides, and in a press conference said on March 26, 1975 that the Middle East was now in "potentially grave danger" and that the broader Geneva peace conference that the United States and the Russians had organized in late 1973 would probably have to be reconvened to seek a way of avoiding a war.

While Kissinger did not blame Israel for the failure, he seemed to suggest the Israelis could have done more to avoid the breakdown. Ford, however, had seemed in his briefings of Congressmen to lay more blame on Israel. Kissinger, in his memoirs, is quite clear in saying that Rabin was at fault for not being more forceful within his own cabinet in pushing for an agreement with Egypt,

At this point, Middle East diplomacy looked hopeless.

But early in July, I was summoned to a briefing by Simcha Dinitz, the Israeli ambassador, along with a few of my colleagues. Dinitz wanted to tell us of his recent trip to the Virgin Islands where he had an unpublicized two-day meeting with Kissinger, who was on vacation at the Caneel Bay Plantation, the Rockefeller-owned resort on Saint John in the U.S, Virgin Islands. The State Department later confirmed the visit but gave little in the way of detail.

But Dinitz told us enough to let us know that a breakthrough indeed had occurred. In fact, events moved fairly rapidly. On August 15, I wrote a story with a Washington dateline that said: "United States and Israeli officials completed work today on the draft language for a new agreement between Israel and Egypt now in the final stages of negotiation. After four days of intensive talks at the State Department, the Americans and Israelis agreed on language for points of agreement already achieved and specified what was still undecided."

Dinitz and Joe Sisco headed the respective delegations.

Kissinger flew to Vail, Col. to report to Ford on the negotiations which was to be announced by Ford. Indeed, Kissinger went out to the region a week later and wrapped up the accord, in which Israel evacuated the Mitla and Gidi passes in Sinai and turned over the Abu Rudeis oil field to Egypt.

In return, the Israelis got pledges from the United States that their oil supply would not be reduced and their security not impaired. U.S, observers could be placed on the passes.

On a personal note, Marie-Jeanne was alone in our house in Washington at the end of summer with our new born son, Michael, and our two-year old son, James, and I was telephoning, sometimes two or three times a day to try and cheer her up.

An important sidelight on that trip for me was that a passenger on that plane was a freshman Congressman from Brooklyn, Stephen Solarz, who was extremely interested in foreign affairs, and had gotten himself onto the Foreign Affairs Committee. Solarz became particularly interested in the fate of Syrian Jews many of whose relatives lived in his district, and worked hard behind the scenes to get Hafez al-Assad to let Syrian Jewish women emigrate to find husbands. He later played an important part in my coverage of the Israeli-Egyptian accord.

When we got back to Washington with the agreement, much of the accord was secret, that is, was not publicly released. Joe Sisco briefed the House Foreign Affairs Committee on the contents, including the "secret" parts. That afternoon, Solarz called me up, and from his notes, read to me virtually all the "secret" parts.

That gave The Times a nice exclusive for a while. Eventually, the State Department released the documents and the Senate approved them. The day my "exclusive" was published, Sisco called me up. He said to me on the phone: "Bernie, one question: Was your source from the committee, or from the department?" I replied: "Joe, I'm sorry, but no comment." Given the mood of Congress, this accord led to weeks of back and forth, with many in Congress worried about the commitment of U.S. personnel.

But Israel also received a number of other benefits that were spelled out in auxiliary agreements. The United States pledged not to have any dealings with the PLO until it recognized Israel. It also promised to sell it various pieces of advanced military hardware. More importantly, perhaps, this was Kissinger's last Middle East agreement. There were no more Middle East shuttles until Jimmy Carter was elected president in 1976.

Sadat came to Washington in November, 1975, and spoke to a joint meeting of Congress, and urged a sympathetic attitude toward the Palestinian cause and to temper its support of Israel.

He was the first Egyptian leader to make a state visit to the United States and Kissinger called it a "historic mission—a sign of rapid improvement in Egyptian-American relations." The fact that the joint meeting took place was the result of intense White House pressure, I wrote, on a reluctant Congressional leadership. The White

House and the Congressional leadership agreed to invite Prime Minister Rabin to speak when he visits Washington early in 1976.

That trip turned out to be Kissinger's last "shuttle" to the Middle East. He traveled in 1976 to Africa, trying to deal with Soviet and Cuban penetration of the area, particularly in Angola. He sought to persuade Prime Minister Ian D. Smith of Rhodesia to agree to a power-sharing arrangement with blacks who made up the majority of his country, and he visited, Pretoria, the capital of South Africa, for talks with Prime Minister John Vorster. It was my only trip to that country and I met a very young John Burns who was then The Times' correspondent there as well as an equally young Robin Wright, who was then a stringer for the Washington Post.

On one of his trips,. to Britain, Iran, Afghanistan, Pakistan and the Netherlands, in August, he was asked if President Ford would defeat Ronald Reagan in the Republican presidential primary which was to take place in a week, and then go on to defeat Jimmy Carter in the election. I wrote: Kissinger replied to the French journalist that "I am confident that President Ford will be nominated and hopeful that he will be elected."

"It was not a statement to win points with Mr. Ford's political advisers who would have preferred a more optimistic public attitude toward November, but it was apparently the best Mr. Kissinger felt he could do. No one was more conscious of the huge lead that Mr. Carter held over Mr. Ford in the polls than Mr. Kissinger.

He must prod, cajole and promise foreign governments while knowing that they must be calculating that anything the Ford administration does now may have to to be re-evaluated next January by a Carter team."

On his trips, Kissinger usually liked to fit in a sightseeing visit. On the stopover in Iran, the Shah had arranged for him and the press corps to visit an Iranian caviar processing plant on the Caspian Sea at the port of Bandar Pahlevi. Kissinger was reported angered and demanded to know why he had to go there.

This reportedly caused gfreat concern to to staff members of the U.S. embassy who had inserted the visit at at the personal suggestion of the Shah. When we all got to the plant it was about 110 degrees outside.

As soon as Kissinger and his wife Nancy and son, David, arrived, a sturgeon was produced and eviscerated with the gray roe removed. Kissinger looked away, paled and seemed extremely uncomfortable. Within the hour, however, everyone was ushered into an air-conditioned room where we sampled some of Iran's finest caviar with blinis and cold vodka.

On that same Iran trip, Iran announced it would spend $10 billion more on U.S. arms and would go ahead with plans to buy eight nuclear reactors, with guarantees not to reprocess the spent uranium in country—an issue, of course that would have reverberations many years later.

After his last overseas trip to the annual NATO ministers meeting in December 1976 in Brussels, Kissinger made a series of farewell appearances in Washington and New York. I wrote a Reporters Notebook, published on January 19, 1977, his next-to- last day in office, headlined: "Now Kissinger Woos His Critics." Abe Rosenthal, the paper's top editor, sent a note around saying this is what a Reporter's Notebook should look like. I regarded this as a very big compliment. I wrote: "As Henry A. Kissinger's term expires, he has been closing out the public record with a round of farewell lunches and dinners. He has used these usually routine affairs to say some unusual things, trying to make peace in the last days with some of the groups with which his relationship has been most uneasy during his tenure as Secretary of State,"

"I am grateful for the opportunity to appear before you today," Mr. Kissinger said ironically and to bursts of laughter at the National Press Club in his farewell to the reporters who had covered him. "It is almost like coming home for we have so much in common—a reluctance to see our names in print, a uniform appreciation of the goodness of mankind, total subordination of ego, a basic reliance on working within the system, and, above all, humility."

At the end of his speech, he turned serious. "Because of my origin, I have perhaps a unique perspective of what

America means to the cause of freedom and human dignity. And I have had no higher aim than to repay in some small measure my debt to this country which saved me from totalitarianism and the world from Slavery. I leave to you for a time, the great domain of public policy," he said ot the press, seeming to choke a bit with emotion.

"I would be hypocritical if I pretended that to part is easy. I envy you the excitement, the responsibility, the opportunities that will be yours. I shall never forget how hard you tested me. I shall always cherish the experiences we enjoyed together. And I will think of you with affection tinged with exasperation."

Nothing exasperated Kissinger during his more than three years as Secretary than his inability to win over the American Jewish community. He was aware that because of his even- handed approach to Middle East diplomacy, his highly publicized embraces with Arab leaders, and his continuous pressure on Israel to make concessions, he was suspect in the minds of many Americans and many Israelis. The low point came during one of his trips to Israel when Israelis shouted at him "Jew-boy go home"—an epithet that was used on the Nixon tapes. Kissinger, himself, was not religious. He did not regularly go to religious services, His second marriage was to a non-Jew. And he was sworn in as Secretary of State on the Jewish Sabbath on a King James bible. He tried to explain himself when he was honored by the Conference of Presidents of Major American Jewish Organizations.

"We have had, of necessity, a very complicated relationship," he said. "From my point of view, probably no criticism has hurt me more than if it came from this community. And probably from your point of view, it was especially painful if disagreements occurred between the Jewish community and the first Jewish Secretary of State in American history."

"I thought it was important for the future of Israel and for the future of the Jewish people that the actions that the United States Government took were not seen to be the result of a special personal relationship, but that the support we gave Israel reflected not my personal preferences alone but the basic national interests of the United States," he explained. With the audience hushed, he added:

> "I have never forgotten that 13 members of my family died in concentration camps, nor could I ever fail to remember what it was like to live in Nazi Germany as a member of a persecuted minority."

Following his speech, the chairman, a rabbi, said:

> "My friends, no words need be spoken, because what we have felt cannot be captured by words.

It belongs to that realm of the intimate which cannot be encompassed by earthbound language. We have sought our brother and we have found him, and we are profoundly grateful for this experience."

CHAPTER 24

Carter's Bold Camp
David Gambit, 1978

As 1977 opened, there was the expectation of change in Washington. The most obvious of course was that the new president, Jimmy Carter, was an unknown to virtually everyone in political circles, including the vast Washington press corps.

We knew his background—governor of Georgia, a naval officer, a peanut farmer. What we did not expect was that this newcomer would put so much emphasis on foreign affairs and in particular, human rights. From the beginning of his term. I can remember that the routine State Department noon briefings were enlivened by statements criticizing the Soviet Union for its actions against one dissident or the other. This was completely different from the past.

Carter himself, in his Inauguration Address, spoke out forcefully on human rights. And by early March, he was urging that the U.N. Commission on Human Rights, which was located in Geneva, move to New York, where it would get more attention. Carter, though, did not stop there. He seemed to want to be known as the voice for his administration's foreign policy pronouncements in the early months, much to the surprise of us correspondents, who were used to more reticent presidents.

In fact, what was odd was that even though Carter admittedly had little experience in foreign affairs, and had appointed two experts to top spots: Cyrus R. Vance, who had been a deputy Secretary of Defense in the Johnson Administration, working under Robert S. McNamara. And who had done special assignments for various presidents since then, was named Secretary of State. Vance insisted, when he took the job that there would be only two spokesmen on foreign affairs, himself and the president.

As we would see, however, that promise from Vance broke down in practice over time.

The other expert was Zbigniew Brzezinski, who Carter chose to head the National Security Council.

I knew "Zbig" which was what everyone called him, from the time he was a graduate instructor in Harvard's Government department. I was enrolled as a freshman in 1953-54 in Government 1 which was a year-long course in political theory. The way the course worked was that a professor gave a lecture and a section man, usually a graduate student, ran a smaller group in a follow-up discussion group.

When the time came to study Marxism, Zbig used his "section" acting as a mock Polish Communist to "convince" his American students on the advantages of Marxism over capitalism. My roommate, Edward Abramson, who had Zbig as his section man, said he was most convincing.

Of course, at the start of the administration, the same problems existed as were there at the end of the Ford term: the Middle East, the problems still remaining between Israel and Egypt and between Israel and Syria, and the Palestinian question. How to complete SALT II with the Russians, and ways to strengthen Europe. Iran then was a surprise waiting in the wings. Carter and Vance thought they could move quickly on the Middle East by dealing directly with the Palestinian question, an issue which Kissinger had avoided in his disengagement agreements with Egypt and Syria in 1974 and 1975. The Times hired Richard Burt to replace Les Gelb, who had joined the Vance team as assistant secretary for Politico-Military Affairs. Burt, who later went on to become Ambassador to Germany, cultivated Zbig, and got some good stories from his office. I covered State and traveled with Vance as I had with Kissinger. Vance had said before taking office that he intended not to travel as much as Kissinger, but that proved impossible to carry out. In his first month in office, he went to the Middle East, covering six countries in six days, something even Kissinger did not attempt. He had a press conference at each stop but there was virtually no news produced. On the plane itself, Vance seemed shy with the press. I wrote in a Reporter's Notebook that: "Vance seems to be feeling his way with the press. He wants to be informative, although his nature appears to urge him to hold back. At the start of the trip last Monday night at Andrews AFB he walked to the rear of the plane and chatted easily with reporters but he has not returned to the press area since then [six days]." I had a long talk with Hodding Carter, who was Vance's spokesman, and complained about Vance's shyness with the press, and tried to provide some guidance for the future.

I suppose what most dramatized the Carter administration's "new" approach was the way it handled the Russians. Not only were the human rights criticisms of the Russians highly publicized, but Carter himself went out of his way to hold a press conference, just a week before Vance was to fly to Moscow to present new proposals to Brezhnev and Gromyko on advancing the stalled SALT talks and to say that Vance would give priority in Moscow to seeking agreement for "substantial reduction in the number of strategic missiles and bombers allowed by each side." Carter added that "if the reduction cannot be achieved the two sides should complete a treaty incorporating the overall level of 2400 missiles and bombers already agreed upon in 1974 and leave disputed issues for subsequent negotiations."

Usually such information is "top secret" and not divulged before the other side sees it. Carter also said that Vance would discuss the human rights situation in the Soviet Union, including the emigration problems of Jews. The latter issue, of course, had been a thorn in efforts to secure a trade agreement between the two countries for years, with the Congress linking free emigration of Jews to normal tariff treatment for Russia.

This was prelude to the fact that when Vance got to Moscow at the end of March 1977, the Russians were primed to reject whatever he offered them. My lead story on March 30 said it all: "Talks between Secretary of State Cyrus R. Vance and Leonid I. Brezhnev on a treaty to limit offensive missiles and bombers carrying nuclear warheads broke down today. The Soviet leader rejected as 'inequitable' both of the United States proposals for breaking a two-year impasse in negotiations for such a treaty,"

Later, Vance said he was "disappointed" but felt overall relations were not impaired. Brezhnev, who briefly met with American newsmen at the Kremlin, looked in poor health, although he was to live for five more years. As experts aboard Vance's plane began speculating on what went wrong, one theme of course was Carter's decision to rub in his human rights concerns about Russia after he had been warned by the Moscow embassy that that would not help the negotiations.

In any event, only a few days after Vance returned from Moscow, Ambassador Anatoly Dobrynin was meeting with him at Moscow's request to set up an advance meeting between the two sides before they were to meet again in Geneva in late May on strategic arms. These talks would continue onwards until finally culminating in a summit meeting in Vienna between Carter and Brezhnev in June 1979.

Carter has gotten considerable praise for pushing to a conclusion a Panama Canal Treaty which ceded ownership of the Canal to Panama. Negotiations had begun in the Johnson administration after riots by Panamanian youths had led to bloodshed and a suspension of diplomatic relations. Credit for the negotiations on the American side goes to veteran diplomat Ellsworth Bunker and former IBM executive Sol Linowitz.

But the foreign policy area that consumed most of the new administration's energy in foreign affairs for the first two years was the Middle East. Carter and Vance had decided, even before assuming office, that it made no sense to continue Kissinger's step-by-step diplomacy, but rather to seek a global solution and to reconvene the Geneva conference that Kissinger and Gromyko had organized in December 1973 in the wake of the October 1973 war but which never did anything but serve as a launching pad for

Kissinger's successful initial deals between Egypt and Israel in 1974 and 1975 and Syria and Israel in 1974. Kissinger, Sadat and the Israelis were distrustful of the Geneva framework because they saw no way to accommodate the Palestine Liberation Organization. And even though the Russians were officially the co-chairmen of the Geneva conference, the Americans, Egyptians and Israelis did not want them to play an active role in the talks.

From the first months in office, Carter began inviting the heads of state from the Middle East to Washington for preliminary talks. Carter, in a press conference in May, 1977, while Israeli Prime Minister Yitzhak Rabin was in Washington, talked about "the right of the Palestinians to have a homeland, to be compensated for losses that they have suffered." He said "They do include the withdrawal of Israel from occupied territories from the 1967 war, and they do include an end of belligerence and a re-establishment of permanent and secure borders." This led, I wrote, to a formal protest from the Israeli government that the drift of Carter's most recent statements had gone beyond anything any Israeli government could accept as the basis for an overall Middle East settlement.

President Anwar el-Sadat of Egypt was next to Washington and then King Hussein of Jordan. Carter himself flew to Geneva to meet Syrian President Hafez el-Assad. The strongest element in all this was the continued emphasis on Palestinian rights which drove the Israelis into disbelief and led the American Jewish Community into strong opposition to Carter. At that time, because I covered the Middle East so extensively, I became very acquainted with the leaders of the American Israel Political Action Committee (AIPAC), which at that time was headed by Morris Amitay, a former Kennedy administration official who became known as Israel's leading lobbyist in Washington.

In the spring of 1977, Menachem Begin, whose right-wing Likud Party, had had no part in Israeli government in the past, was elected to rule the country, shocking Washington, because it feared an end to diplomacy.

Vance continued to make trips to the region but no breakthrough seemed in the wind. Then suddenly, in early November 1977, Sadat announced that he wanted to go to Israel and speak to the Israeli Knesset in Jerusalem and lay out the Arab views on Middle East peace. This was such a startling proposal that he was condemned by many Arab states and he could get no leaders to volunteer to accompany him.

Even though this was a repudiation of the Carter administration's push for a Geneva meeting, the administration backed Sadat's initiative.

With American prodding, Sadat got an invitation from Begin and arrived in Israel for a 36 hours visit beginning on November19. His Foreign Minister, the pro-Western Ismail Fahmy resigned in protest, as did Mohammed

Riad, the designated replacement. Ironically, as I wrote in my lead story in The Times about Sadat's trip, the Carter administration was still hoping somehow to turn this into a second Geneva conference.

"Officials privately conceded that Mr. Sadat, a close friend of the United States, stood the risk of becoming politically isolated in the Arab world as the result of his trip to Israel. If that happened, officials said, efforts to convene a Geneva conference on the Middle East—a major goal of the Carter administration—would collapse and Mr. Sadat's own future and that of American influence in the Arab world would then be thrown into question."

The mood in Washington during this period was one of near panic. No official believed Sadat's trip to Israel was going to sway Begin to change his mind about the Palestinians, or to stop building settlements in the Sinai and the West Bank. Nor did they think it would improve his standing in the Arab world. So all efforts were made to protect Sadat at all costs and to make sure that Begin was as hospitable as possible. In fact, while Sadat had originally planned only a one-day visit to speak to the Knesset, Begin invited him for three, making it more of a state visit.

After the New Year, Carter flew to Egypt to meet with Sadat and ostentatiously read a statement saying the Palestinians should be enabled "to participate in the determination of their own future." In Israel, Begin said he was pleased a Palestinian state was not mentioned, but rejected the idea of self-determination for the Palestinians. "To us, self-determination means a Palestinian state and we are not going to agree to any such mortal danger to Israel."

Meanwhile, a foreign ministers meeting was set for Jerusalem involving Israel, Egypt and the United States. Other Arab states were invited but none accepted. In one of the ironies of these negotiations, the press corps preparing to fly with Vance was sitting in a bus at the State Department at 8:30 p.m. on January 14, 1978 waiting to be driven to Andrews AFB for a 10 p.m. departure when Hodding Carter announced the trip had been postponed, at least a day, because of a disagreement on what to call the pending meeting. Carter called the issue to be discussed: "The West Bank--Gaza Strip-Palestinian issue." The Egyptians, I wrote in The Times, "are understood to favor calling it simply 'the Palestinian question' while the Israelis want the item under discussion to refer to the 'Palestinian Arabs of Judea, Samaria and the Gaza District.'"

We newsmen were of course looking forward to substantive results following on Sadat's historic visit to Jerusalem in November 1977, although the vibes from Israel were not very promising.

The first day of talks began in the Jerusalem Hilton Hotel and the diplomatic atmosphere was good., at least from the official briefings. But the fireworks started at the elaborate dinner in the large ballroom of the Hilton hosted by Mr. Begin. In all the Middle East shuttles I had gone on, this was one of the rare moments to sit at a table with members from Israeli and Egyptian delegations. I remember that sitting at my table was an Israeli who told me he was an amateur expert in the origin of names. So I said, "My last name is 'Gwertzman.'" He said. "Oh, it comes from the Bible, referring to the Maccabees spreading flowers and species on the steps of the Temples." I said: "Oh, I just thought it came from my ancestors who might have sold spices in East Europe." He replied: "That's possible too," [Gvertz means spice in German and Yiddish].

The dinner took a sudden rocky turn when the speeches came. Instead of the usual platitudes of welcome, Begin ripped into the Egyptian guest unexpectedly. Foreign Minister Kamel, Begin said, "told us on arrival under what circumstances peace cannot be established." Begin clearly was irritated by Kamel's tough reiteration on Sunday and Monday of Egypt's demands for Israel's total withdrawal from all Arab lands taken in the 1967 war and self- determination for Palestinians. After being sternly lectured to by Begin, Kamel said he would keep his comments to the negotiating room. The next day, after negotiations began again, it was announced that Sadat had recalled his delegation to Cairo. So all the good will created by Sadat's visit to Jerusalem was gone.

Back and forth it went throughout the year without much apparent progress. Finally in July 1978, the United

States was able to persuade the Egyptians to resume direct talks with the Israelis – this time in London. Originally, they were supposed to meet at the luxurious Churchill Hotel located near the American Embassy in central London. But the British government, fearful of a terrorist attack, urged that the talks be held elsewhere. So at the last minute, they were moved to Leeds Castle, outside of London. From the skimpy briefings we reporters received after each of the two day sessions, we did not get the impression much was accomplished, but Vance said that although "major differences remained" he felt that enough progress had been made to justify his returning to the Middle East in about two weeks.

What we reporters did not know, of course, was that Carter had decided that once Vance returned to Washington to have him go to Jerusalem and Cairo and issue invitations to Begin and Sadat to come to Camp David in early September for a three-way conference to work out an Egyptian-Israeli framework for peace and a Palestinian autonomy accord. Originally, Vance had hoped to continue the three-way foreign ministers meeting started at Leeds in July, but Sadat had decided not to continue that procedure in a public statement in early August. Vance told us of the invitations and the acceptance by both sides on the plane ride home. I filed a story, but the Times as all other New York newspapers went on strike that night in an 88-day pressman's strike.

I was hoping the Washington bureau would be allowed to operate and that we could file our stories through the News Service. But that was not allowed. I and a few other colleagues were hired as free lancers by my former paper, the Washington Star, to write news analyses on Camp David. At first, Abe Rosenthal, the Times' executive editor, wanted to forbid this, but he was talked out of it and relented. I began writing for The Star, which was now owned by Time magazine. The old families that used to run the paper had sold it in the mid-seventies.

The editor of the paper was Murray Gart, formerly chief of correspondents for Time. He was assisted by Sid Epstein, my former city editor at The Star. They were very kind to me and told me to just cover the news as If I were working for The Times. I got paid minimum salary as I recall. And during the early days of the Camp David talks, I joined the herds of journalists and drove out religiously from Washington to Thurmont, Md. Where Camp David was located, to the Edward C. Creeger Jr. American Legion Post 168 which was serving as the press center for the summit. There we received what amounted to daily "no news" briefings."

I had no idea, of course, when I started that the strike in New York would close all newspapers for 88 days, but I stuck it out with The Star and wanted to be in on the action. Finally, on Sunday afternoon, September 17, a very rainy day, we were told at the press center that the talks were over, and that there would be ceremonies at the White House that night.

Sure enough, there were two broad agreements. One was an outline Egyptian-Israeli peace agreement and the other, a framework agreement for the future of Palestinians living on the Israeli-occupied West Bank and Gaza Strip. I wrote what I consider today a penetrating analysis of that initial accord, demonstrating that what it amounted to was a sell-out by Sadat of his lofty stated goals for the Palestinians. I wrote that Sadat "under President Carter's prodding, decided to do just what his critics had warned ever since the Jerusalem mission [the previous November] that he would do just what he had denied he would do."

"He has agreed, in effect, to a separate peace treaty with Israel, which regains for Egypt all of the Sinai lost to Israeli in the 1967 war but which guarantees nothing for Jordan or Syria which also lost territory to Israel in that war," I wrote that "the mood of Arab journalists at the White House last night was one of disbelief that Sadat would go back on Egypt's demands and apparently extract so little from Israel."

Reading over this in 2018, it is remarkable how little has changed politically in the Middle East. Despite years of diplomatic efforts, there still is no Palestinian "country," the Syrian borders have now been torn asunder by a violent civil conflict, but Israel still controls the Golan Heights.

And Jordan no longer has any control over the West Bank of the Jordan River or of East Jerusalem.

As the strike in New York was nearing its end, Murray Gart and Sid Epstein took me to lunch and made me an offer to stay at The Star. I could have any title I wanted: World Editor; Foreign Editor; etc. I could get a great salary if I would join the Star. I thanked them but decided to stay with The Times. Little did I know that like all other major afternoon newspapers in the United States, The Star would close down forever in August 1981. I might add parenthetically that in June 1978, the Washingtonian Magazine named me one of the 50 top journalists in Washington.

CHAPTER 25

Securing the Israeli-Egyptian Peace Treaty

Although Camp David set out the outline for an Egyptian-Israeli peace treaty, it did not wrap it up. It took longer to do so than the Americans, Israelis and Egyptians thought., much longer than President Carter, in particular thought reasonable. The so-called "Framework for the Conclusion of a Peace Treaty Between Egypt and Israel" called for the two sides to make a good faith effort to conclude the peace treaty within three months—by December 17,1978.

Of course, in the immediate aftermath of Camp David, The New York Times, the newspaper of record, was silent. It did not resume publishing again until the strike of pressmen ended in November.

But if the Carter administration officials thought that they could quickly move on to an Egyptian-Israeli peace treaty they were wrong.

Sadat quickly realized that he was being accused of selling out the Palestinians by pushing for his own peace treaty with Israel, and was insisting on elevating the second Camp David accord, the one dealing with Palestinians, to a higher place, and incorporating that into the peace treaty.

Secretary Vance, in his memoirs, noted that "as the treaty negotiations proceeded, our conclusions that linkage of the implementation of the treaty to the autonomy talks would be the most difficult issue proved correct." He said the Egyptians wanted to link the two accords "in order to respond to Arab criticisms that they were signing a separate peace with Israel." That of course was what was evident to most observers, including me, from the start.

The Israelis, Vance said, understood what the Egyptians were trying to do and would not agree to anything that implied that implementation of the peace treaty was tied to progress on the Palestinian issues or the question of a comprehensive peace."

The dispute led Carter to rap both the Egyptians and Israelis in a press conference. He called on both of them to stop debating over details and agree to compromise language that would link the peace treaty to an overall Middle East settlement.

That was on November 9, 1978.

A month later, with still no progress, he asked Vance to go back to the Middle East to try and get agreement directly with the two sides.

This was to be one of the more bizarre Vance trips but we would only learn about how bizarre it was much later. He arrived first in Cairo and got Egyptian agreement to much that was unresolved but ran into a brick wall when he showed them to Prime Minister Begin. He then telephoned the White House and all we were told at the time was that Vance was ordered by the White House to return to Washington. It made no sense to any of us on Vance's plane. We only learned upon arrival in Washington that Carter wanted Vance there when he announced the decision taken in secret to launch formal diplomatic relations with Beijing beginning January 1. The decision was worked out on a trip taken by Brzezinski and kept secret from the State Department.

This irked Vance because he had an important meeting with Gromyko set for Geneva later in December to complete the SALT II negotiations. What made matters worse apparently was that Brezhnev sent a note to Carter expressing concern about the U.S. decision to open formal relations with China but that Carter chose to say in a television interview that Brezhnev's note had been "very positive in tone."

I accompanied Vance to Geneva and the members of his team said as they flew home after three days of talks that "the Russians were probably unhappy about the impression fostered by American officials, including President Carter, that the Soviet Union was unconcerned, and even supportive of the Chinese-American relationship." As it was, Carter and Brezhnev finally met in July in Vienna for a summit to sign a Salt II accord.

Meanwhile, the drama over the unfinished Egyptian-Israeli peace treaty continued apace. Finally, in early March, 1979, Carter decided he would go to Cairo and Jerusalem and try to wrap it up personally. The Times decided to send a large contingent with Carter, including me. Up until then, I had not flown on Air Force One, the President's plane since I had been in the pool flying with President Johnson from Melbourne to Canberra in 1966 for the Washington Star.

That trip in 1966 was a very pleasant one. We sat up front near the president and could chat with him. The White House pool, I learned under Carter, was quite different. That's why, I suppose my colleagues volunteered me for the "honor." I was sitting next to an old acquaintance, Leslie Stahl of CBS. We were cramped, knocking knees almost the whole time in the very back of the plane and we never spoke to the president.

We went first to Cairo. Carter and Sadat took a 120 mile train ride to the northern Mediterranean city of Alexandria where they continued their talks. They were cheered by vast crowds along the train route which clearly energized the Carter party including the journalists aboard. Carter, in his memoirs, said "we particularly enjoyed a trip from Cairo to Alexandria, moving slowly through the beautiful farming regions of the Nile Delta on a fine old train built in 1970. Our car was completely open on both sides and we felt that we were right in the midst of the hundreds of thousands of people along the way."

"There were no apparent worries about security. In Alexandria. We were welcomed by the largest and most enthusiastic crowds I have ever seen. As I told Sadat, describing my reception would be one time a politician would not have to exaggerate."

The Americans stayed overnight for a banquet and then flew back to Cairo where Carter addressed the Egyptian parliament the next day. So far so good. The Times ran a charming piece from a Cairo coffee house written by Earleen Tatro. It was one of the best pieces from the area in the paper all year.

"The repeated applause that interrupted President Carter's speech to the Egyptian parliament today worried the men who had crowded around the small television set in the Zahrit Bab el-Louq coffee house.

"Will President Carter understand? Will he think we are impolite?" they asked each other. One man said, "He is not used to this. I have never seen people applauding in the telecasts of the American Congress."

Sadat had given Carter a "yes vote" on his peace proposals and now he needed to get them approved by Begin.

But when he met privately with the Israeli leader Carter was shocked to find out that Begin told him the proposals would have to go first to his cabinet and then to the parliament—a long process. After two days of making no progress, Carter, Vance and Brzezinski decided that there was no longer any need to stay in Israel and "we made plans to leave the following day," Carter wrote in his memoirs. Meanwhile, Jody Powell, the White House spokesman, had been instructed to give a high level briefing to the top American media people in Jerusalem in which he was told to blame the impending "failure" completely on the Israeli side.

Thus, the early evening newscasts on CBS and NBC both had reports of Carter "failing" in his mission. Hedrick Smith, the Washington bureau chief for the The New York Times, was also briefed, and in his news analysis datelined March 12 from Jerusalem, he quoted one of Carter's aides saying the trip had ended up "a debacle."

Because we had so many correspondents covering the trip, I had been chosen to cover the news story this day, and I was waiting for the last possible moment to file. I, of course, knew about the raucous debates in the Israeli parliament assailing the U.S. and Egyptian proposals. And I knew of the negative White House briefing.

But as I was getting ready to write my story in the press center in the King David Hotel, I was approached by an Israeli press official whom I had met in the past and who had been helpful. He asked me what I was going to write. I said it was probably going to say that the trip was ending on a negative note, with the Israeli side rejecting the Egyptian-American ideas.

He then told me that I was being too negative. He informed me that as we were talking, Foreign Minister Moshe Dayan was again meeting with Vance to work out a last minute compromise. This allowed me to call New York and tell them that the possibility of a last minute deal existed, and not to believe the pessimism on the newscasts.

Ironically, the deal was only announced when the Carter team arrived in Cairo and Sadat and Carter were able to speak by phone with Begin who told them that his Cabinet had approved the deal.

How did this come about? I was able to write on March 14, 1979, a lengthy story for the March 15th paper, a so-called tic-toc. After learning from Brzezinski at about 9 pm after the last meeting with Begin that the American side was planning to depart the next day in frustration, Ephraim Evron, the Israeli ambassador to Washington met with Foreign Minister Moshe Dayan and asked that one more effort be made to strike a deal. In fact Dayan and Vance reached agreement on key points and in the morning the two sides met over a long breakfast, and they seemed to have an accord. But Begin still was not definite. He did not give his final "yes" until Carter was in Cairo at the airport with Sadat.

Finally, Sadat and Begin and their teams flew to Washington and after some last minute haggling, finally agreed to the final wording of the peace treaty and its accompanying protocols.

I was given the privilege of writing the lede story for the Times on March 26, 1979 for the March 27th paper:

"WASHINGTON, March 26—After confronting each other for nearly 31 years as hostile neighbors, Egypt and Israel signed a formal treaty at the White House today to establish peace and "normal and friendly relations."

"On this chilly early spring day, abut 1,500 invited guests and millions more watching television saw President Anwar el-Sadat of Egypt and Prime Minister Menachem Begin of Israel put their signatures on the Arabic, Hebrew and English versions of the first peace treaty between Israel and an Arab country.

"President Carter, who was credited by both leaders for having made the agreement possible, signed, as a witness, for the United States. In a somber speech, he said. "Peace has come.""

Needless to say that framed front page is one of my proudest moments but, of course, the hopes that were spawned with that peace treaty never were put into life. To this day, except for a subsequent peace treaty with Jordan, Israel still has no other peace treaties with Arab countries, and is still trying to work out a deal with the Palestinians.

On March 23, 1986, Samuel W. Lewis, who had been U.S. Ambassador to Israel from 1977 to 1985, took note of the 7-year anniversary of the peace treaty in this gloomy assessment:

> "Seven years later, the Egyptian-Israeli peace treaty appears a lonely relic of shattered dreams. Anwar el-Sadat is gone, [assassinated in 1961], Menachem Begin in seclusion, Jimmy Carter far from power. Their successors do, on occasion, politely commend their achievement, but today's preoccupation is elsewhere. In both Israel and Egypt there is widespread disillusionment with the peace, though few in either country speak of overturning it."

CHAPTER 26

The Iran Crisis

During the Camp David talks between the Egyptians and Israelis in September 1978, which were moderated by President Carter, the only other foreign news that attracted much attention were wire reports about "riots" in Iran against the Shah's regime.

We were aware of anti-Shah sentiment, but I don't think we in the press corps took it seriously enough. But Vance, in his memoirs, says that "on September 8, the Shah declared martial laws in a number of cities that had been centers of unrest. In clashes between the military and the demonstrators, a large number of demonstrators were killed, presaging a new spate of protests and strikes.

Vance says that the Shah was depressed by his inability to restore order and uncertain what he should do next. Vance says he urged President Carter to call the Shah to reaffirm support, which Carter did. Also, President Anwar el-Sadat of Egypt did the same. But the crisis continued,

Thus, even as we in the press were trying to cover the finale of Camp David, we had from afar a very big crisis brewing, which would take another year to mature fully—that of Iran.

Because President Carter laid so much emphasis on human rights in foreign affairs, this caused concern in the mind of the Shah, who was well aware of the growing sentiment in the U.S. Congress against selling more arms to Iran because of its alleged human rights abuses.

Vance in his memoirs, "Hard Choices" says that he had gone to Tehran in early May 1977 to attend a meeting of the Central Treaty Organization (CENTO), a dying body, set up in the Eisenhower years and also to meet with the Shah to reassure him of American backing,

"I met the Shah on May 13 in the Niavaran Palace in Tehran. He was an intelligent, quiet yet imperious man, Although apparently decisive, I had a vague feeling that he was insecure. I opened the meeting by delivering a presidential invitation to visit Washington in November. The Shah was delighted." Vance then outlined the U.S. plans to deal with Soviet ambitions in the region, and the Shah promised to do all he could to support a just settlement of the Arab- Israeli dispute. Vance said: "I emphasized that we wanted to continue our military supply relationship with Iran and I informed the Shah that the president has decided to go ahead with the pending sale of 100 F-16 advanced fighter aircraft, despite the serious political problems that would pose with Congress, We would also, I told him, seek congressional approval of his request for the sophisticated and costly airborne warning and control (AWAVS) aircraft."

On human rights, Vance said he stressed "their importance as a key element of our foreign policy. I emphasized that the president was committed to reaffirming the primacy of human rights as a national goal."

My editors and I still had confidence that the Shah's problems were not that serious. I was focused on Vance's trip to Geneva later in May 1977, when he was to meet with Gromyko for a second round of talks on strategic arms reduction, after the first attempt in Moscow in March had gotten nowhere. Charles Mohr, a veteran Times correspondent, covered Vance's trip to Tehran in May, but learned little of his talks with the Shah because Vance, per his custom, revealed almost nothing,

Underscoring the importance the editors attached to the Geneva meeting, I was joined there by Chistopher S. Wren, the Times' Moscow correspondent, who had briefly served as my deputy there when I was correspondent in1969-71, My story on May 19 was on the front page because it said that Vance and Gromyko "were reported today to have made progress toward breaking a deadlock in negotiating a treaty to limit long- range offensive nuclear weapons systems."

And in fact, the conclusion of what became known as SALT II became a major accomplishment of the Carter administration. It was signed by Carter and Brezhnev in Vienna in the spring of 1979.

Meanwhile, the Shah's trip to Washington was on schedule for November 1977 and in advance of his arrival, I reported on November 14 that Carter officials said that the Shah had informed the United States that Iran, in contrast to past practice would not take the lead in seeking an increase in oil prices at the year's end OPEC meeting in Caracas.

But the true significance of the Shah's trip—or rather its insignificance at the time—was shown by the front page of The Times on November 16, 1977. The lead story with a multi-column headline was from Jerusalem. It reported that Prime Minister Menachem Begin had formally invited President Sadat of Egypt to come to Israel to address the Knesset, something Sadat had stunned the world a few weeks earlier by offering to do just that. That led the paper obviously.

My story on the bottom of the page was pegged to the Jerusalem story and reflected the Carter administration's persistent hope that there could still be another Geneva conference on the Middle East bringing all parties, including the Palestinians, together, something of course that has never happened, as late as 2018.

The Shah's arrival in Washington did get front page treatment because of the unusual circumstances surrounding it. It was written by Linda Charlton and it noted that it was marred by tear gas that had wafted in from its use by Park Police breaking up fights between pro and anti Shah demonstrators near the White House. It was the first time anyone could remember this type of thing ever marring a White House ceremony. The Times ran a front page picture showing President and Mrs. Carter dabbing their eyes, reacting to the tear gas, while the Shah stood ramrod.

Later, inside the White House, Carter tried to make light of the tear gassing and fighting that upset he usual protocol arrival. In an inside story, on page 12, I wrote "President Carter assured the Shah today that the United States would continue to honor its long-standing relationship with Iran and praised the Shah for maintaining a "strong, stable progressive Iran under his leadership." Carter added later: "I want to apologize to the Shah for our temporary air pollution problem."

According to William Sullivan, the U.S. Ambassador to Iran, who was in Washington for the visit, the Shah returned home in good spirits from his talks with Carter and other officials in Washington. He enjoyed the White House dinner in his honor and his appearances on Capitol Hill. Iran remained a debating point on the Hill, but top officials did not pay too much attention to it.

And much to the Shah's pleasant surprise, Carter added Tehran to his end of the year world tour for a stop-over on New Year's Eve, 1977-78. Originally, Carter wanted just an informal evening, but the Shah insisted on a white tie affair, with speeches and dancing. And in a way that became the high point of relations. In an impromptu toast to the Shah, Carter said the Shah was "dearly beloved by his people and sustaining an island of stability in his part of the world." Ambassador Sullivan said that toast "would later come back to haunt the record of the Carter administration in subsequent days." Vance said in his memoirs that the President's words "would come back to haunt us."

We all know, of course, that early in 1978, there were violent protests against the Shah's regime in various cities around Iran. They were goaded in part by sermons that were recorded in Paris by the Ayatollah Ruhollah Khomeini, who was determined to overthrow the Shah. At first, there was considerable disagreement among Westerners as to whether Khomeini could be negotiated with or not. Sullivan, who was in Washington in the summer of 1978 on home leave, told Vance that the Shah had a tough road ahead and proposed establishing contact with the religious opposition, The Shah, in late summer began calling for more liberal policies, early elections and a general loosening of restrictions.

But at the same time, his own situation worsened, and he began considering leaving the country just as Carter was assembling the top leaders from Egypt and Israel to Camp David for talks that would eventually lead to an Egyptian-Israeli peace treaty signed on the White House lawn in March 1979. Both Carter and Sadat called the Shah from Camp David to boost his spirits, but eventually, the Shah departed Iran on January 19, 1979, not to the United States where he had originally planned to go, but to Egypt, to be close in case the military was able to restore order quickly.

During this period, I was covering Middle Eastern affairs intensely. I was covering Camp David for The Washington Star while The Times was on strike and then traveled with Vance as he tried to wrap up the details of the Egyptian-Israeli peace treaty, which took longer than anyone expected. I went with Carter to Egypt and Israel and for the final and decisive talks in early March 1979. I covered he actual signing of the peace treaty on the White House lawn on March 26, 1979.

As this was happening, events were worsening in Iran. The Shah had appointed as prime minister Shahpur Bakhtiar, but three days after the Shah had departed for Egypt, The Times from Tehran ran a lead story by R.W. Apple, its distinguished London correspondent, reporting that "A Million Marchers Rally for Khomeini in Tehran

Streets." All the signs were that Khomeini was going to return to Iran in triumph shortly and he did on February 1.

And that was followed by the collapse of the Bakhtiar government and its replacement by the Bazargan government picked by Khomeini. For a while there were two rival governments and Washington intended to recognize the Bakhtiar one, but it resigned on February 11. And the military high command virtually collapsed under attack. Vance, underscoring divisions in the U.S. government, says that "on Brzezinski's instructions and without my knowledge, David Newsom [undersecretary of State] called Sullivan from the White House situation room to ask for an assessment of the chances for an immediate military coup. Sullivan, under immense strain trying to save Americans in the embassy, gave a colorful but unprintable reply"

On Valentine's Day. February 14, 1979, everything seemed to come to a head, both in Afghanistan and in Iran. I was called into action early and was at the State Department all day and night. Carter was due to fly to Mexico for a state visit on February 16 and if the crisis in Iran had not been resolved, he would have had to postpone his trip.

The Afghan crisis developed first. The U.S. Ambassador Adolph Dubs had been kidnapped and taken by force to the Hotel Kabul where he was being held by unidentified captors demanding the release of Afghan prisoners. Vance was involved early and reportedly urged the Afghan authorities to be cautious. But instead, the police stormed the hotel and in the shooting Dubs was killed.

In Tehran, the embassy was under siege for about two harrowing hours by hordes of protesting students. After the crowds left, the U.S. Government thanked the Tehran authorities for moving quickly to rescue the embassy. My friend Hodding Carter, the department spokesman, said the actions in rescuing the embassy staff were "both effective and prompt."

Both events were over before most people in D.C. woke up in the morning.

But instead of alerting Washington that the embassy was in a very precarious situation, the short-lived take over led officials to believe the worst had passed. Sullivan retired from the Foreign Service that summer, as did his Number Two.

Bruce Laingen was sent out to replace Sullivan, but the Iranians would not accept him as an ambassador so he stayed on as a diplomat in charge of the embassy. Vance met with Iran's Foreign Minister Ebrahim Yazdi at the United Nations for a general talk in September and on November 1, Brzezinski flew to Algiers and met with Prime Minister Barzagan and with Yazdi, who was also there for the Algerian Independence day holiday.

Meanwhile, the Shah's health was deteriorating badly. He had gone from Egypt to Mexico where he was diagnosed with cancer of the liver. He then sought to enter the United States for medical treatment. This produced a period when such luminaries as David Rockefeller and Henry Kissinger lobbied President Carter to allow the Shah into the United States for medical help.

Carter was reluctant, but finally agreed when under pressure from Kissinger who said he would not support the recently signed SALT-2 accord unless the Shah was admitted. On October 22, 1979, the Shah was allowed into New York Hospital-Cornell Medical Center to undergo surgical treatment. The Shah was later taken by U.S. Air Force jet to Kelly Air Force Base in Texas and from there to Wilford Hall Medical Center. Medical complications ensued and he was required to have six weeks of confinement at the hospital before he recovered.

He finally left the United States on December 15, 1979, and went to Panama where by all accounts he was treated poorly and his health deteriorated,

Finally, he sought the support of Egyptian President Anwar el-Sadat who again welcomed him. He returned to Egypt in March 1980, had another series of operations and his health steadily worsened. He died on July 27, 1980. President Carter had been warned by his advisers that the admission of the Shah to the United States might lead to another attempted takeover of the U.S. embassy in Tehran. And that occurred on November 4, 1979 when some 300

Iranian youths were able to break through the fortified American embassy and take all those inside prisoner.

The Times led the paper with a one column Reuters story saying the students had seized the embassy and would hold it until the Shah was returned to Iran.

I had an accompanying front-page story that day saying Iranian government officials promised they would do what they could to free the hostages, but indicating that no one was putting much faith in those promises.

Little did I know then that the prime minister and foreign minister would both resign the next day and that Khomeini would take full charge of the situation. Nor did I know that I would be writing almost a story a day for more than a year on the hostage crisis,

Indeed, the first story I wrote on November 6, 1979 was that the United States was "stressing diplomacy" in efforts to free the hostages. George H.W. Bush, who had been CIA director and head of the Chinese liaison office, who had thrown his hat into the 1980 presidential face, said the possible use of force should be considered. A State Department official said such talk was irresponsible because it endangered the hostages. Of course, Gary Sick, who at that time was Brzezinski's Iran specialist on the National Security Council staff, in his book, "All Fall Down" notes that from the first NSC meeting on the crisis, military options were considered.

The hostage taking had caused a national furor, It dominated the TV and radio waves. On November 9, there were large-scale marches in Washington against the hostage takers although there were also some pro- Iranian marchers as well. In Iran, John Kifner of The Times was reporting marchers to the American Embassy shouting "Death to the Americans."

I was asked to write the lead story for the Sunday Week-in- Review section on November 11, 1979, summing up the first week. "The past week was. In President Carter's own words, 'the worst I've had in office.' 'It's tough going,' said Secretary of State Cyrus R. Vance, his face showing strain and fatigue after long, fruitless hours in search of a solution." Of course, when those words were written, no one thought the crisis would last some 444 days, that it would see a failed U.S. rescue attempt, the resignation of Mr. Vance and Mr. Carter's failed re-election campaign as a result.

Adding to the problem facing Carter and Vance was the situation in neighboring Afghanistan. There, suddenly on December 27, 1979, even while Washington was grappling with the hostage crisis, it awakened to find the Soviet Union had begun a round-the- clock airlift to Afghanistan, and had ousted and executed the hard line leader, Hafizullah Amin. The new leader of Afghanistan was Babrak Karmal, a former deputy prime minister who had been living in exile in Eastern Europe. Apparently,

Soviet troops had been involved in fighting in the city center of Kabul, the Afghan capital.

All this came as something of a shock to President Carter, if not to Brzezinski. In an end of the year briefing for White House reporters, Carter warned the Soviet Union to withdraw its troops from Afghanistan, or face "serious consequences" in its relations with the United States. Brzezinski was hoping that perhaps the Iranians would be alarmed by the Soviet presence in Afghanistan and release the hostages, but that did not come to pass immediately. The Ayatollah was not going to change his colors quickly.

And the Soviet move into Afghanistan seemed to genuinely shock Carter. After all, it was Carter, who at the start of his administration, had seemed a bit naïve when he told Ambassador Dobrynin in their first meeting: "I've heard great things about you and your great service in Washington. I hope to have a great relationship with Mr. Leonid Brezhnev."

I wrote in a week-in- review piece on January 6, 1980 after the Afghan invasion, that his comments "mirrored in a way, the attitude of President Franklin D. Roosevelt."

"I have a hunch," Roosevelt was said to have told an aide in 1942, "that Stalin doesn't want anything but security for his country and I think if I give him everything that I possibly can and ask nothing from him in return, noblesse oblige, he won't try to annex anything and will work for a world of democracy and peace," I wrote. "It has been a point of historical controversy what would have happened if Roosevelt had lived to deal personally with Stalin's refusal to live up to some of the agreements made at Yalta."

It also came as a shock to Vance. I interviewed him in his office on January 14, 1980, and Vance said that Carter had given the Russians until mid-February to withdraw their troops from Afghanistan or face the likelihood of an American boycott of the summer Olympics scheduled for Moscow that year. The boycott took place.

In the weeks after the Soviet move into Afghanistan, there was a stepped up effort to get a negotiated deal to free the hostages. It was all done in secret. Gary Sick lays it out in his book. "All Fall Down." The American negotiators were Harold Saunders of the State Department and Hamilton Jordan, Carter's aide. But in the end, their efforts failed because Ayatollah Khomeini blocked them. As a result, Sick notes in his book,: "A dangerous new phase was about to begin."

As someone who had covered the hostage crisis from day one, I had been pretty certain that a military solution was unlikely. So, I was as surprised as anyone when Carter said at a televised news conference on April 17, 1980 that "some sort of military action" against Iran would seem to be the only alternative if economic and political sanctions failed to produce the early release of the American hostages." At that news conference, he announced new sanctions and a ban on travel to Iran by anyone except journalists. He did not say what kind of military action might be undertaken.

I was sound asleep at home in Washington on the night of April 24-25, 1980 when I was awakened by a phone call from the foreign desk alerting me to a story moving on the wires saying that there had been an abortive attempt to rescue the hostages. I was startled and said I would check it out. Usually when you call a place like the White House press office at 1 a.m. there is nobody there. But this time, the office was humming and someone was ready to read me a statement about the failed attempt. And so, I then dictated a story to the foreign desk that told of the abortive attempt to free the hostages by helicopters that never got to Tehran, I was stunned to hear the details of the operation which seemed so difficult to accomplish.

We had not heard from Vance during this period.

That weekend on Sunday, I got a call from the foreign desk again, saying that Newsweek was reporting that Vance was resigning in protest over the hostage rescue operation. I then started calling Vance aides and quickly confirmed Bruce Van Vorst's scoop.

Vance had been on vacation when Carter summoned his NSC to approve the operation. Warren Christopher, his deputy, was sitting in for him, and relayed the decision to Vance when he returned. Vance appealed to Carter and also to the NSC. When he could not turn the decision around, he resigned. Eventually, Carter got Senator Edmund Muskie of Maine to replace Vance.

I later interviewed Vance in his law office in New York in December 1979 on his reasons for quitting. He said the mission was "immensely complicated and difficult" and that even if the rescue team had reached Tehran, "a number of hostages would probably be killed in the process of extricating them."

"And even if they were extricated successfully, the Iranians would probably seize foreigners the next day, either other Americans in the country or other foreigners." And further, Vance said, "the bloodshed that would take place in connection with the operation and the consequent death and injury to Iranians could well lead to a wider explosion across the Persian Gulf which might divide the Islamic world from the West, pitting the Islamic peoples on one hand and the West on the other. And finally, this would tend to drive the Iranians toward the Soviets rather than separating them, so certainly this wasn't in our interests as well."

I had become friendly with Gary Sick as a "source" during the Iran crisis, and I forget exactly how it came about, but he tipped me off that a seemingly routine visit by Warren Christopher to West Germany in early September 1980 was more than that. It seemed that the Iranians had decided to negotiate the release of the hostages secretly. They used Sadedegh Tabatabai, a brother of Khomeini's daughter-in-law, as his emissary, He had been press attache in Bonn under the Shah and spoke German. Iran sent an advance copy of the four points that Khomeini made public the next day, to show their new interest in negotiations.

Thus began the negotiations that Christopher and the Iranians carried out until the day that Ronald Reagan was inaugurated, I was happy to have my byline on the off-lead of the paper on January 21, 1981: "52 U.S. Hostages in Iran Fly to Freedom After 444 Days."

CHAPTER 27

The Reagan
(and Haig and Shultz Years)

Although Jimmy Carter may have had hopes of being reelected as late as the last week before the election, my father, Max Gwertzman, a life-long Democrat, told me in the summer of 1979, after Carter's "malaise" speech in which he said the country was going to hell and he fired some of his best cabinet members, that he was going to vote for Reagan, a Republican, for the first time.

For us newsmen, the arrival of new faces was almost a relief since by January 1981, we were worn out by the tensions of whether the hostages would be released and in what condition. So when they all showed up in Wiesbaden, West Germany in relatively good shape, we were all delighted. It later turned out that in the White House those early days, some of Reagan's top advisers urged him to break the contract to repay the Iranians the billions of dollars owed them for returning the Americans but that Haig stood firm in insisting that the United States had to live up to its commitment.

Of course, there were many differences. When Carter took office, he personally plunged into foreign affairs with a passion, talking almost every day about human rights violations in the Soviet Union, or the need to do something about Palestinian rights.

The Reagan administration took over at a time when tension with the Soviet Union was still high because of the Soviet invasion and occupation of Afghanistan at the end of 1979.

This had led Carter to put off Senate ratification of the pending arms control agreement with the Russians. In short overall relations were very tense at the outset of the Reagan term with the Brezhnev regime.

There was also a war of sorts brewing in Lebanon between Syria, which had moved troops into the region to protect Palestinians from Israelis, who had crossed into that country as part of an expanding Lebanese civil war.

But the Reagan administration also showed that it was not necessarily consistent. It had inherited from the previous administration a ban on the sale of grain to the Russians, something that was viewed with contempt by American farmers since Russians could buy grain elsewhere on the world markets, By April, Reagan had decided under pressure from his political advisers to end the ban.

I wrote an article on April 25, 1981 about the lifting of the embargo:

> "Hours after the decision was disclosed, Secretary of State Alexander M. Haig Jr. inveighed, as he has done repeatedly since taking office, about the Soviet Union's posing 'the greatest danger' to the world. He promised that the United States would never accept Soviet intervention in countries such as Afghanistan."

> "But his aides acknowledged that Mr. Haig's speech seemed to have a hollow ring because of the decision to end the grain curbs."

Moreover, the first months of the administration were enlivened by several events. One was Haig's unhappiness with the White House's decision to put Vice President George H.W. Bush in charge of "crisis management" in the administration. Haig seemed to be at odds with Ed Meese, Richard Allen, and other White House aides, who blocked him from having private time with the president.

The other, and much more significant event occurred on March 30, 1981, when John Hinkley Jr., a youth, trying to impress the actress Jodie Foster, attempted to assassinate President Reagan as he was leaving the Washington Hilton Hotel after having given a luncheon speech.

Reagan was wounded seriously, but survived after surgery at Washington Hospital Center. His press secretary, James Brady received a crippling head injury.

The attempted assassination shook the country, but Reagan's rapid recovery was also remembered well.

Haig was forever remembered, however, in the aftermath for having taken the stage at the White House Press room and saying "I am in control." He seemed to feel that until Vice President Bush could get back to Washington by plane, he should be seen as the country's leader. His own colleagues apparently laughed behind his back when he did it. "Constitutionally, gentlemen, you have the president, the vice president and the secretary of state, in that order, and should the president decide he wants to transfer the helm to the vice president, he will do so. As of now, I am in control here, in the White House, pending the return of the vice president and in close touch with him. If something came up, I would check with him, of course."

Legally, the Secretary was no longer third in line, but fourth, and for days, Haig's actions only reinforced the image of his being power-crazy.

Despite his age, Reagan was able to return to work fairly quickly and that allowed Haig to continue on his planned overseas trips. His first was to the Middle East, which was delayed because of concern over a crackdown in Poland and a massive Soviet military movement around the country, suggesting that Moscow might intervene, a la Czechoslovakia in 1968. That did not happen and so Haig went on as scheduled to the Middle East. Haig met with Sadat in Egypt, Begin in Israel, King Hussein in Jordan, and with the Saudis and then went on to various allied countries in Western Europe to discuss mainly relations with Russia and deployment of U.S. missiles on their territory.

I wrote a news analysis on April 12, 1981, at the end of the trip which noted that Haig had told reporters at the outset of the trip —his first as secretary of state—"he was convinced that the measure of his effectiveness would not be who was in charge of crisis management or his behavior the day President Reagan was shot, but what he would accomplish. When the report card was rendered, it would be rendered on substance, he said." I noted that Haig, "whatever his political standing in Washington, seemed to be highly respected by foreign leaders." I noted that "their spokesmen referred admiringly to his vigor and forceful manner, his tough approach to the Soviet Union, his loyalty to friends and his knowledge of the issues."

I tempered the praise by noting:"Clearly, Mr. Haig, after his embarrassing public rows with the White House, hoped that this trip would create a positive impression of him as a statesman. But this aim was complicated by the general nature of the mission itself. Its goals were broad, and there were no specific negotiations undertaken, such as a resumption of talks on West Bank autonomy. "Partly, too, impressions may have been colored by Secretary Haig's dealings with the press. Despite his long experience in public office, he often seemed tense and uncertain in talking with reporters.

"They sometimes felt he viewed their questions as hostile when they were only seeking to pin down details or get fuller explanations.

"It is not essential, of course, that Mr. Haig win journalists' popularity contests; secretaries of state are not paid to be stand-up- comedians. His unease only becomes a serious drawback if it creates uncertainties about what the policies are."

On June 7, 1981, Israeli jet planes bombed an Iraqi nuclear reactor that was being built by the French 10.5 miles southeast of Baghdad, causing an international stir. At that time, it was not commonly known that Israel had already built its own nuclear weapons. The Israelis claimed they did it for their own defense. A few days later, Haig left on another trip, this time to the Far East, the principal stop Beijing. But he was still preoccupied by worries about Poland. My first story on his Asian trip, datelined Hong Kong, reflected this:

"HONG KONG, June 12—Secretary of State Alexander M. Haig Jr. held a news conference here today to express concern about 'the seriously deteriorating situation in Poland.'

'Within hours of his arrival for a rest stop on his way to Peking, where he arrives Sunday, Mr. Haig decided to speak out about his apprehension that the Soviet Union might go beyond its threatening letter this week to the Warsaw leadership and intervene to stop the independent trends in Poland.'"

The trip to China was a highly successful one for Haig and the administration because despite Reagan's well-known admiration for Taiwan, his administration had already decided to lift trade restrictions against China and to open talks during Haig's trip on selling arms. In fact, on the last day of his talks, Haig and Deng Xiaoping, the Chinese leader, said their talks had gone "very well" and that Taiwan had not been much of an issue.

On a personal note, this was my third visit to China since going with Kissinger in 1973 on his first trip as Secretary of State. I would make many more visits to China in later years, particularly when my older son James lived and worked in Shanghai. When I was a young reporter for the Washington Star just beginning to cover the State Department, I remembered the tales of some Old China hands talking fondly of the Peking dumplings they used to consume in quantity in China when they had lived there in pre-Communist days. I have since loved Chinese food just as much.

There was an odd aspect to the ending of Haig's Asian trip, which should have been viewed as a major success. As we were winding up a visit in Wellington, New Zealand, I and a colleague from the Wall Street Journal had asked one of Haig's aides—I think it was Richard Burt, who used to work with me on The Times, how Haig dealt with non-Asian issues on the trip, since, he tried to emulate Kissinger in taking the State Department with him. That led to a briefing at a table in a hotel bar where Burt went over with us in some detail how Haig had succeeded in watering down a Security Council resolution that the U.N. Ambassador Jeanne Kirkpatrick was going to let go through which would have sharply condemned Israel for the June 7th bombing of the Iraqi nuclear installation. This forced Haig a day later to make a public statement disavowing any criticism of Mrs. Kirkpatrick.

I ended up with a news analysis noting that "Haig and his advisers were growing uneasy and more than a bit defensive about the growing number of columnists and others, most notably former Secretary of State Cyrus R. Vance, who have complained about the lack of a meaningful foreign policy." [Vance had recently criticized the decision to sell arms to China]

"It's true that we have not come out with a grand conceptual design a la Kissinger or Brzezinski or somebody else, and it's true that the President has focused his primary attention on getting the economic mess at home straightened out," Haig said in Manila. "But do not delude yourselves. It doesn't mean that he does not have a foreign policy or we don't know precisely where we're going because we do."

What was surprising to me in late summer 1981 was the way the Reagan Administration changed its attitude toward the Russians ever so finely. President Reagan in his first press conference on January 29, had accused Soviet leaders of reserving "the right to commit any crime, to lie, to cheat." And Haig, in that early period was also unsparing in his criticism of the Russians.

But on August 11, in a speech to the American Bar Association in New Orleans Haig surprised me and other journalists by saying that the administration's military buildup would encourage Soviet moderation and that the United States sought fair agreements with Moscow that recognized legitimate interests on both sides. Haig said "We offer a reduction in the tensions that are so costly to both our societies. We offer diplomatic alternatives to the pursuit of violent change. We offer fair and balanced agreements on arms control. And we offer the possibility of Western trade and technology."

And on August 23, Haig said on a television interview show that the Reagan Administration was ready to meet the Soviet Union half-way and was "anxious for an improvement in the dialogue." Haig said he would be meeting Gromyko in New York in September during the annual U.N. General Assembly Session even though he did not expect any "wowing breakthroughs." These were to be the first high-level Soviet-American meetings of the Reagan administration, and Haig said he hoped that they would eventually lead to a Reagan-Brezhnev summit.

After two meetings totaling nine hours and a considerable amount of press buildup, the two sides wound up their talks with no surprise improvement in relations but on the other hand there was no worsening. There would be more talks in Geneva on limiting medium range missiles by the regular arms control experts and Haig and Gromyko planned to meet again in 1982.

For me, this was becoming something of an old record. I was wondering if there would be a real breakthrough any time soon, But we were shaken from our collective boredom by the events in Poland.

The really interesting East-West story was in Poland where the Polish Communist Party seemed desperate to keep the Soviet Union from repeating a "Czechoslovakia" or "Hungary" on it.

John Darnton, the Times' correspondent was filing wonderful copy from Poland, and when the authorities cracked down by initiating martial law on December 13, 1981, he filed through the mail as a "letter." He won a Pulitzer Prize for his reporting. The Reagan Administration briefly reacted strongly, blaming Moscow for the crackdown. But it soon seemed to lose interest as did Western Europe.

I, of course, had fond memories of Poland, dating back to my first visit in 1959 as part of the Lisle Fellowship Group that went on to Russia for two months, and to my solo visits for the Star In the 1960s when I wrote about the liberal trends there, how My Fair Lady was being performed in Polish and how everyone was studying English and listening to the Voice of America.

On January 8, 1982, I was reporting on the front page that "State Department officials said today that the Polish crisis had prompted new consideration within the Administration of a possible meeting between President Reagan and Leonid I. Brezhnev." I then quoted "an aide" to Haig saying that while he would not rule out the idea of a summit, "he was very skeptical that one would occur any time soon."

This apparent softness toward Moscow led Kissinger to break with the Reagan administration in an Op-Ed piece in The Times on January 17.

Howell Raines, a White House reporter in the Washington bureau of The Times, ran a piece on February 5, reporting that Reagan was proposing to Moscow his own plan to eliminate "medium-range nuclear missiles in Europe" by both super-powers.

And even though the U.S. economy in 1982 was not very robust, I reported on February 24 that Reagan, at Haig's urging was planning to ask Congress for more than $1 billion in economic and military aid to Caribbean countries, mainly aimed at bolstering El Salvador against incursions from rebels based in Nicaragua, helped out by Cuba. Earlier in the year, Hedrick Smith, the Washington bureau chief, had reported that Richard V. Allen, who had been Reagan's National Security Adviser since inauguration, had resigned over a minor scandal involving taking some money from a Japanese magazine. He was replaced by William P. Clark, an old Reagan hand, who had been Haig's deputy secretary of state. Smith erroneously reported that Clark would "reduce friction and in-fighting at top levels of the administration." Instead it only worsened.

On April 2, 1982, the Argentine military junta, faced with a deteriorating economy at home, decided to invade the Falkland Islands which had been a British Crown Colony since 1841. This became a war in slow-motion since it would take Britain weeks to assemble an armada to retake islands invaded by Argentina. What I considered bizarre was that Haig decided on his own to try to mediate the conflict that was brewing and to head it off rather than send some experienced Latin American hands or jurists.

Haig took no press on his plane and we learned from his memoirs that he felt that he was close at the end of his mission to getting a deal, but the Argentines pulled back at the last minute. For Haig, it was a personal setback. In his memoir, "Caveat," Haig recalls, "In the few days since my last trip to Buenos Aires, my prediction to my wife that the Falklands might be my Waterloo, had taken on the character of a prophecy." He noted that with the collapse of the peace efforts, his "image had suffered." He claimed that during Reagan's first trip to Europe, a 10-day swing that included an economic summit at Versailles in early June 1982, "it became plain that the effort to write my character out of the script was underway with a vengeance."

As it turned out, Haig did become the second consecutive secretary of state to resign from office, although in his case, "resignation" is stretching the truth. What happened is that as the Reagan team returned from Europe, fighting erupted in Lebanon, primarily between Israel and PLO forces, but also involving Syrian forces. Haig sought to send instructions to Phillip Habib, the special Middle East envoy in Beirut, but needed to have Reagan's approval. He sent them to William Clark at the White House, but Clark did not show them to Reagan right away. This led Haig to send Habib instructions directly. Later, this apparently infuriated Reagan. But he did nothing at first.

A week later, however, on June 26, Reagan handed Haig an envelope, which included a note, saying he had accepted his resignation with regret, even though Haig had not formally resigned. Reagan told him he would ask George P. Shultz to replace him. Later that morning, Reagan stunned the White House press by announcing the "resignation" personally and that afternoon, Haig read his own "resignation" letter.

My own impressions of Haig were quite mixed. I did not get to know him well. Even though I traveled on all his overseas trips in which he took reporters, I cannot say I knew him intimately. He was clearly trying to emulate Kissinger, but lacked having a Nixon as his boss. Reagan simply did not indulge in the kind of intimate foreign policy planning that Nixon did. Shultz fitted in better with Reagan but even he suffered from the same problems of getting his ideas through to the boss, as we shall see.

I was amused by an Op-Ed piece written by Richard Holbrooke in The Times on June 30, 1982, comparing the Vance and Haig resignations, Holbrooke, whom I had known when he worked in the Carter administration as assistant secretary of State for East Asian and Pacific Affairs, compared Vance to Sir Thomas More, who left over one issue—the attempt to rescue the Iranian hostages by force.

"In fact, the circumstances surrounding Mr. Vance's departure could have justified a broader rationale,

"Holbrooke wrote. "The previous nine months had seen a series of bitter setbacks to his hopes in several critical areas, especially U.S.-Soviet relations."

"Mr. Vance could thus easily have said, as Mr. Haig did last week, that the foreign policy on which we embarked together was shifting. But that would have been wholly out of character for Cyrus Vance, who like More, preferred to depart alone."

"On the other hand, Mr. Haig, like Martin Luther, seems to have attacked the foundations of his own church......We should not trivialize these departures by attributing them to minor causes or isolated events. They illuminate the dilemma of men trying to maintain personal dignity and consistent policy values while fulfilling public ambitions. Their dilemma was created in large part by a grotesque foreign policy structure that can be made to function, although still imperfectly, only when a President truly leads his Government."

(Holbrooke was named special ambassador for Pakistan and Afghan affairs by President Obama, but he died in 2010.)

It took a while for Shultz to take over the reins of power in the summer of 1982. For some strange reason, Reagan had asked Haig to stay in charge while the Lebanon war was going on, and he ran it, partly from his Seventh floor office, and later, from the Greenbrier resort in West Virginia where he could play tennis every day.

Shultz took over at the end of July after relaxed confirmation hearings. He was well known on the Hill. Soon after Shultz became Secretary, Reagan from California on September 1, 1982, read his own "peace proposal" for the Middle East over a local radio station. He gave it after the latest fighting in Lebanon had died down and PLO forces had been evacuated from Beirut, thanks to the work of U.S. Marines and Ambassador Philip Habib. In his address, he called upon Israel to allow the Palestinians in the West Bank and Gaza to have "full autonomy over their own affairs" for five years after elections for a self-governing Palestinian authority. Reagan also called on Israel for a "settlement freeze" to provide confidence for further negotiations. He said that he favored self-government for the Palestinians in association with Jordan.

The Reagan plan was immediately rejected by the Begin government in Israel and by the Arab states. In other words it was a flop on day one. It did not have much of a build-up in advance, and it was not "sold" to the parties privately.

It became the subject of Shultz's first major public speech, however, which I covered at the Helmsley Palace Hotel, in New York to a cross-section of some of Israel's strongest financial backers in the United States. I quoted a United Jewish Appeal spokesman as saying that each of the 300 national leaders at the dinner had given a minimum of $100,000. There were about 150 demonstrators outside the hotel protesting Reagan's position on the Middle East, but Shultz's speech was received warmly inside.

Acknowledging there were major differences, Shultz said there was no need for the parties to agree now on any principle but that of "the need to come together at the bargaining table."

"To talk," he said, "To talk about differences: to talk about aspirations: to talk about peace. But in all events, to talk." But Shultz, as we were to learn, did not share Kissinger's activism, nor even a bit of Haig's. After Reagan's September speech, he did not go out to the region to try to "sell" it. Instead, he waited several months before going to the Middle East and that was largely due to a crisis over Lebanon.

Shultz also met for the first time while in New York with Andrei Gromyko, the dean of foreign ministers at that time, but with U.S.-Soviet relations still in a deep freeze over Afghanistan and Poland among other issues, there was not much to agree upon. Soviet-American relations were in a deeper freeze than usual, in part because of the serious illness of Leonid I. Brezhnev, the leader. No one could talk about it publicly but officials all acknowledged that at most he came to work one hour a day or so.

With things looking quiet, I crossed my fingers and decided to go to San Francisco to take part in a meeting of a Young U.S.- French Leaders Group to which I had been recently nominated (my wife Marie-Jeanne's father was

French and in fact was working for the French embassy in Washington). No sooner had I gotten to the Bay City, however, then I had to turn around because of the news that Brezhnev, whose rise to power I had charted back in 1964 for the Washington Star when he helped oust Nikita S. Khrushchev and whose speeches I had covered endlessly for the Times in Moscow in the early 1970s, had died on November 10.

I did a piece in the Times on "Kremlinologists" in the U.S. Government and gave a well-deserved plug to my long-standing friend, Paul K. Cook, who had been the State Department's top Soviet watcher for more than 20 years, and was in Moscow during my tour there. He noted in an article I quoted that "Our prediction rate in recent years is not good." But the consensus was correct this time. The favorite among the experts was that Yuri V. Andropov, 68, the former head of the KGB, would replace Brezhnev at the top of the Soviet Communist Party. And indeed, he did. He met with Vice President George Bush and Shultz, who represented the United States at Brezhnev's funeral. Both sides talked about a desire for better relations. But of course, nothing much happened. Shultz made his first trip as Secretary to Europe in December, which included the usual NATO meeting in Brussels, where I as usual, loaded my bags with chocolates for my family, from a charming little store called "Mary's" which was near our hotel. I also, as usual, loaded my stomach with mussels. Reagan had already lifted most of the sanctions against the European allies that had been levied over their participation in a Russian pipeline venture. And there was discussion of lifting sanctions against Poland if the draconian crackdown was lifted as predicted on the anniversary of the martial law imposition on December 13. But for much of the new year of 1983, the attention was on the Middle East and in particular, on Lebanon. Israel had moved its troops into southern Lebanon to counter PLO forces, and Syrian troops, increasingly bolstered by Soviet military aid, were increasing their hold on parts of the country. Shultz decided to go the region in late April 1983, with a planeload of reporters along, to see if he could work out a deal to end the fighting in Lebanon. Shultz's initial goal was to work out an agreement between Lebanon and Israel which would allow the Israelis to withdraw its troops, but the Israelis would only agree to do so if Syria was also a partyto the accord.

We spent the month of May 1983 shuttling around the region. Shultz had set a sort of arbitrary deadline of May 9 by which time he was to be in Paris for a ministerial meeting. On that date, I wrote a wrap-up story with the help of young Tom Friedman, then the Beirut correspondent, and David Shipler, the Israel correspondent, on how a tentative Israeli-Lebanese accord had been worked out, but it all hinged on Syria also pulling out of Lebanon. That did not happen. And in fact on May 17, Friedman wrote a long piece about Lebanon's prime minister pleading for Shultz to return to get Syria to join the accord which had just been ratified by Lebanon's parliament.

Of course all the plans for dealing with Andropov went out the window when he, too, died early in his term, on February 9, 1984, just 15 months into office. He was replaced by Konstantin U. Chernenko, who in Russian terms, was an "apparatchik," an aide to Brezhnev, who talked glibly about wanting to resurrect the era of détente in relations. Meanwhile with Reagan seeking reelection, and both countries preaching better relations, there was clearly an improvement in relations. But Chernenko himself died on March 10, 1985, turning the reins of power over to Mikhail S. Gorbachev, who at that time was virtually unknown in Washington. Chernenko had the distinction of being the leader in power for the shortest time in Soviet history.

Gorbachev was, of course, to turn out to be the most fascinating of Soviet leaders in the seven years he was at the helm. I was still a reporter when he began, and wrote, I thought, some penetrating analyses about the changes that took place in Reagan's thinking due in part to Gorbachev. Serge Schmemann, who was in Moscow, of course, wrote incisively from the scene. I have to say that later on when I became foreign editor, Serge and I worked very comfortably together as a team, but I am getting ahead of myself.

I became caught up with Gorbachev in October and early November 1985 as plans were being discussed for the first Reagan summit meeting with a Soviet leader. Reagan had in a way frightened the Russians with his so-called "Star Wars speech" in March 1983 in which he talked about devoting funds to building defenses in outer space to defend against missile attacks.

The Russians had nothing like this, and were constantly inveighing against it. Because of the Soviet invasion of Afghanistan during the Carter administration, the United States had in effect ended any serious cultural exchange program with the Russians. A new program had been drafted and was to be signed during the Reagan-Gorbachev summit that was to be held in Geneva on November19 and 20. I pointed out in a Week-in-review piece that ran on November 15, the parallel with the important Big Four Summit held in Geneva in 1955, 30 years earlier when President Eisenhower, Prime Minister Nikolai Bulganin, Communist Party Leader Nikita S. Khrushchev, and heads of the British and French governments met in the first post-Stalin "thaw" summit and out of the that meeting came the first Soviet-American cultural exchange agreement, to which I was a participant in the summer of 1959 as a member of a an exchange of "youth." I spent the summer in the Soviet Union that year and wrote a series about Soviet teen agers for the Washington Star where I had worked and would work when I finished my graduate work.

The Geneva summit went extremely well. There were no major agreements signed other than the cultural exchange accord, but the two men both praised each other publicly. Gorbachev in a televised 80-minute speech to the Supreme Soviet said his talks with Reagan had been a success even though he had failed to get an agreement for a moratorium on nuclear testing.

The thinking then was that Gorbachev would come to Washington for a summit meeting, but nothing happened until August 23, 1986 when a Soviet employee of the United Nations, Gennadi F. Zakharov, was arrested for trying to buy secret jet engine designs. A week later, the KGB arrested my good friend Nicholas S. Daniloff, whom I had known well in Washington as a colleague covering State Department for UPI, but who now was in Moscow for US News and World Report (he had previously been a UPI reporter there), and who spoke fluent Russian from a long Russian heritage. This was clearly an attempt by the Russians to set up a prisoner trade, and it eventually occurred. Nick eventually wrote a book about his experiences and later headed Northeastern University's Journalism Department for many years.

One result of the prisoner exchange was an agreement for a sudden two-day summit in Iceland on October 11 and 12, advertised as a "preliminary" summit to a major one in Washington the following year. The idea for Iceland came from Gorbachev in a letter to Reagan. The Iceland location caught the media world by surprise and by the time the New York Times assembled its team, it was virtually impossible to find commercial airline seats to Iceland since the networks had taken them all. The publisher of The Times, Arthur Sulzberger, known as "Punch" came to the rescue by contributing the Times' corporate jet, a modest sized plane which took the half dozen correspondents to Reykjavik in style. We took over a small inn, which luckily had good phone connections. We were helped out there because during the year, an Icelandic journalist working in New York for the year, who had used the Times for assistance, volunteered to help. She said her husband ran a car agency there and would be happy to serve as our driver. And he did.

It was a most unusual summit. There was a news blackout until the last day. Maureen Dowd, one of the Times' White House correspondents, later a well-known columnist, had a field day writing how Raisa Gorbachev dominated the scene in the absence of Nancy Reagan who had not gone to Iceland. Iceland was not really geared for this kind of summit, but they handled it as well as they could. Finally, on the last day, after a very long final meeting between Reagan and Shultz and Gorbachev there was a press conference by Shultz for the Americans and Gorbachev spoke elsewhere to the Russian correspondents.

In my lead story, I quoted Gorbachev as saying: "We missed a historic chance. Never have our positions been so close." The issue of course was the same that had split the two sides in recent years. Ever since Reagan announced the plan to start research into defense in outer space against missiles, called "Star Wars" for short, the Russians had made that their prime goal to stop. As it turned out, this was my last summit meeting I covered as a reporter. I would attend another one as an editor, and that would be it.

We had a long discussion back at the inn on whether the summit produced positive results or was a setback in relations. The initial wire reports gave the meeting a negative appraisal. I believed that this was a strange summit since the two sides came close to getting rid of all long range missiles even if the end result did not show much. There was a good discussion about what happened, with a lot of pressure from New York which, of course, had to decide how to play the story.

The eight-column headline that The Times put on my lead story I thought was fair: "Reagan-Gorbachev Talks End in Stalemate/As U.S. Rejects Demand to Curb 'Star Wars'" Any doubts about the way the meeting went were dispelled in the next couple of days by Shultz. At a press conference two days later in Washington, he said "We almost got to the point where what would have to be described as the most sweeping bargain ever made was possible, but we couldn't quite make it." And later in the week, talking to the National Press Club, Shultz joked: "Many people have asked why I seemed and looked so tired and disappointed immediately after the meeting ended in Reykjavik," I quoted Shultz as saying. "The answer is simple. I was tired and disappointed."

A personal note here. On May 3, 1985, I turned 50. Marie- Jeanne threw a big birthday party for me at our house in Washington and it was a lot of fun. My colleagues, my parents from New York, my brother, and all sorts of friends came to celebrate with me. But afterwards, I fell into a bit of a funk. I felt that at 50, my reporting days were numbered. I had a feeling that I was getting too old to be a reporter. But I had no ambition to do anything else. Little did I know how my life would change in the next year.

In October 1986, Max Frankel became the next Executive Editor of The Times, and many changes were announced. Howell Raines was replaced as deputy Washington editor, the Washington bureau chief, Bill Kovach was replaced by Craig Whitney, and I was initially asked to become the chief White House correspondent. I asked not to be moved from diplomatic correspondent on the grounds that Reagan, a lame duck in his final two years in office, would not be very interesting to cover.

Then, Joe Lelyveld, whom I had known when he was based in the Washington bureau, and who had now been named foreign editor, asked me to come to New York to be his deputy. Coincidentally, Marie-Jeanne had been urging me to look for a bigger house in Washington so the boys could each have his own bedroom. So I asked her if she would mind looking for a house in the New York area instead of Washington.

She surprisingly said no. But before I could move to New York, there were still some very important foreign policy stories I wanted to complete, and it was only October when my appointment was announced.

I was hoping I could spend my final months as a reporter writing about plans for a Gorbachev-Reagan summit in Washington to sign a significant arms reduction treaty. But instead, I would be thrown into a real "scandal" in the final months of my reporting career, the so-called "Iran-Contra" affair.

I thought helping run the foreign desk might be an interesting change in my life at that time, so I accepted the offer. The Times was generous in finding me an apartment near Lincoln Center which it paid the rent on for the five or six months until the family could move from D.C. And the Times extended me a loan to help pay for the house we eventually bought in the Riverdale section of the Bronx. Both James and Michael were accepted at Horace Mann School which was walking distance from our home.

CHAPTER 28

On to New York, and Communism's Collapse

The Iran-Contra scandal came as a complete shock to all of us covering Shultz since we never expected him to be out of the loop on such a development. It was a case of the National Security Council Staff, principally Robert McFarlane and later John Poindexter, working with the Israelis, and being persuaded by the Iranians, that if they could sell them some sophisticated military hardware, the Iranians could secure the release of Americans who had been taken prisoner in war-torn Lebanon. Although the first deal-making, involving McFarlane had occurred in 1985. We did not hear about it until the wire services reported on articles appearing in Lebanese periodicals and later in Iranian press reports.

A few hostages were actually released, but millions of dollars of equipment were turned over by the Israelis to the Iranians for use against the Iraqis violating the strict U.S. embargo the against sending arms to Iran. It became doubly worse when it turned out that McFarlane was then using the money he got from Iran to finance the rebels in Nicaragua which was banned by Congress. This led to considerable confusion. Did Shultz know about this? If he did, how much?

He went before Congressional committees and asserted that he was lied to, and that the President, in effect, did not know what was going on.

The head of the CIA. William Casey, died before he could testify.

Reagan gave an evening speech to the nation, denying everything, and then later reversed himself.

A special prosecutor ended up indicting several top officials, but President George W.S. Bush. who succeeded Reagan as president in the 1988 elections, pardoned everyone. Despite the scandal. Reagan ended up being a very popular president.

He did sign a nuclear limitation treaty with Gorbachev, and he left office on a high note of détente.

Meanwhile, shortly after New Year of 1987, I moved to New York. The Foreign Desk, namely Marie- Courtney, the administrator for many years of the foreign desk, found me a nice rental near Lincoln Center, a short subway ride to The Times.

Marie-Jeanne and the boys stayed in D.C. so they could finish the school year. I arranged with real estate brokers to show me condos in mid-town Manhattan that we might buy, and Marie-Jeanne came up on a few weekends to look at the few that were within our price range and to look at houses.

I remember well that on the first weekend she came up, at the end of January on Martin Luther King's birthday, a rainy dismal day, we rented a car and headed to Riverdale for the first time. it was cold and rainy and nothing looked good, and she broke down in tears at night.

Both Max Frankel and Jack Rosenthal, who I knew well and had also moved to New York from Washington and both settled in Riverdale, an upscale part of the Bronx over-looking the Hudson River. Jack was particularly persuasive because of the presence of three very good private schools, Horace Mann, Fieldston and Riverdale Country Day. His son went to Riverdale Country Day.

My sons chose Horace Mann. On a more sunny weekend, we found a house in Riverdale which needed some work, but the price was right and we bought it, and in fact at this writing we still live in it.

On my first day at work, Joe Lelyveld introduced me at lunch to Orso's, a very nice Italian restaurant on 46th street off of 8th avenue. It later became one of our favorite restaurants in New York. The Times building then was on 229 West 43d Street and the paper was actually printed in the basement and the first edition hit the streets about 1030 p.m.

Trucks would pull up in the street on 43d street to receive the papers as they came out of the chutes. The linotype machines were upstairs and copy was sent to the printers by compressed air.

I found I liked the work immensely. The initial stories I was charged with were of course those within my expertise, those dealing with the Soviet Union, the Middle East and with the on-going scandals involving the Reagan administration before Congress.

In those days, reporters sent in "skeds"—they informed the foreign desk of their stories ahead of time with a paragraph or two so that it reached the foreign desk before 1 p.m., and then they sent in a longer summary which was due by 4 p.m. and the full story by 6 p.m. We on the desk would alert the top editors of our front page candidates as early as possible, and the front page would be drawn up at a meeting in Max Frankel's office at 5:30 p.m.

I was looking forward to seeing my parents more often. They were living in Hackensack, N.J., having sold their house in New Rochelle, N.Y., and living part of the time near Palm Beach, Fla. One night, I had dinner with my parents and my brother Steve and his wife, Sheila at the NYU club, which my father liked He went to NYU law school). But tragically, my father died in his sleep early in March. He was buried in Kensico Cemetery.

Unfortunately, my mother, whose memory had been slipping never recovered. She ended up shuttling between Steve and our houses for the next couple of years until we finally found a good nursing home for her in New Jersey where she lived until she passed away in 1993.

I got to know all the editors fairly quickly. Kevin McKenna and Tom Feyer were top aides along with several astute women editors, such as Jeanne Pinder and Helen Verongos. My family moved up to Riverdale after school ended. We actually drove up on James's birthday, June 17 in our family Peugeot. We spent the first night in a motel in Yonkers. My brother Steve, who lives in New Jersey, and is a collector of cars, sold me one of his cars, and I began using that to drive to work, as we had a two car garage in our new house.

I of course was fascinated by the continuing Iran-Contra hearings in which Shultz in late July 1987 lashed out at William Casey, the head of the CIA, and at Poindexter and McFarlane for lying to him repeatedly as well as withholding information from President Reagan. He also revealed that he had tried to resign three times over this issue but had been turned down. This was of course the low point in Shultz' long and honorable career. For a while, these stories put a hold on the major international story—the seeming rapprochement between Moscow and Washington that had begun with the Reagan-Gorbachev summit in Geneva in November, 1985.

By the end of 1987, the way finally was cleared for Gorbachev to come to Washington for a summit meeting in which he and President Reagan signed the first treaty reducing the size of their nations' nuclear arsenals. It was the first time the top Soviet leader had come to Washington in some 14 years, since Leonid I. Brezhnev visited in 1973. Reagan and Gorbachev seemed in very good humor. They insisted on using their first names, "Ron" and "Mikhail" in the negotiations.

But apparently there was a lively if unproductive discussion on human rights issues.

The next year, in June 1988, Reagan made his long-awaited return visit to Moscow. I accompanied our correspondents to Moscow. My first time back since my days as bureau chief. It was a mirror to Gorbachev's visit to Washington seven months earlier, and likewise, was the first visit by an American president since Richard Nixon had come in 1974. Americans on the trip were surprised by Gorbachev's defensiveness, due in part by the criticism leveled at him by several Communist Party leaders led by Boris Yeltsin, the Russian Repubic leader.

The Gorbachevs made another trip to the United States in the waning days of the Reagan presidency, in December 1988, so that he could address the General Assembly. Actually, Celestine Bohlen, who followed Raisa Gorbachev around, had a more interesting story, recounting Raisa's enthusiasm in talking about New York, and visiting

Estee Lauder's Fifth Avenue headquarters for lunch and meeting with Nancy Reagan and Barbara Bush.

But as 1989 came upon us, the ever growing story was the student demands in China for democracy, as demonstrated by the take over by as many as 100,000 students in Tienanman square in the center of Beijing early in the year. It was fanned by the arrival in May by Gorbachev, making a historic visit to patch up Soviet-Chinese relations which had been strained to the breaking point for some 30 years, ever since Khrushchev's anti-Stalin policies. The students used his visit to put posters up in Russian saying "glasnost"—openness. Of course, a month later, Chinese troops would be opening fire on these same students in the square shocking the world with their brutality.

The Times was fortunate in having Nick Kristof and his wife Sheryl WuDunn as our correspondents in Beijing to cover these events. Keller accompanied Gorbachev to Beijing on his trip.

But as Keller, the Moscow bureau chief wrote in September 1989, in a very perceptive news analysis that we had encouraged. "One of the great contradictions of Mikhail S. Gorbachev is that while the outside world grows more and more captivated by his skill and charm, much of his own country seems increasingly immune to the magic." He pointed out that just that weekend, Foreign Minister Shevardnadze was having unusually warm sessions in Wyoming with Secretary of State James Baker, and Gorbachev was being hailed as a bold visionary by Prime Minister Margaret Thatcher with whom he spent four hours. Keller wrote that "The Baltic republics are defiant, Armenia and Azerbaijan are reported close to civil warfare, consumers look ahead to winter with something near panic, and Mr. Gorbachev is openly blamed for not waving a wand and making the hard times go away."

In July, 1989, I took some vacation. Marie-Jeanne and I and our two boys, James and Michael, flew to England to be tourists, and then took a channel boat to Dunkirk where we met Marie-Jeanne's cousin, Christine, and her family who lived there. While in Dunkirk, I got a phone call from Max Frankel offering me the job of Foreign Editor, since Joe Lelyveld was being promoted to Managing Editor. I accepted the job with great pleasure and set about planning to ask Jim Markham, then the Paris bureau chief, to be my deputy. When we finally got to Paris, and I had lunch with Jim at a nearby cafe, he at first accepted it with pleasure. But the next day, he changed his mind, and explained that he had conflicting romantic problems in Europe. But after talking it over and over, by the time we were to leave Paris, we had a joyous farewell dinner at the Tour D'Argent restaurant with Jim and his daughter. He was to join me in New York after Labor Day. Toward the end of August, however, I got an early morning call from Youssef Ibrahim in the Paris Bureau telling me Jim had shot himself in the head.

To this day. I have pangs of guilt for having persuaded Jim to come to New York, despite his doubts. Max, Joe and I flew to a memorial service for Jim in New Hampshire.

One of my first actions as foreign editor was to send out a message to all correspondents in early August letting them know that the paper was hungry for stories; that now was the time to send us that feature they had been putting aside for the "rainy day" in the future. Markham, still in Paris, sent me a note in early August saying that there had been an interesting wire service story from Budapest, Hungary, about several East German tourists camping out at the West German embassy in Budapest and refusing to leave until Hungarian officials allowed them to leave for Austria—and the free world. Until then, tourists from Communist countries could move freely across borders of Communist countries, but could not go to the West without permission. This looked interesting so I asked Serge Schmemann, our Bonn correspondent, to cut short his family vacation in Canada and head to Hungary and take a look. Celestine Bohlen, our Budapest correspondent, was on home leave. But she soon returned. Also sent to the scene was veteran East European reporter, Henry Kamm, who was my boss when I joined him in the Moscow bureau in 1969. Henry was German born and was a great asset to our team.

We gave great play to the story from Hungary, particularly to Serge's story datelined September 10 from Budapest which said that "Hungary announced today that it is allowing thousands of East German who have refused to return home to leave for West Germany. It was another chapter and a dramatic one, in a summer-long exodus through the new Hungarian gap in the Communist frontier."

We immediately sensed what was happening and I sought out all German-speaking correspondents on our staff to send to Central Europe. That included David Binder, who was in the Washington bureau, and had been our Bonn bureau chief for years, and Craig Whitney. What we all could see was that the Russians had decided under Gorbachev not to try to prevent these events from transpiring. Again, as Serge wrote in a week-in-review piece: "What few expected was that the gap in what was once known as the Iron Curtain would touch off an extraordinary chain of events: the flight of thousands of East Germans. Hungary's rejection of a 30-year pact with East Germany and ultimately the revival of the most fateful question hanging over Europe, the reunification of Germany." In East Germany, Erich Honecker, its 77-year old chief was seriously ill, while the exodus made clear the popular disdain for his rule. As Schmemann wrote: "Until recently, it had been a matter of faith that Moscow would draw the line at any challenge to the leading role of an allied Communist Party and of any hint of neutrality in the Warsaw Pact. But when Poland jettisoned the Communists and when Hungary defied the East Germans the Soviet Union did not intervene."

According to our reporters, the turning point came on October 7 when Honecker, from his sick bed ordered security forces to be prepared to open fire on demonstrators in Leipzig —a "Chinese solution"—to the rising tide of dissent in East Germany. But this was avoided when Egon Krenz, the Politburo member charged with security, flew to Leipzig on October 9 and cancelled Honecker's orders, allowing the protestors to march unmolested. Krenz became the new party chief on October 18 following bitter internal party discussions. Despite party efforts to assuage the people, huge demonstrations persisted, which we covered at the time. On November 4, Krenz announced that East Germans who wanted to settle in West Germany could travel freely through Czechoslovakia. More than 10,000 a day began surging across the border. That same day more than a half million East Germans demonstrated for democracy in the largest protest that East Berlin or East Germany had ever seen.

Back in New York, I was on the phone with Serge constantly. It was quite obvious that the Berlin Wall was going to be opened at some point, but just when was anyone's guess. We knew that the East German Politburo was meeting on this question and Serge had gone to a press conference in East Berlin there. In the era of no cell phones and no internet, we really had to wait until he got back to his hotel room at the Kampinski to hear from him.

Meanwhile, The Times, as usual had its 5:30 p.m. front page meeting in Max Frankel's office to discuss what should be on the next day's front page. My best offering was that it seemed likely the Wall would be opened. So Max dummied it on the page that way but we weren't sure. Our front page deadline was about 9 pm and about 8:30 pm Serge called from his hotel room to say the Wall was open. How did he know? His East German assistant Victor Homola had walked in to his hotel room after having gone through the Wall. Serge and I, 20 years later, went through all this on the Council on Foreign Relations web site in 2009 when I was working at CFR.

Nancy Kenney, who had just been hired as a copy editor in 1989, recalled for me the atmosphere around the foreign desk in those days:

"What a time we had. Sitting in that drab office with those old metal desks and stained carpeting was like being at the center of the universe! Everyone on the desk was working 60 to 90 hours a week, the adrenaline rushing as we closed the first edition and then the second and third with seconds to spare. For months we ran tracks across the top of the pages titled: 'Upheaval in the East.'"

Meanwhile, with all attention focused on Germany, I began to think about the other countries in East Europe.

When I was diplomatic correspondent in Washington in the 1970s, I was friendly with some Bulgarian diplomats and had even visited Sofia on one of my trips to Eastern Europe. I realized that Clyde Haberman, our Rome bureau chief had reported on Bulgarian Turks fleeing Bulgaria back in August, so I asked him to "drop in" on Sofia and see what's doing there. My assumption was that Todor Zhivkov, its long-time Communist leader, was doing fine, and I was looking for some articles on how he was able to avoid the turmoil affecting the rest of Eastern Europe. Clyde protested that he had better articles lined up in Italy, but finally agreed to go. And of course, on the day he arrived, Nov. 10, 1989, not only had the Berlin Wall just been opened, but Todor Zhivkov, Eastern Europe's longest serving leader resigned as president and head of the party. Only a few weeks ago, Clyde and I had a laugh about this, how I was regarded as a genius for predicting all this, when of course I had no idea this would happen at all. It may have been the first time Bulgaria graced the front page of the New York Times.

At about the same time the Berlin Wall was attracting all our attention, Czechoslovakia was on the brink. R.W. Apple of the Washington bureau was there, but on the day of the "big story" he was not in Prague and we had to use an Associated Press story, "The largest anti-Government rally in more than 20 years ended in violence today [Nov.

17]when riot police officers attacked demonstrators trying to march to downtown Wenceslas Square."

During the rally, protestors shouted, "Dinosaurs resign" and "we want freedom and free elections," "Communists get out." Among those who were clubbed was Paula Butturini, the fiancée of John Tagliabue. She was working for the Chicago Tribune in Warsaw but had gone to Prague to cover the demonstrations. She required 15 stitches in her head but was released from the hospital.

The protests continued. On November 20, 200,000 Czechs marched in Prague for freedom. A story by John Tagliabue said that "More than 200,000 marchers called today for freedom and a change in government in the largest and most vociferous public demonstration since the euphoric Prague spring that preceded the 1968 Soviet-led invasion of Czechoslovakia."

Four days later. Steven Greenhouse reported from Prague that the Communist Party's leadership had resigned. For the eighth straight day, some 350,000 people had crowded into central Prague and this time they heard from Alexander Dubcek, whose liberal regime had been overthrown by the Soviet invasion in 1968,. Greenhouse wrote: "After the news of the resignations of the old leaders spread, there was singing and dancing and scenes of jubilation throughout the center of Prague where just a week before the police had clubbed demonstrators in a vain effort to put down the protests."

Finally, on December 29, Vaclav Havel, the Czechoslovak writer whose insistence on speaking the truth about repression in his country repeatedly cost him his freedom over the last 21 years, was elected president by the parliament in an event celebrated by the throng outside the chamber as the redemption of their freedom, wrote Craig Whitney. It was a highly colorful ceremony, one of the highpoints of the end of Communism in Eastern Europe.

But just as light was shining on Czechoslovakia, a large- scale anti-government uprising broke out in the Rumanian city of Timisoara in western Romania, not far from the border with Hungary. There were reports of as many as 10,000 protestors. These were the first reports of anti-government demonstrations in Romania, and we had no correspondents in that country since we had not been able to get visas for some time. Tom Friedman wrote our story from Washington and it was played under the fold. Nicolae Ceausescu, the Romanian leader was in Iran on a state visit when this happened. Our story quoted a State Department analyst as saying: "It looks like Romania's time may have finally come. I would emphasize the word 'maybe' though. Ceausescu has a pretty tight lid on the place. But it will happen sooner or later."

I asked people like John Kifner, who had done so well in covering the fall of the Shah in Iran, to try to get to Bucharest, I asked Celestine Bohlen to do the same, and also Clyde Haberman. The easiest way was via Yugoslavia. I messaged John Tagliabue, who was in Germany visiting with his children from his earlier marriage, not to try to get to Bucharest until the airport was open, but John had already headed toward Romania with two journalist colleagues by car. In the early morning of December 24, I was awakened by a call from the foreign editor of the Chicago Sun Times informing me that John had been wounded in Timisoara and that he had been dropped off in a local clinic. The other people in the car had gone on toward Bucharest. I was startled, first that his companions would just dump him there, and secondly, frightened as to how we could get him out of there. I immediately called Serge in Bonn where he had gone for Christmas, and he stopped everything to get to Tags' side. He did it by flying to Belgrade and driving to Timisoara. Serge's Bonn office manager had also arranged for the German Red Cross to arrange a plane to fly to the Timisoara airport to evacuate Tags. By that time, Paula, Tags' fiancée, who herself had been badly hurt in Prague, had joined Tags and Serge in Timisoara. They all flew together to Munich where Tags spent many weeks in a hospital. Paula says in her book, "Keeping the Feast" that the Romanians let the Red Cross plane take Tags because they feared he would die from infection from his wound since they did not have necessary antibiotics to treat him. David Binder, back in Washington from Germany, wrote the lead story about Romania until we could get someone into Romania.

Meanwhile, our small detachment of correspondents finally arrived in time to cover the overthrow of the Ceausescu regime, the execution of Nicolae and his wife by a kangaroo court, with John Kifner writing the lead story. Celestine Bohlen and Clyde Haberman writing first hand reports from Bucharest, and Tom Friedman from Washington. We were also receiving many phone calls about Tags because his older brother was the commissioner of the National Football League.

At the same time that there was the unexpected explosion in Romania, U.S. forces suddenly invaded Panama to overthrow the dictator General Manuel Antonio Noriega, who for years had cooperated with the CIA in many of its plans in Central America. This competed for front page space with East Europe as well. Lindsay Gruson, who had spent much of the year reporting on the civil conflict in Salvador, was in Panama, and wrote a gripping account of his being taken prisoner, along with a dozen other Western correspondents, from the lobby of the Hilton hotel, and threatened with death, and finally released. Within a couple of days, the U.S. troops had overthrown Noriega, and he went into hiding, taking refuge in the Vatican's embassy. He eventually surrendered to U.S. authorities and stood trial, where he was convicted and sentenced to imprisonment until 2007.

He was then extradited to France which in turn sent him back to Panama where he died ias a prisoner in 2017.

Also competing for front page space was the impending secession of Lithuania, Latvia and Estonia from the Soviet Union. They had been forcibly incorporated under the Stalin-Hitler pact of 1939. And on December 21, Esther Fein reported from Vilnius that the Communist Party of Lithuania had voted to break away from Moscow and to declare independence. It declared the goal was an independent Lithuanian state. Gorbachev was on record as opposing this, but it was deemed unlikely he would do anything; indeed he did not. Roughly two years later, the entire Soviet Union fell apart. Two days later Gorbachev announced he would go to Lithuania to reason with the Communists there to persuade them not to secede, but he was being criticized for being too weak. And when he did arrive in Lithuania, his words had no effect.

CHAPTER 29

1990: Another Very Busy Year For Us

And while our attention was so focused on places like Eastern Europe and the Soviet Union and Panama, we on the Foreign Desk were somewhat caught by surprise by the copy coming from Chris Wren and John Burns in South Africa reporting on the very dramatic changes taking place there.

In fact, February 1990 was to be one of the most important months in African history. We were almost giddy with excitement, if you can picture that. Joe Lelyveld, who had served there in his youth and won a Pulitzer for a book he wrote about apartheid, of course was keenly interested, as was everyone else on the paper. We led the paper on February 3, 1990 with a story from Wren reporting that South Africa's President F.W. de Klerk, who had just been elected, "today lifted a 30-year ban on the African National Congress, the movement that has been fighting to bring down white minority rule in South Africa, and promised that Nelson Mandela, who has been imprisoned for nearly 25 years would be freed soon."This was all done in a speech at the opening of parliament.

Burns, an an accompanying article from Johannesburg, wrote a largely color story reflecting the mood of excitement among the opponents of apartheid, not only blacks, but the major newspapers in the city. But at the same time, he was also reporting that the police were using tear gas in the streets as well as clubs to break up a march near the city center. I had first met Burns in 1975 when I had accompanied Kissinger on his trip to South Africa when he was trying to work out a deal on Rhodesia and had gone to South Africa to seek Pretoria's help. Burns was an incredible correspondent. Little did we know that Burns would soon wind up in Bosnia where he would be holed up with others in Sarajevo for weeks at a time under fire in that very bloody civil war which was to break out shortly

Burns was coming off a period in New York where he had been treated for cancer at Sloan-Kettering, during which time The Times rented for him and his wife an apartment in a comfortable town house on Manhattan's East Side while he he went in for his weekly treatments. Marie-Jeanne and I used to visit him and his wife weekly to keep their spirits high.

Meanwhile, we were preoccupied with Gorbachev and his efforts to keep the Soviet Union whole, while republics like Lithuania, Latvia and Estonia—the Baltic states that were forcibly incorporated into the USSR as part of a deal between Hitler and Stalin—and other non-Russian republics like Georgia, Ukraine, Azerbaijan and Armenia began making moves for independence. They all saw what was happening in East Europe and so they thought "why not here as well?

It was a wonderful time to be running the foreign desk then. The New York Times was doing very well financially; its pages were overflowing with advertisements and its circulation was the highest it had ever been. I was told that I had essentially no limits on the space I needed to tell the unfolding dramas going on around the world and I could hire part-time correspondents if I needed to. Such fearless young ladies as Donatella Lorch, who trapsed through Afghanistan, and Brenda Fowler, who helped cover breakaway parts of Eastern Europe were on the team. (Lorch later became a valuable staff writer in Africa).

On May 2, 1990, as an example of the unusual character of what was going on, we ran a front page story from Moscow with a lead from Bill Keller saying: "President Mikhail S. Gorbachev and the Kremlin leadership were jeered today by throngs of protestors who were allowed to march through Red Square at the end of the annual May Day parade. The Soviet leaders watched in evident amazement from the top of Lenin's mausoleum as a shouting, fist-shaking column milled underneath waving banners that condemned the Communist Party and the KGB and supported Lithuania's declaration of independence." We ran a picture of someone holding a handmade placard in Russian saying: "Gorbachev, the People Don't Trust You: Resign.

The background for all this had occurred in March 1990 when Lithuania declared its independence from the Soviet Union. That announcement caused shockwaves around the world and led to Gorbachev making threats against Lithuania, and imposing sanctions on that republic.

Finally on June 29, the Lithuanian parliament voted to suspend its declaration of independence for 100 days in return for Moscow's end of its economic boycott and an agreement to negotiate. These negotiations went on and on, with fits and starts.

Meanwhile, in the spring of 1990, I received a plaintive message from Sheryl WuDunn, Nick Kristof's wife, our second correspondent in Beijing. Her problem was that she had forgotten to renew her press card in time and the Chinese press office was refusing to renew it so she could not file any stories. Clearly this was punishment for stories filed a year earlier during the Tienanman Square days. She thought perhaps if I made a personal appeal, it might help. I agreed, and so in July 1990, Marie-Jeanne and I headed first to Tokyo to meet with Steve Weisman (who would later become my deputy foreign editor when Mike Kaufman left) and then we arrived in Beijing.

As I anticipated, my meetings with various press officials on Sheryl's behalf did no good. I was told: "If you do not renew your driver's license in New York, you cannot drive." But I told them, "You can apply after after the deadline and it will be okay." Eventually, she got her press card when Bill Safire, the New York Times columnist, visiting Bejing, told the Chinese that his friend, President Nixon hoped they would give back her press card,

While I was in Beijing, I got a phone call from Joe Lelyveld in New York telling me about the Iraqi invasion of Kuwait and telling me that I ought to get back to New York. When I told him that I had a meeting planned in Hong Kong with Asian correspondents he gave me a few days more to stay abroad. I still remember a final dinner with my colleagues at a Szechuan restaurant in Hong Kong in which the aroma of the cooked spices was so thick in the air it was hard to breathe.

Once back in New York, we went on a "war footing." We sent correspondents out to the field. The U.S. military began sending its forces to Saudi Arabia, but the Saudis were not too eager to have American correspondents roaming around. So we had to be careful. Johnny Apple went to Riyadh and became our chief correspondent along with Malcom Browne, both of whom who had extensive Vietnam experience. Judy Miller went to Riyadh, and Alan Cowell to Amman. Chris Hedges we asked to "roam" and he did the best he could.

Months went by and the main story was really in Washington. The Bush government was trying to make sure it had lined up every government on its side in the pending war, and it did just about. What we lacked was a correspondent in Baghdad, CNN, which at that time was just starting out, had Peter Arnett, and he was able to give eye-witness accounts of U.S. bombing raids over Baghdad which were quite heavy leading up to the eventual invasion which only lasted for three days. CNN also ran live the daily briefings by General Norman Schwartzkopf from Saudi Arabia which had the only "news" of the day, and that was an early harbinger of what the internet would hold for us in the next decade.

Hedges got himself captured after the war had ended by Iraqis and it took a bit of effort but we got him released without too much trouble. The war was a lopsided victory for the allies but it left Saddam Hussein still in power. As the Iraqi war was going on President F.W. de Klerk announced he was abolishing the last laws supporting apartheid. But in Moscow, Keller was reporting further signs of Gorbachev's failure to live up to his reputation abroad as a liberal by his backing down in Lithuania and allowing his hardliners to force those seeking independence there into a situation where they were faced with a loss of their economic wherewithal.

I had gone on vacation one with my wife and two young sons to Bar Harbor, Maine in early August 1991 and we drove back to our house in Riverdale on a Saturday night, August 18. Marie-Jeanne and I had planned to take a week of vacation in the city doing a bit of sight-seeing before I went back to work.

But as soon as we got home, I got called from the desk, informing me that there was a "coup" in Russia and Gorbachev had been ousted while on vacation in the Crimea by hard-liners from the Kremlin. The announcement was made at 6 am Moscow time on Sunday which allowed us time to put a banner story on the front page of the Sunday paper.

CHAPTER 30

The Collapse of the Soviet Union

I couldn't believe at first what had happened, knowing the iron-clad security provided the Soviet leaders, but again, I knew these were not "normal" times. We were fortunate that the coup was announced at 6 a.m. Moscow time, which was seven hours ahead of New York time, giving us plenty of time to put a solid front page up. The banner headline was cautious: "Gorbachev Is Ousted In An Apparent Coup". And Frank Clines' lead was also tentative: It said Gorbachev "was apparently ousted from power today by military and KGB authorities while he was on vacation in the distant Crimea."

We were lucky to have a great team of experienced Russian hands in Moscow at the time. The bureau chief was Frank Clines who was not a Russian expert, but was a seasoned correspondent, and a good leader. Also there were Bill Keller, who had taken time off to write a book about Russia, which he never finished; Serge Schmemann, probably our most seasoned Russian expert, the son of a Russian Archbishop; and Celestine Bohlen, the daughter of a former ambassador to Russia, Charles Bohlen. I called them affectionately our "Chudesny Kvartet"[wonderful quartet].

As it turned out, the "coup" was very short-lived. In a remarkable turnaround, Boris Yeltsin, who was head of the Russian Federation, and who was a major opponent of Gorbachev, cut short his trip to Kazakhstan when he heard about the coup against Gorbachev, rushed back to Moscow and was able to convene the Russian parliament in the so-called "White House" building on Monday. He was also able to gain the loyalty of troops assigned to arrest him and was able to take control of Moscow.

Thousands of Muscovites thronged the streets, and by Wednesday it was clear that the so-called coup had failed, Gorbachev was released and flew back to Moscow and Yeltsin, standing on top of a tank which was symbolically standing guard in front of the parliament building was giving speeches blasting the coup.

Serge wrote some of his finest pieces during the month of August about the collapse of the Soviet Union. In the paper of December 15, 1991, we ran a "Special Report" that began: "Looking back now, the August coup was both Mikhail S. Gorbachev's finest moment, and the start of the final act in his tumultuous reign. The collapse of the pathetic coup was his victory. It demonstrated that the freedoms he had loosed had taken root, and it brought out the qualities of courage and determination that brought about the end of the cold war"

"Now, the man who set out almost seven years earlier to reform the world's biggest empire finds himself on the verge of being swept aside by the very forces he set loose. And although his Foreign Minister Eduard A. Shevardnadze was still calling on him today not to resign, it seems more and more certain that he will have to give up the role he has played in exchange for some unknown future."

I asked Serge to in effect write the Soviet Union "obituary" as well, which we ran on Christmas Day as a Special Report, "End of an Empire:" "The Soviet state, marked throughout its brief but tumultuous history by great achievement and terrible suffering, died today after a long and painful decline. It was 74 years old." He wrote that "The end of the Soviet Union came with the resignation of Mikhail S. Gorbachev to make way for a new 'Commonwealth of Independent States.' At 7:32 p.m., shortly after the conclusion of his televised address, the red flag with hammer- and – sickle was lowered over the Kremlin and the white –blue-red-Russian flag rose in its stead" Frank Clines wrote the lead story.

As I write these words in, 2018. I am trying to remember the optimism I felt in late 1991. After all in that year, the United States had led a coalition that decisively defeated the Iraqis and forced them out of Kuwait. The Soviet Union was now no longer a powerhouse to be feared. And the former Soviet satellite states in Eastern Europe were now independent. And 1992 was to be the year in which Secretary of State James Baker was going to try to get the Middle East peace conference working. And China and Asia seemed quiet.

What we did not expect was the terrible bloodshed about to occur in the Balkans.

CHAPTER 31

My Final Years In Print Journalism

In the aftermath of the collapse of the Soviet Union, and the realization that there no longer was a Cold War to worry about —or so it seemed at the time—I became a bit philosophical and brooding about the fate of foreign reporting.

It seems ridiculous today. But it led me to write a lengthy memo to the foreign staff at the end of 1992:

> "What has spurred this memo, of course, has been the breakup of the Soviet Union and Gorbachev's resignation last Christmas which followed so closely upon the collapse of the Communist system in Eastern Europe two years earlier. Not only have these developments drastically altered the world's political map, but they have had an inevitable impact on how we as reporters and editors do our job. As most of you know from

first hand experience, this has forced us to think in somewhat different terms about our reporting and to diversify our coverage considerably."

I was urging my colleagues in the field not to worry too much about East-West issues or about conflicts and to concentrate on social problems and more intangible issues. But of course I was too premature.

Just a half year earlier on May 22, 1991, Barbara Crossette was reporting from Madras, India, an eyewitness, first-hand account of the assassination of Rajiv Gandhi at a campaign stop 25 miles southwest of Madras. She was riding in his car and interviewing him and asked him if he was afraid of this style of campaigning. He said he did it before he had been elected prime minister and now that he was no longer prime minister he saw no reason not to do it again. "A minute or two later, Rajiv Gandhi was dead, killed by a bomb explosion about 10 yards from this reporter."

Meanwhile, Jane Perlez who is still, in 2018 reporting for The Times, had gone to Somalia to report on the famine situation there and wrote some gripping accounts, so gripping in fact that President George H.W. Bush in his last year in office sent in U.S. forces to help. A big headline in The Times on December 9, 1992, said "U.S. Forces Arrive in Somalia/On Mission to Aid The Starving." But Somalia unfortunately, in that period will forever be remembered not for the rescue mission but for the military fight in Mogadishu that began on October 3, 1993 that led to the most serious American military firefight involving American servicemen since Vietnam.

Some 18 American soldiers were killed and more than 70 wounded in 15 hours of ferocious fighting. More than 500 Somalis—not all of them combatants by any means— were killed and more than 70 wounded. There were no U.S. reporters on the ground at that time. We were not there. As a result, it took us a while to catch up fully. The Somali strongman, Mohammed Farah Aidid actually survived in power until 1996. That battle later known as "Blackship Down" after the name of the U.N. helicopter that was hit by a rocket was later made into a movie. It led to President Clinton's withdrawing U.S. troops from there earlier than planned.

As I was writing these memoirs I asked Jane about how she got involved in the Somalia famine story and why she wasn't there when the Blackhawk helicopter went down. In 2016, from Beijing, she replied:

> "I was based in Nairobi, and in the spring of 1992, I ran into the Swiss ambassador on the street and he painted a compelling, little known portrait of terrible famine in Somalia.

I went to see the International Committee of the Red Cross. I had quite good relations with them, and by June 1982 they were at their wits end about what to do about the lack of attention to the fighting and the hunger in Somalia. So they arranged for me and a photographer, Fiona McPherson, to fly up to Mogadishu on one of their tiny planes, about a 90 minute ride as I recall....The local ICRC picked us up at the airport and drove us to Baidoa, the epicenter of the famine.

"We got to Baidoa as the sun was setting on a Friday evening, and bedded down at the ICRC house. The next morning, we got up and drove through the mist on a road with bodies lying on the side to a Unicef feeding camp. At the camp, a little outdoor shelter there was just one jerry can of very thin gruel and graves had been dug on the perimeter to bury the dying children. One small child died while we were there, and was buried. I remember when I gave the mother some money in sorrow, she and her husband fought over the meager notes. I was lucky. The ICRC guy in Baidoa was very experienced and compared the situation to Ethiopia in the 1980s, asking how could the world let this happen again. That caught people's attention.

"That story created quite a stir, and then, a little later, as I continued to write stories, George Bush wrote in the margin of one: "We must do something about this." Even though Bush was in the middle of his re-election campaign (which, of course, he lost to Bill Clinton) he was touched by the Somali crisis....Bush sent the Air Force with aid, and then the arrival of U.S. troops around Christmas in 1992. By early 1993, I had been assigned to Warsaw (I had been in Africa for more than four years) and the interest in the famine and the clan fighting was dropping dramatically."

A much more serious story was the slaughter that would occur in Rwanda beginning in April 1994 when Hutu troops went on a rampage slaughtering Tutsis, the latest example in the long standing civil strife that had afflicted that country.

Our African correspondent, Donatella Lorch, based in Nairobi, who filed an early story about the Rwanda crisis from her outpost in Kenya, went with three or four other correspondents and chartered a small plane which was diverted from Kigali to Bujumbura. There, they persuaded the International Red Cross to let them go with them in a medical convoy to Kigali. There they were holed up in the Mille Collines Hotel, and terrified of being overrun by mobs. They had phone connections with us in New York, and I was on the phone with the United Nations authorities. Finally, some U.S. forces under U.N. command got to the hotel and evacuated them. One of the officers told her that she had "high-level" backing, I guess that meant me. She did file a story datelined April 13, 1994 from Kigali. Lorch was able to go back and forth to Rwanda over coming months by different ways, eventually coming down with malaria while on holiday in Paris. My wife and I paid a call on her, in fact, in a Paris hospital on our way home from a visit to Moscow and Warsaw.

I still have momentos of that hair-raising day. On April 14, I sent her a note:

> "Donatella, we have been through so many of these episodes, starting when you were or inveterate Afghan stringer, posing as the mujahadeen's wife, that I should learn never to worry, but needless to say, I never learn. I always worry. And happily, we had a wonderful, happy ending to the latest chapter in the Perils of Donatella. Thanks for some very professional stories, written with great self-restraint and compassion which told the story very well."

She returned my message from Nairobi:

"Bernie: Your note made my day. For all of us stranded in Kigali, our real savior were not the UN or the Belgians but the NYT Foreign desk.

"As we all sat on the floor of the hotel lobby yesterday listening to the mortars getting closer and closer, I was the great envy of my colleagues for having a boss like you."

The Russian story, of course, never went away. In June 1992, Yeltsin came to the United States, addressed Congress, signed a surprise arms control treaty with President Bush, made a surprise statement that American Vietnam POWs were in Soviet prisoner camps, something that turned out to be untrue, and then went back home to face increasing dissension.

Yeltsin found himself faced with the same kind of struggle he had had with Gorbachev in 1991-92. But this time, the situation was much worse. Over the summer of 1993, a situation of dual power had developed in Russia. The Supreme Soviet pursued its own foreign policies. Izvestia wrote on August 13: "The President issues decrees as if there were no Supreme Soviet, and the Supreme Soviet suspends decrees as if there were no President."

On September 21, Yeltsin, in an apparent breach of the constitution, announced on television that he was disbanding the Supreme Soviet and the Congress of People's Deputies by decree. He said he would rule by decree until there was a new election. The next night, the Supreme Soviet declared Yeltsin removed from the presidency by virtue of his breaching the constitution and Vice President Rutskoy was sworn in as the acting president. Over the next several days, Yeltsin faced popular unrest.

Corruption was rampant, violent crime was skyrocketing, medical services were collapsing, food and fuel were increasingly scarce. Moreover Yeltsin was getting the blame increasingly. But by early October, Yeltsin had secured the support of Russia's army and ministry of interior forces. In a massive show of force, Yeltsin called up tanks to shell the Russian parliament house, the White House which Yeltsin had made famous in August 1991 when he stood outside it on a tank to defy the coup against Gorbachev.

Schmemann's article on October 5, 1993, under a two-line banner headline, was quite dramatic: "Tanks and troops loyal to President Boris N. Yeltsin today crushed an armed uprising by his opponents with a potent show of force that left their white riverside stronghold battered and in flames."

"The Parliament building, known as the White House, was shaken by huge explosions from 125-millimeter shells fired from T-72 and T-80 tanks. As crack airborne troops conducted a floor by floor assault, hundreds of legislators, defenders and supporters began filing out of the building… Their leaders followed."

The opposition leaders were jailed and Yeltsin closed many opposition newspapers, including Pravda, the former organ of the Communist Party. It was a strange contrast to 1991. Then, the army was heckled when it surrounded the parliament building and urged not to fire. On this day, young people were urging them to fire on those inside.

Celestine Bohlen, who was still reporting from Moscow, wrote a follow-up story, noting that "flags flew at half-staff across Moscow today even from atop the charred parliament building, as Russia observed a national day of mourning and families held funerals for those who died in the violence that engulfed the capital on Sunday and Monday."

At this point in my narrative, I called up Serge in 2015 and asked him to recall what it was like filing stories for the foreign desk in those days, nearly 25 years ago.

"First of all, I don't know how much you can praise yourself in your book but I'll go ahead. I think it was terrific that you were foreign editor precisely at that time…The point is that you were a reporter. You always started off by asking, 'What's up old man?' instead of telling me what to write…I think a good foreign editor is one who first of all listens to the people out there and finds out from them what's going on and bases the reporting on that...We were a really good team because I felt I had ownership of the story and you were going to tell me if I'm off. I remember I wrote a lousy story and you said. 'I don't think it works.' And you killed it. And I was fine with that because I knew I could trust you and I think the other thing you brought to the desk is your appreciation of history. You are fascinated by these processes not only as journalism but as a historical process.

"We had a feeling that we are participating in something that was part of history, that would remain part of history and that we were writing the first draft."

I mentioned to Serge that I thought in that period when he was German bureau chief and later went back to Moscow that the Times had plenty of money in its budget for foreign news. I told him that "I remember assembling every correspondent who could speak any German and we sent them out there. We dispatched David Binder, who had been Bonn bureau chief for years, but had lately been a desk editor in Washington. Craig Whitney, the London correspondent, was active and we hired some young stringers like Brenda Fowler, who spoke German and went off to help cover Slovakia when it broke off from Czechoslovakia. She later became an expert on the "Iceman" discovered in a cave and wrote a book about him. And of course my old colleague from Moscow, Henry Kamm, a native German speaker, was called into action.

Serge remembered fondly the work done for us by Esther Fine, who is the wife of David Remnick, who was then the Washington Post man in Moscow, and is now, of course the editor of The New Yorker. She spent a good deal of time covering the Lithuanian story for us. Serge added;

> "I think The New York Times was at its absolute peak in those years and I think what made it fantastic for all of us was that it was a good story. This was not a disaster or a catastrophe. There was no blood in the streets, no airplanes going down, no war. It was a good story."

I also asked Nancy Kenney, who we hired on the foreign desk in late 1989. She was very young and had come to New York from the Paris Herald-Tribune. She listed for me the desk editors she remembers to this day: Dave East (slot), Gerry Cassidy, Ian Macauley, Bob Kanasola, Joel Simons, Don Bachellor, Tom Mashberg, Lusita Lopez, Carolyn Curiel, Helen Verongos, Kal Lindenberg. She notes: Later, Ed Marks, Joe Gregory, Kathy Rose, Lawrence Lew, Jeanne Moore, Vinnie O'Brien, Barth Healy, Bill Hampton, and Vinnie O'Brien.

The backfield—the editors who assigned and first handled copy: Tom Feyer, Jeanne Pinder, Tom Kuntz, Dean Toda, Pat Stewart. She says that she and some others eventually moved over to the backfield. Mike Kaufman, an expert on Eastern Europe was my first deputy editor, and he was later succeeded by Steve Weisman, Jim Clarity was weekend editor.

Nancy was quite complimentary also: "I really do marvel now at the welcome I received on my first day," she says. "You took me to lunch at Sardi's. I remember your pointing out Barbara Walters as she walked past, and introducing me to Clifton Daniel [a former managing editor and Washington bureau chief] just before we left the restaurant." She added that "today, copy editors at The Times do not report to a department head but to a central copy-editing czar, which gives them far less of a sense that they matter to the editors who assign and shape the news. You gave us a sense that we were a team and a family whether we were copy editors or in the backfield." My own philosophy as an editor was as she pointed out and as Serge noted, to work as team, to make sure the correspondents in the field always felt we were there for them and pulling for them.

The story that resonated for many years in the 1990s was the Serbian story. After the breakup of Yugoslavia, the Bosnian Muslims living in Sarajevo, were determined to have their own state called Bosnia. The Serbian forces were equally determined to keep Bosnia within Serbia. John Burns, whom I got to know well from his time in New York recuperating from treatment for a cancer treatment in a rented East Side town house the Times provided him and his wife while I was deputy foreign editor, had asked him to go to Bosnia to cover that story. I had first met him in South Africa when I was a correspondent covering Henry Kissinger during his one trip to South Africa, and he was The Times South African correspondent in Pretoria. Burns would later go back to South Africa and cover with Chris Wren the end of apartheid in the 1990s. I am sure John would have preferred staying in South Africa but grudgingly moved to Sarajevo, just as the fighting began to get quite hair-raising. We supplied him with a cell phone with an attachment that allowed him to seek out satellites in the sky to file his stories. John won a Pulitzer Prize for international reporting in 1992 for his reporting from Sarajevo. The story that we supplied the jurors began this way:

> "Sarajevo, Bosnia and Herzegovina, June 7— As the 155-milimeter howitzer shells whistled down on this crumbling city today, exploding thunderously into buildings all around, a disheveled, stubble-bearded man in formal evening attire unfolded a plastic chair in the middle of Vase Miskina Street. He lifted his cello from its case and began playing Albinoni's Adagio.

"There were only two people to hear him, and both fled, dodging from doorway to doorway, before the performance ended.

"Each day, at 4 p.m. the cellist, Vedran Smailovic, walks to the same spot on the pedestrian mall for a concert in honor of Sarajevo's dead.

"The spot he has chosen is outside the bakery where several high-explosive rounds struck a bread line 12 days ago, killing 22 people and wounding more than 100. If he holds to his plan, there will be 22 performances before his gesture has run its course….."

The Bosnian War, of course, continued until 1995 when a peace agreement was worked out in Dayton, Ohio through U.S mediation. At the same time that hope was being generated for a possible easing of East-West relations, suddenly in September 1993, there was word of a breakthrough in Israeli-Palestinian relations worked out by Norwegian diplomats in secret talks in Oslo between Israelis and Palestinians. Throughout the history of the Middle East negotiations going back to 1948 this was the missing link. Israel had been willing to deal with Arab states but not directly with the Palestinians.

During the 1970s, when I was diplomatic correspondent, making frequent trips to the Middle East with the secretaries of State the United States never negotiated with Palestinian leaders.

And since Israel itself had absolutely refused to deal with the Palestine Liberation Organization, which the Arabs saw as representing all the Palestinians, no progress had seemed possible. The Camp David agreement worked out by President Jimmy Carter with Egyptian President Anwar el-Sadat and Israeli Prime Minister Menachem Begin in 1978 had two parts, one dealing with the outline for an Egyptian-Israeli peace treaty, which eventually led to the treaty signed by the two leaders at the White House in March 1979 after much negotiation.

The second part, dealing with the outline for a Palestinian accord was never put into effect. Ironically, at the end of his presidency, Carter appointed Sol Linowitz, who had helped negotiate the Panama Canal Treaty, to be his Middle East envoy to try to get a Palestinian deal worked out.

I knew Linowitz because we used to have occasional lunches to discuss world affairs when I was diplomatic correspondent in Washington. He called me at home in December 1990, after Ronald Reagan had won the election defeating Carter's re-election bid. He said over the phone that he would have been able to get a Palestinian deal if

Carter had won. But with Reagan as the next president, it will not be possible.

In any event, we pulled out all stops when Arafat and Rabin both came to Washington and signed on the South Lawn of the White House a Declaration of Principles of Palestinian Self-Government in Israel-occupied Gaza strip and West Bank. The Times gave it a two-line banner headline, with a big picture showing President Bill Clinton looking on as Rabin and Arafat shook hands. For Rabin, that picture would cause political problems in Israel as the right wing would angrily call it a sell-out. He would be assassinated in November 1995 by a right-wing assassin after a peace rally.

But in 1993, we were thinking only positively. We ran a long special report from Clyde Haberman from Jerusalem telling everyone how the secret diplomacy came about. And probably there was no more concerted string of "good news" from that region for some time.

I asked Haberman in March 2016 what his personal views were at the time of the agreement. "I was an optimist back then," he replied. "Though, I too found the suicide bombings unsettling [there had been a string a suicide bombings against Israelis in retaliation for an attack by an Israeli that killed 29 Muslims and wounded many more praying in a Hebron mosque in February 1994]. But I thought that with the Oslo accords Israel and the Palestinians had achieved a fundamental psychological breakthrough....I proved of course to be wrong. By the time I returned for several months of reporting in 2001, the situation had deteriorated to the point where no progress could be made."

In early March of 1995, as Yeltsin had become deeply involved in his war with Chechnya, a Muslim province that was trying to break away from Russia, his office invited Lelyveld to visit the Kremlin for a group interview. He asked me to go instead, and so I made my farewell visit to Moscow as a member of The Times foreign desk. The interview with Yeltsin was held in a Kremlin conference room and lasted nearly an hour. There were two editors from Britain, and one each from the United States (me), France, Italy, Germany, Egypt, and Japan. We were supposed to be briefed on Chechnya, where fighting continued, but little was said about Chechnya. The main story was about his desire to have President Clinton attend the annual May Day parade in Moscow, which this year would mark the 50th anniversary of the allied victory in Europe. He promised that there would be no Russian tanks and hardware in the parade. Clinton and other allied leaders did show up for the parade on May 9, the day it is normally celebrated in Russia. In the West. May 8th is the usual day for noting the anniversary.

Needless to say, I enjoyed seeing my byline once again on a story from Moscow on the front page of The New York Times. It was to be my last front page byline.

In late 1994, Joe Lelyveld, who by this time had become Executive Editor of The Times, took me to dinner and asked me to think about what I wanted to do next. He pointed out that in 1995, I will have been foreign editor for some six years, which by Times standards was a long time. He was most complimentary of my work. He asked if I would be interested in being Paris Bureau Chief, knowing of Marie-Jeanne's background as a French interpreter. I demurred, pointing out that my mother was then in a nursing home in New Jersey and I really needed to stay in the New York area.

That led me to relate to him that in 1993, I had visited my older son, James, then a sophomore at Harvard majoring in computer sciences, and he took me to his computer science workshop to see his work station. He then showed me an early version of the Library of Congress web site probably on a Netscape browser. I remember remarking to James that since it had pictures and text, I didn't see why the New York Times couldn't be on the web as well. He said that it was not practical, that the web sites he knew of needed more bandwidth and speed than was currently available. I put it in the back of my head. And I began subscribing to web services such as Netscape, and America Online.

In 1994, AOL came to The Times and made an offer to carry the Times on its service, offering a considerable payment to the paper, but Max Frankel, as I recall, was opposed. Oddly enough, the New York Times News Service eagerly lobbied for it, and the publisher accepted the offer, and that led to @Times being carried on AOL. The Times hired about five editors to supervise the culling of stories and to make sure they were put on the AOL site. AOL also included the ever-popular Times crossword puzzle. AOL also added a forum where readers could write letters commenting on articles.

Since so many of the letter-writers were commenting on articles in the foreign section, I volunteered to comment on criticisms etc.

I told Lelyveld that I would like to become involved in the field of web journalism which was just beginning. The Times itself had just assigned a small group led by Kevin McKenna who had been on the Foreign Desk earlier, and Bill Stockton and Steve Luciani to look into it. They were to hire Ron Louie as a designer later on. And Martin Nisenholtz was hired by the publisher to be the president.

Lelyveld announced my pending departure from the Foreign Desk with a rather flowery statement to the newsroom staff:

"I remember saying more than eight years ago when I invited Bernie Gwertzman to join me on the foreign desk that I was confident he'd be a 'tower of strength.' It wasn't an original phrase and self-quotation is a vice. Still, I'm proud to repeat it, for a tower of strength is exactly what Bernie proved to be in what became the longest run that anyone has had in the top foreign desk positions in the last thirty years.

"As we all know, it's not just longevity he has to his credit, for his time as foreign editor spanned the greatest run of foreign news since World War II—huge, transforming events like the fall of Communism, the breakup of the Soviet Union, the end of the cold war, the flaring of the Gulf War, majority rule in South Africa, Arafat greeting Rabin and the return of murderous ethnic conflict in Western Europe.

"Through all of this, Bernie was the indomitable captain on our deck and while the proud array of framed front pages in his tiny office won't win any awards for interior décor, they're a tribute to some of the most glorious newspapering The New York Times has seen, ever. What more can you say of an editor than that he kept his paper firmly on top of the greatest stories of our time and, in the process, won the loyalty and love of all who worked with him? Those words, I think, do not in the least exaggerate Bernie's achievement in these years. My personal debt to my old foreign desk sidekick is simply enormous."

I began my new job by writing memos on what other news organizations were doing on the web, but for the most part, I really did not have much to do. I did not have an office, but worked from a desk and computer in the wire room without much privacy. Eventually. Arthur Sulzberger Jr, then the deputy publisher, suggested I join McKenna and the others who had just set up their own office at the Hippodrome Building on 44th street and 6th avenue, about a block and a half north of the Times building. And thus started my new career.

CHAPTER 32

The NYT on the Web
And The Internet

Looking back, I don't think any of us who were involved at the ground floor of The New York Times' entry into the world of the internet could have foreseen in 1995 the impact this new technology would have on the world of journalism. But it did not lack in enthusiasm. All the participants in the new venture except its leaders were very young and willing to work long hours at night to see the new project succeed.

When I became editor of the The York Times on the Web in 1996, I had just turned 61. I was nearly 40 years older than most of my staff.

How did all this come together? First of all, Arthur Sulzberger Jr. who had just become publisher in 1992, was interested in the internet, and I saw him at a workshop at Harvard in the summer of 1995, soon after I had taken on the title of senior editor for Internet matters. That same summer, he suggested that I join the small team that the company had set up to explore the setting up of a web site of its own. This was suggested by McKinsey, the consulting firm, as necessary to protect real estate advertising. Joe Lelyveld, after naming me as senior editor, had asked me to do a survey of what other papers were doing, but had not given me any specific marching orders. So, when invited, I moved with alacrity to join Kevin McKenna, my old colleague from the Foreign Desk, Bill Stockton, from advertising, Steve Luciani, from technology, and Ron Louie, who had been hired to design what The New York Times on the Web would look like.

I had been interested in the world of computers and the internet since 1982 when I was with my older son James, who was then 9 years old in a toy store in Bethesda, Md. And I bought him one of the first computers built for the commercial market, the Sinclair ZX81.

It had to be hooked up to a TV and I let him play around with it. He always had a hankering for things mechanical and he soon enough began learning the codes needed to do things with it.

Soon, I was persuaded to buy an Apple II after considerable hectoring from my son. I bought an early modem and installed it and found to my delight that I could file stories to the New York Times from home without having to go to the office. We also started going to meetings of the Washington Apple Pi society which used to meet every Saturday at Bethesda Naval Hospital. There, computer enthusiasts used to hand out floppy discs with their latest programs on them.

By the time we moved to New York, and I became deputy foreign editor, I was a computer hobbyist and I had signed up for Compuserve, Delphi and Prodigy besides America Online, which was the giant at the time. Through AOL, one could get an internet connection. It was useful to me because I could get the latest AP news from Compuserve at home so I could see what the Foreign Desk knew without bothering the late editors.

This background, of course, helped me persuade Joe Lelyveld to nominate me as Senior Editor for Electonic Media when my time as foreign editor came to an end in the spring of 1995. Joe had first proposed the Paris bureau chief job, knowing Marie-Jeanne was a French interpreter, but I deferred because my mother by then was in a nursing home in New Jersey.

Originally, the web planning group was located on the seventh floor of the Times building, but by the time I joined them they were on the sixth floor of 1120 Sixth Avenue, at the corner of 44th street, a block north of The Times building on 43d street. The building is called the Hippodrome building. Martin Nisenholtz was hired by Sulzberger to be our first president.

As I recall, our first hire was Naka Nathaniel who had been an intern in the graphics department at the paper and had expressed an interest in the web project. Another very early hire was Elizabeth Osder, who had been working for Knight newspapers, and had put up an early web site for the Cleveland Plain Dealer in connection with the opening of the Rock n Roll Hall of Fame. And she ran the forums debating the top five songs.

The New York Times took note of the debate and this led Kevin McKenna to call her and ask her to come to New York for an interview and he hired her to become Content Development Editor, responsible for material not taken directly from The New York Times.

I hired Jean-Claude Bouis, a senior writer at the Associated Press, to be our breaking news editor, in charge of putting out reports every day at noon and 5 p.m. on the news of the day, This sounded good on paper, but in practice if important news broke, it was very hard to wait to put it out. I hired Meredith Artley in the spring of 1996, soon after we launched the site. I interviewed her recently and she recalled that I told her that I didn't think much of journalism schools, and she thought she was sunk because being a recent graduate of Missouri that was her only qualification.

But I hired her, she says, because "I had an email address and was willing to work late hours so you hired me." I told her later, "It was an amazing group of people we hired. Anybody who knew anything about the web, we hired."

Meredith, who later went on to become editor in chief of the International Herald Tribune's web site and later, that of CNN, said: "It was an incredible group of really impressive people who really didn't know what the future held in terms of what was going to happen with the web or the internet or what was going to happen with journalism on the web site." She and Naka took me to lunch in 1998 to tell me that they had gotten engaged. They were our first married couple from the web.

By the end of 1995, when we were getting ready to launch, there already were several newspaper sites online.

In fact, in 1994, when AOL launched its full-scale operation it offered The New York Times a prime spot on its portfolio of newspapers available to subscribers.

But Max Frankel, the editor of The Times at the time was opposed. But The New York Times News Service agreed to it, and was able to persuade the publisher to do so. It hired a small team led by Elliott Rebhun to process New York Times articles onto AOL. They also managed forums and arranged guests who answered questions. I participated in some of these when I was foreign editor. AOL of course charged for its access to the internet and it was often overloaded and users in the early days often faced busy signals when they tried to dial up AOL.

Our site would rely on users having their own access to the internet either through their place of work or through the now growing number of commercial internet providers. In New York City there were already a few.

In the summer of 1995, Martin, Kevin and I visited "Nando," the web site of the News and Observer from Charlotte, N.C. an early web site that carried mostly wire service stories but did it very well. It is now a very healthy full web site. The San Jose Mercury News, in Silicon Valley, was also an early leader. We were in a way in awe of those pioneers who had a lead on the rest of the pack. Ben Grabowski was hired to make sure whatever we did got published, and by the fall of 1995, we decided to have a trial run while Pope John Paul II was in New York City. We hired some freelancers and we succeeded in publishing a web site with a picture of the Pope on the center of the home page just as future home pages would look for the next two years.

We published our first edition for public consumption on January 22, 1996. We had quietly published a few "dry runs" ahead of time. The Times took note of this in a story inside the paper with a headline that said: "The New York Times Introduces a Web Site". What was interesting to me and some others was that in the early days, the Times treated the web site as sort of a cousin, not as a prodigy. And for whatever reason, the psychology of the Times newsroom toward the web was unusually cold and aloof toward the young people on the web site, rather than warm and welcoming.

In part, the fact that the web site was located a long block and a half away, and it was described as "a wholly owned subsidiary of The New York Times Company" contributed to this attitude. Nisenholtz later explained that this was the idea of Russell T. Lewis, who at that time was the president and general manager of The New York Times, and who felt that the web site to survive had to be independent of the Times financially. To this end, they set out to have a stock offering of the Electronic Media Company by the spring of 2000.

At launch, the web site was free to users in the United States, but everyone had to "register," that is give their email address and password so we could see how many people were regular "users." We allowed overseas users to access the site free for 60 days but after that, even Canadian users had to pay $35 a month. We also charged everyone to use the crossword puzzle online which infuriates users to this day, but it was immensely popular since we published the puzzle in the evening, so rabid users could do it before they went to sleep.

I used to joke that the only people paying to use the web site overseas were Japanese stockbrokers, figuring they could afford it. I also suspected that in places like Tel Aviv, one subscriber's password went "a long way," meaning there was considerable cheating. In any event after 18 months,

Nisenholtz ordered an end to charging people overseas. He recalls that in 1998, when we stopped charging "we got more registered users in about an hour than we had subscribers in the last 18 months." I had also urged an end to charging once I had heard that the American Embassy in Germany had ordered its people not to subscribe since the Washington Post site was free.

The first real test of the fledgling web site was on Election Night, 1996. President Bill Clinton's re-election against Bob Dole, the Republican candidate. The election forced us, of course, to have breaking news all night. To be able to do so, we had created an elaborate set-up thanks to John Freed, who was later to become my deputy editor. Then he was editorial production manager, and several weeks before election night, had worked out a plan to give our site what neither the paper nor television could provide: continuous 15-minute updates ot the presidential, senate and house races, state- by-state as well as local ones in the New York region. John was able to run wires from AP into our own computers that allowed continuous updates. Kevin McKenna worked from the newspaper newsroom and kept us abreast of what the paper was doing.

J.C. Bouis assisted by Mo Krochmal updated the web site around 8 pm to report that Clinton was surging ahead of Dole in exit polling. And around 10 p.m, armed with the story filed by Richard Berke and an analysis by R.W. Apple, we put up a very strong home page declaring that

Clinton had been re-elected. The producers led by Will Tacy, Sean Driscoll, and Naka Nathaniel smoothly put up the revised web site. Virtually every web site that night had trouble keeping up with the the number of people seeking access to their sites. In addition, we found ourselves under assault from an unknown attacker sending so many false commands to our computers that at times our speed was cut back even further. But Ben Grabowski, our systems chief, together with the IBM systems people, kept us functioning.

When the results were totaled for the evening, we found that we had 711,000 "page views," a record for us, surpassed the next day when we had 741,000. Translated into "hits," that is actually more than 3 million. But translated into people actually using the site, the number was much more modest, perhaps as many as 70.000, a far cry from the more than 1 million who bought the printed version. Nevertheless, it was an important bench mark for us. Our reach, though small, extended around the world, even to Beijing where our service was featured at an American Embassy party.

In a memo for the staff later, I wrote: "The internet is young, the media is still clunky and in years to come, veterans will certainly look back on Election night 1996 with a fond nostalgia. Sort of the way old-timers today may recall the linotypes on 43d Street."[They had been replaced by computers which set type]. Of course, in June

1997, the presses on 43d street ended their run as newspaper production was shifted to a new plant in Queens.

I can still remember, on a snowy day in January 1996, soon after we had started our work at the Hippodrome Building, walking toward the Times building where my car was parked in a garage next door. I kept thinking how expensive it was to publish the The New York Times newspaper compared to the New York Times on the Web, when I watched the newspaper delivery trucks pulling up to receive the papers coming off the presses. But of course, we produced virtually no income to The Times company and that was to be the continuing problem for us.

Another major moment occurred on Saturday, August 31, 1997, an otherwise sleepy night at the end of summer. At that time we were following the practice of closing down our operation when the newspaper did. Will Tacy was our night editor and he called me at home around 10:30 at night with a bulletin informing me that Princess Diana, who had been divorced for a year from Prince Charles, had been injured in a car crash in a Paris tunnel with Dodo Fayad and a driver. I said something like "Good story. Lead the site with it." Luckily for us, before the site closed up shop for the night, a bulletin appeared that all three occupants of the car had in fact been killed in the crash. So Tacy and the crew stayed up all night updating the story well after the paper closed for the night. That led us to make sure that we always made sure that we did not leave the web site unguarded in the early morning hours. But we did not actually hire a permanent late person until 2000 when we hired Jade Walker, who has made a living by being late editor for different publications. At this writing she is late editor for the Huffington Post.

We kept the original home page design throughout 1997. In fact, we published and distributed a color poster that we circulated widely showing 24 of our favorite home pages of the year. What is striking when one looks at those pages is how little news is on them. For instance, the home page of February 26, 1997 had Deng Xiaoping's death as the lead story, and his picture on the home page and the only other story, a Cybertimes feature on an international phone scam. We stayed with that format until 1998 when with the assistance of IBM, we loosened the format and had many more headlines on the home page, an approach much closer to the current set up.

The loosened format was also made possible by the sense that more people had faster internet connections as well, and had more bandwidth to play with at home as well as in the office.

Recently I asked Rob Fixmer, who was the first editor of Cybertimes, to talk about the first days of the Cybertimes site. He said "My marching orders when I went over there were to experiment with the platform and find out what innovations we could bring to our reporting and to try new things. At the same time, we had to invest a lot in getting the [technological] news out every day....A lot of times, we were just playing. We were having a whole lot of fun. Martin wanted Cybertimes to cover the new media, while you guys covered the rest of the news. When I look back on my career, all the newspapers I worked for and the magazines, it was the most fun I've ever had."

We still suffered from the Times' newspaper view of the web site as a very poor cousin. Not every reporter or editor held that opinion, but so many did that it was something of a morale problem for my very young staff. And it hurt in our ability to cooperate with the paper. Early in the web site's time, I paid a visit to the Washington bureau where I had spent many years, of course, as a correspondent. At a lunch with the staff, I explained what we were trying to do, and at one point I said: "Let's say about 10 a.m. there is a shooting in the Senate, and a senator is shot. We'll go with a wire story. But as soon as a staff writer has enough material, he or she should file something for us right away."

Everyone seemed to nod their heads. Then one reporter asked: "Say I get a tip from the FBI exclusively in the afternoon on who was behind it all? I should hold it for the paper, right?" I answered: "No, wrong. You should give the exclusive to the web site. We are the same paper."

But in 1997-1998, the view that we were the same paper was hard to comprehend. Reporters on the paper feared that if they had an exclusive, it would be lost to the winds if they put it out on the web site first. Even sports writers were reluctant to allow the web to publish their early stories on the web for fear of the competition stealing some exclusive material.

Finally, in 2008, the newspaper broke the story of Governor Elliott Spitzer's use of prostitutes on the Times' web site, and that ended the reluctance of the paper to publish exclusives on the web. I was gone by then from the Times.

Meanwhile, as more and more readers became familiar with the internet, and our web site remained free, our readership began to increase. And by 1999, our web site had won several awards for excellence, and we took private credit for helping the paper win a Pulitzer Prize for National Reporting on Race Relations in 2000 with a number of feature articles that were generated by the web site led by Meredith Artley.

Meanwhile, around this time, according to Martin Nisenholtz, there was a a lively debate within the New York Times corporate walls as to whether the NYT on the Web should be a separate company or not. I don't think that any of the web staff could envisage the web site standing as a unique company, but that is what was being proposed, with its own stock offering. Nisenholtz, in an interview later, said.

"Obviously, the folks at the newspaper were not happy about losing control of their web site, which in many ways, I don't blame them. But it was determined that we would become a separate digital operation, much like many of the other operations that existed at the time." He added that "we would pursue a public offering of the stock, which again, other operations were doing at the time." The effort to have a stock offering came to an ignominious collapse in 2000.

Nisenholtz relates that "we were working with Goldman Sachs" in the latter half of 1999 and into 2000. "AOL had just acquired Time Warner." Deals were in the air. "We were sitting in a room with our bankers…I believe it was April of 2000. Taking a company public, you work very closely with your bankers. You've created this thing. It was actually a tracking stock. We created this document called an S3 which is like an S1 except for a tracker. We were rehearsing the road show at that point. At that time, I think people were still carrying beepers. Remember those little beepers? They started to go off all in unison. The Goldman folks basically said 'there's some issue.' I think the market was actually diving hundreds of points that day. They went back to Goldman, but they said, 'We'll be back tomorrow to rehearse again.' We never saw them again because the dot com boom was over, so there was no IPO [Initial Public Offering]"

I don't know how much money I would have made from that IPO but from what Martin implied, as a senior executive, I would have been handsomely rewarded. In passing, my son Michael was a staff writer for a web magazine called "Bolt," which was aimed at young women, and it too was planning a stock offering, and he, too, was excited about becoming wealthy at the age of 25. But Bolt also had to drop its stock plans, and Michael a couple of years later was laid off and the online magazine soon folded.

I was enjoying myself as editor. I particularly liked working with the young people who joined the editorial side with very little experience. I used to bring the night editor of the day to the daily front page meetings of the paper, as well as the photo editor, to listen to the newspaper editors kick around their discussions of the news of the day. We would then go back to our office and between five and six o'clock have our meeting and discuss how prominent we wanted to play stories and what extra treatment to give them—what video or audio was available for instance.

One day in March 1999, I got a telephone call from Henry Kissinger, who I had of course covered intimately when I was diplomatic correspondent in the 1970s and he was Secretary of State. He had just published volume three of his massive memoirs, "Years of Renewal," and was curious why it had not been reviewed yet in The Times Book Review section. I explained that was the responsibility of the Book Department and I was sure it would not neglect his book. I told him I was now editor of the web site, and no longer had responsibility for the printed paper. I arranged to do an interview with him together with Bill Goldstein, the Book Editor of the web site. My first question was one I was always eager to ask: Which of the world leaders he had met would he love to have at a world summit? His answer: Anwar Sadat, Yitzhak Rabin, Charles deGaulle, Zhou En-lai, and Richard Nixon." It was actually one of the most interesting interviews Kissinger had ever given. For instance, talking about the collapse of the Soviet bloc, he said that "starting in the last year of the Ford administration (1976), I expected the satellite orbit to collapse. I did not expect East Germany to collapse. I thought the Russians would not let that go without making more of an issue of it."

Kissinger said that "in early 1989 I was going to Moscow to a conference. George H. W. Bush had just been elected president and he asked me what I thought his biggest foreign policy problem was going to be... I said your biggest foreign policy problem will be the collapse of the satellite orbit over the 8 years of your presidency. He gave me a letter to Gorbachev to explore that with him on an informal basis.

So I went to see Gorbachev and I said, 'Look, I think maintaining the orbit is going to be too expensive and we ought to use the arms control negotiations to arrange an exit. He wouldn't hear of it. This was January 1989. A year later he was out of all those countries. But I absolutely did not expect the end of the Soviet Union."

The year 2000 was greeted in New York with great enthusiasm. Large crowds filled the streets. Martin invited spouses and boyfriends and girl friends to the office to celebrate New Year's Eve. Marie-Jeanne came down with me to the office and we went to Times Square together to watch the ball fall from a distance. We stayed the night at our friends the Sweedlers who had an apartment on Central Park West.

Meanwhile, the web site moved from the Hippodrome to larger quarters at an office building at 500 Seventh Avenue where we had two floors in a building formerly used almost completely by the clothing trade. It was a few blocks south of The Times building. The size of the staff increased to more than 200, with many more on the business side. The circulation of the web site increased each year. There was a new sense of optimism around The Times.

Around Labor Day, 2001, there was a big party saying farewell to Joe Lelyveld who was retiring as Executive Editor of the New York Times. He was being replaced by Howell Raines, who I knew well from the Washington bureau, and later from the London bureau. He had replaced Jack Rosenthal as Editorial Board chairman and was now promoted to lead the newspaper. It would be momentous several months for the newspaper.

On the evening of September 10, 2001, Marie-Jeanne and I went on a press party aboard the private boat of the owner of Forbes magazine which was arranged by Robert Lenzner, an old friend of ours who was then a columnist for Forbes. The boat went around New York harbor. It was a foggy, rainy night, but we both remember seeing the World Trade Towers that night.

The next morning, as I was preparing to leave my house is Riverdale to drive to the office, I got a phone call from my younger son, Michael, who lived on the lower East Side. He said a plane had just hit one of the Towers and you could see it on TV. And of course, while I was watching the drama unfold, I saw the second airliner hit the other tower. I was on the phone with the office, and soon learned that I could not make it into Manhattan because all roads were closed and all transportation was stopped.

Fiona Spruill was the day editor. I asked her for her memory of that day.

"I came in right between the first and second plane [crash]. Jade Walker and Dan Bigman [the business editor of the web site] were the only people in the office on the news side. I was immediately thrown into the middle of this crazy story....We then began having serious technical issues. It became very difficult to publish the site. We had a lot of trouble. We never officially went down. It took a while for people to get into the office. It was a very scary period where we couldn't find Naka. Naka filmed the second plane hitting and then we couldn't find him. I sat down at my desk at 9 am and got up once to go over to 7th avenue and saw streams of people walking up 7th avenue covered in dust. I left my desk at midnight and it was weird. The only sign of it, even though I had been living it all day long was a police car covered in dust speeding down 7th avenue. At that point, the wind hadn't shifted. Even in Times Square you couldn't tell anything had happened."

"There were a lot of very stressful moments. It was the first time in my memory that the newsroom at the paper really thought about getting information onto the web site in a kind of proactive way," she added. Fiona said she was on the phone constantly with Terry Neilan, who was the contact person in the Times newsroom for the web site. "And then began a period of a crazy two to three months where we just never stopped. We dealt with the anthrax attacks too." Fiona added that she felt personally threatened. "I have vivid memories of when the second tower collapsed, wanting to crawl under my desk. I didn't know if I could take it anymore."

As soon as I got into the office after 9/11 I started looking at the emails which had started pouring into our forums from overseas. They were by and large 99 percent "keep your chins up Yanks" type of messages. They brought tears to my eyes. There were so many emails. I assigned three editors just to sort through the mail to get them into the forums. One writer for instance said: "I've never much cared for you arrogant, pushy and noisy New Yorkers. But after Sept. 11, I'm using adjectives that are much more appropriate descriptors like 'courageous' and 'resilient.' "The headlines in the first days said it all: "Vacant Rooms and Scared Tourists," "No. 1 Anthem: 'God Bless America'

I can't leave 2001 without remembering the baseball season. I have always been a diehard New York Yankees fan, and the baseball season was suspended for a week because of 9/11 and when it was resumed, there was a special passion about the Yankees winning the American League pennant, which they did, and then going on to face the Arizona Diamondbacks in the World Series. The Yankees lost the first two games in Arizona, then won the next three in New York. The next one in Arizona was won by Arizona but the last game had the Yankees winning 2-1 going into the bottom of the ninth inning with Mariano Rivera, the great closer on the mound, but he blew it, losing the game 3-2.

In 2002, with Howell Raines as Executive Editor of the newspaper, I had little direct contact with him. In April, I received an unexpected summons to go to the publisher's office. I did so, and once there, Sulzberger Jr. informed me that since I was now 67, the Times wanted me to accept a buyout at attractive terms, which included two years salary and a good solid pension plan. If I wanted to stay in the organization, he said that he was sure Howell could find something for me in the newsroom. But when I went to see Raines, he did not have any ideas. In short, he was keen on my leaving. He wanted me replaced, it seemed, by a friend of his, Len Apcar, who had been a deputy business editor. He had had no previous web site experience. I accepted the buyout reluctantly and announced it to the staff which was shocked, Many of the original team had already left for other jobs, or were about to. Meredith Artley became the web editor of the International Herald Tribune in Paris [and now is the web editor for CNN in Atlanta]; Will Tacy left for Mother Jones on the West Coast, and now is working for a publication called Good. Unlike my farewells from reporting and from the Foreign Desk we had no big farewells. I had a cookout at our house. Later Arthur Sulzburger had a formal farewell for me on the 14th floor of the newspaper in early September after people had returned from their summer vacations.

Eventually, Les Gelb, an old friend, dating back to New Rochelle High School, who had worked with me on the Times Foreign Desk, and who was now in his last years as President of the Council in Foreign Relations, asked me to serve as a consultant for the Council's new web site. It evolved into my doing more than 1,000 interviews over the next 12 years.

CPSIA information can be obtained
at www.ICGtesting.com
Printed in the USA
LVHW041340141118
596836LV00011B/264/P